Servant Songs

Reflections on the History and Mission of Southeastern Baptist Theological Seminary, 1950–1988

Servant Songs

Reflections on the History and Mission of Southeastern Baptist Theological Seminary, 1950–1988

By
**W. Randall Lolley, Morris Ashcraft,
Thomas H. Graves, and Others**

Edited by Thomas A. Bland, Jr.

Smyth & Helwys Publishing, Inc.
Macon, Georgia

ISBN 1-880837-94-3

*Servant Songs: Reflections on the History and Mission
of Southeastern Baptist Theological Seminary, 1950–1988*
Edited by Thomas A. Bland, Jr.

Copyright © 1994
Smyth & Helwys Publishing, Inc.
Macon, Georgia

Printed in the United States of America.

The paper used in this publication meets the minimum
requirements of American Standard for Information Sciences
—Permanence of paper for Printed Library Materials,
ANSI Z39.48–1984.

Library of Congress Cataloging-in-Publication Data

Bland, Thomas A., Jr.
   Servant songs / reflections on the history and mission of
Southeastern Baptist Theological Seminary, 1950—1988
/ by   Randall W. Lolley, Morris Ashcraft, Thomas H. Graves,
and others ; edited by Thomas A. Bland, Jr.
   xii + 244pp.   6 X 9' (15 X 23cm.)
   Includes bibliographical refences and index.
   ISBN 1-880837-94-3
   1. Southeastern Baptist Theological Seminary—History—20th
century. 2. Baptist theological seminaries—North Carolina—
History—20th century. I. Ashcraft, Morris. II. Graves, Thomas
Henry, 1947–   . III. Bland, Thomas A. IV. Title.
BV4070.S85L65 1994
207'.775655—dc20   94-4441
                                              CIP

Contents

Preface

As early as spring 1988—the semester following the takeover of Southeastern Baptist Theological Seminary by ultraconservative trustees —faculty members and administrators discussed the possibility of chronicling the history of the school, including the events that led to its demise. For a variety of reasons, this project could never get off the ground—until now.

In January 1993, I approached Randall Lolley, Morris Ashcraft, and my father with the idea of compiling a group of essays relating to Southeastern from its founding to the arrival of Lolley's successor, Lewis Drummond, as president in April 1988. These three, along with other former professors and administrators whom I subsequently contacted, readily approved of and pledged their support to this challenging but redemptive undertaking. This book is the fruit of their efforts.

While we all realized that sufficient time had elapsed to allow for rational reflection on what *was* Southeastern Seminary, we were also painfully aware of attempts by some to revise history to make Southeastern in the years 1950–1988 appear to have been what it was not. Criticism of the school's character and record for that period is, of course, nothing new. There always was a small, sometimes vocal, minority of ultraconservative students who either could not come to terms with Southeastern's intellectual and theological openness or could not fully identify with the socially progressive servant model of ministry that the old Southeastern espoused. Ironically, however, perhaps the crudest expression of this viewpoint in recent memory came from someone who never attended the school. At an October 1993 Bible conference in Rockville, Maryland, that purported to bring independent Baptists and Southern Baptists together for dialogue, Jerry Falwell said: "Southeastern Seminary in Wake Forest has corrupted the land for so many, many years, putting out preachers to the left of Gorbachev on everything."[1] Incidentally, of current Southeastern President Paige Patterson, who also attended the meeting, Falwell remarked, "Of all the people in America to bring in as president of Southeastern, they brought in Dr. Paige Patterson. Paige is to the right of me. I mean he is way out there."[2]

The fallacies in such visceral criticism are obvious. But when criticism recently has bled over into carefully crafted revisionism, friends of the old Southeastern have had some cause for concern. An effort at such revisionism was evident in Ed Young's inauguration sermon for Patterson in October 1992. Young, president of the Southern Baptist Convention and a 1962 graduate of Southeastern, said that the advent of the Patterson era marked a return to the founding purpose of Wake Forest Institute (later Wake Forest College): "Dr. Patterson, with your inauguration, certainly this piece of dirt has come full circle."[3] Apparently failing to recognize that any sort of formal theological education for ministers was considered by many Baptists in the South in the 1830s to be evidence of extreme liberalism,[4] Young lamented the Baptist State Convention's approval of Wake Forest College's move to Winston-Salem, a process that began in the 1940s and culminated in 1956. Young attempted to portray present-day Wake Forest University as a bastion of ultraliberalism. Completely misunderstanding or ignoring context, he cited a sentence from the current catalog of the university as evidence of how much the school has changed over the years. The sentence that he quoted reads: "No matter what field you choose when you graduate, a decision to come to Wake Forest is to choose liberal learning as a way of life."[5] Young went on to argue that Southeastern Seminary, which began in a building on the Wake Forest College campus and took over the rest of the facilities when the college moved, was conceived and nurtured in the same liberalism that, in his view, has so thoroughly corrupted Wake Forest University. He recalled how in his student days at Southeastern he and his friends would pray for revival at the seminary, because "we doubted our salvation, questioned our call from God, and wondered what kind of Bible we had left to preach."[6]

This book shows convincingly, I think, that—though Southeastern Seminary *was* founded as a progressive Southern Baptist institution of higher learning; though it *did* attempt to fulfill its educational mission somewhat differently from its sister seminaries, primarily because of some unique cultural circumstances in the region that it served; though it *was* characterized by a climate of warm ecumenism and intellectual honesty; and though, somewhat in the great "pro humanitate" tradition of Wake Forest University, it *did* seek to mediate redemptively between the world and the Word—it *did not* set out to destroy the faith of its students or to denigrate the Bible or to champion the cause of theological liberalism over the cause of Christ. But the honest, heartfelt reflections collected herein will speak for themselves on these and other matters.

The book divides very neatly into three separate sections containing four chapters each. Chapters one through four tell the history of the school and provide an in-depth account of the events in the mid- to late-1980s that brought about its downfall. Chapters five through eight deal retrospectively with the personalities and materials that made each of the four curricular areas (Bible, History, Ministry, and Theology) sound. Chapters nine through twelve provide broader missiological, feminist, historical, and educational perspectives on Southeastern between 1950 and 1988. Regrettably, there simply was not enough space to provide more observations from others who are also well qualified to reflect meaningfully upon the Southeastern experience during those years.

Each contributor demonstrates in some way, I think, his or her awareness that Southeastern Seminary during those years was far from being a perfect institution managed and staffed by perfect people. All of us recognize that no approach to theological education is either completely flawless or totally without merit. It is not our purpose, therefore, to glorify Southeastern as it was or to condemn the school as it now is, though several of the chapters necessarily address events that have taken place since 1988. Ironically, the reader will find that in most essays a healthy kind of self-criticism balances a natural tendency toward some sentimentality. Moreover, the diversity of perspective and opinion among the writers may surprise some readers. Throughout the book, though, is also a clear, pervasive sense of gratitude that such a seminary once existed and repeated expressions of sorrow that it is no more. All who really knew and loved Southeastern rejoice, however, that the Southeastern founders' dream of truly excellent, enlightened theological education is finding new life at Baptist Theological Seminary at Richmond, at the Baptist House of Studies at Duke University Divinity School, and gradually elsewhere.

I chose the title *Servant Songs* for several reasons. First, it seems clear to me that Christian servanthood was, very consciously, the governing biblical metaphor for Southeastern from 1950 to 1988. All kinds of ministries, from missions and evangelism to biblical interpretation and preaching, were taught and practiced as imperfect but faithful expressions of the kind of servant ministry that Jesus himself enfleshed and empowered perfectly. No Southeasterner ever gave more profound written expression to this vision than did Edward A. McDowell, Jr., in the first stanza of the "Seminary Hymn":

Ordained of God, His Prophets rise,
They seek not gain nor earthly prize,
They heed the challenge of Christ's call,
They seek to give and spend their all.

Second, the title seemed appropriate because in these essays the reader can hear and see something of the words and work of so many great Christian servants, living and dead, who helped to make Southeastern the special place that it was. Over the years they have strived individually and collectively to embody in some limited, human way the sort of ministry spoken of in Isaiah's "servant songs" (Isa 42:1-4; 49:1-6; 50:4-9; 52:13-53:12). Theirs has been the kind of ministry that has attempted to promote "justice" (42:4), has proclaimed in a wide variety of ways Jesus Christ as "a light to the nations" (49:6), has struggled "to know how to sustain the weary with a word" (50:4), and has modeled itself after him who was not high and mighty on earth but who "has borne our infirmities and carried our diseases" (53:4 NRSV).

Third, the title reflects the profound gifts of the contributors themselves, all of whom, in the spirit of their forebears at Southeastern, sought to proclaim and to practice loving, servant ministry even during those unspeakably painful last years. Many times when I was a student at Southeastern from 1986 to 1989, I saw and heard them and their colleagues uphold even in the most difficult of circumstances. Jesus' own sublime standard of servant ministry, which he set when he washed his disciples' feet (John 13:1-20).

I am deeply grateful to Cecil Staton, Jr., publisher of Smyth and Helwys Publishing, Inc., and of Mercer University Press, who agreed from the beginning that this book needed to be done. I am also profoundly indebted to Scott Nash, senior vice-president of the book division, and to his excellent staff, who saw to it that the book was done well. My gratitude to the contributors, all of whom have had to revisit events that have brought them great sadness in recent years, defies adequate expression. I am also grateful to some good friends in whom I confided about this project early on, and who encouraged me even then. I cannot say enough good things about the church where I am pastor, Sharpsburg Baptist Church, a wonderfully supportive congregation that has given me the time and the affirmation that I needed to finish my work. Finally, for my wife Pat, I reserve my profoundest thanks for all her assistance and love.

Thomas A. Bland, Jr.
Sharpsburg, North Carolina
January 1994

Notes

[1]Bob Allen, "Independent fundamentalists and Southern Baptists meet," Associated Baptist Press, *Biblical Recorder*, 23 October 1993, 3.

[2]Ibid.

[3]Quoted in Norman Miller, "The Destiny of Dirt," *Outlook* 41/4 (Winter 1992): 9.

[4]See, for example, H. Leon McBeth, *The Baptist Heritage* (Nashville: Broadman, 1987) 235–39; Walter B. Shurden, *Not a Silent People* (Nashville, Broadman, 1972) 39–41.

[5]Miller, "Destiny," 8.

[6]Ibid., 9.

—————— Chapter 1 ——————

In the Beginning

Thomas A. Bland

This essay will be devoted to aspects of the story of Southeastern Baptist Theological Seminary from its opening in September 1951 through the administrations of President Sydnor L. Stealey (1951–1963) and President Olin T. Binkley (1963–1974). To tell the story, it will be necessary to return to early Baptist beginnings in the South and to look with care at events in the half decade 1945–1950.

I was not present in the beginning years of Southeastern Seminary. My services with the seminary began in 1956 and continued for thirty-seven years. I have been a very active participant-observer in the life and work of Southeastern Seminary since July 1956 when I joined the faculty. I shall seek to write with a large measure of objectivity, but I make no claim to detachment. I gladly join other colleagues in offering this volume of reflective and interpretative essays, because we all think the Southeastern story needs to be told.

The Beginnings Viewed Historically

Southeastern Baptist Theological Seminary is located in the geographical heartland of Baptist beginnings in the South. State conventions and a number of Baptist institutions in the Southeast predated the founding of the Southern Baptist Convention in 1845.

The beginnings of theological education in this region were in the Baptist colleges. In the early years of the nineteenth century, pioneer Baptist mission leaders such as Samuel Wait promoted the idea of an educated ministry. Wake Forest College (now University) was founded in 1834, with Samuel Wait serving as president. Southeastern Baptist

Theological Seminary's campus was the home of Wake Forest College for 122 years.

By 1845, when the Southern Baptist Convention held its organizational meeting, sentiment for a central theological seminary emerged. The Southern Baptist Theological Seminary opened in Greenville, South Carolina, in 1859. Due to the dire poverty that existed in the South following the Civil War, it became necessary for Southern to relocate. In 1877 that school moved to the city of Louisville, Kentucky. Consequently, there was no Baptist theological seminary on the eastern seaboard of the South between 1877 and 1951.

By the middle of the twentieth century the Southern Baptist Convention had theological seminaries located in Louisville, Kentucky; Fort Worth, Texas, and New Orleans, Louisiana. Persons in the Southeast who attended a theological school had to travel to one of these states, go north, or attend a school of non-Baptist affiliation in the South. While many made the sacrifices required by these circumstances, the absence of a Baptist theological seminary in the Southeast contributed to the reasons that large numbers of pastors in the region never attended a theological seminary.

By the end of World War II efforts began to open a theological seminary in the Southeast. The Buncombe Baptist Pastors' Conference in the Asheville, North Carolina, area prepared in 1945 a proposal sent as a Memorial to the Executive Committee of the Southern Baptist Convention in which that committee was requested to consider the assembly grounds at Ridgecrest Baptist Assembly as a site for a new seminary. W. Perry Crouch, then serving as pastor of the First Baptist Church of Asheville, North Carolina, and C. C. Warren, pastor of the First Baptist Church of Charlotte, North Carolina, presented the Memorial at a meeting of the Executive Committee of the Southern Baptist Convention on 14 December 1945. A committee of three persons was named to study the matter. This grass-roots initiative from western North Carolina precipitated a series of events that eventually led to the birth of Southeastern Seminary.

Briefly stated, between 1946 and 1950 special committees thoroughly studied the need to establish a seminary in the Southeast. In St. Louis, in May 1947, the executive committee recommended to the convention in session that a committee of nine persons be appointed to study theological education, including the question of the establishment of a new theological seminary. The committee made a progress report to the 1948 convention meeting in Memphis and requested continuation for another year.

In 1949 the committee requested, and the convention in session in Oklahoma City approved, the recommendation that "two new seminaries, one in the West and one in the East, be established as soon as suitable sites can be had and adequate plans can be made for financing the same without injury or impairment to our existing seminaries." Another recommendation called for setting up an enlarged committee on theological education, with a member from each state, "authorized to recommend sites, enlist financial support, draw up charters, and perform other necessary duties pertaining to the carrying out of the recommendations."

On 10 May 1950, J. W. Storer brought the report of the Committee on Theological Education to the convention in session in Chicago. The convention voted to adopt the recommendation that the new seminary in the East be named "The Southeastern Baptist Theological Seminary, Incorporated"; that its location be in Wake Forest, North Carolina; that the convention purchase the campus and buildings of Wake Forest College for $1,600,000; that the convention adopt the Articles of Incorporation; and that the trustees of the school be elected.[1]

The preceding paragraphs describe the process by which Southeastern came into existence. It was born out of the need to plant a theological seminary in the oldest part of the Southern Baptist Convention. On the crest of a wave of population growth, Baptist church growth, and the availability of larger numbers of young people who were ready to enter an institution in which to prepare for a church-related vocation, the time was at hand for the actions taken. Moreover, the three seminaries in operation prior to 1950 were overcrowded. The appeal of the Southeast was sharpened by the recognition that approximately one-third of the churches with one-third of the total membership of the Southern Baptist Convention were located within the six coastal states of the Southeast plus the District of Columbia. Furthermore, growing numbers of unchurched persons were in these southeastern states and in the great population centers to the north. The evidence is conclusive that both the need and the desirability of the establishment of Southeastern Seminary had been convincingly demonstrated prior to the 1950 actions of the Southern Baptist Convention.[2]

From Paper to Institution

The newly elected board of trustees convened briefly on the platform of the meeting place of the Southern Baptist Convention upon adjournment on 10 May 1950. There they elected C. C. Warren temporary moderator and agreed to meet in Wake Forest on 20 June 1950 for the first regular meeting.

The board of trustees met on the campus as agreed. The officers of the board elected on 20 June 1950 were C. C. Warren, chairman; J. Leo Green, vice-chairman; John W. Kincheloe, Jr., secretary; and William L. Wyatt, treasurer. The board organized for business. The major accomplishment of this first meeting was to name a search committee to nominate the first president of the seminary. W. Perry Crouch chaired the committee. Other members of the committee were Claud B. Bowen, Fred Brown, Marshall Craig, and Harold Seever. This committee, composed of well-known and highly regarded pastors, began their task.

At this juncture the seminary was "a paper seminary." A president was needed who could secure a faculty, raise funds, recruit students, establish a library, and start classes in September 1951. Chairman Crouch later wrote of "the many months of work and many meetings" before a president was secured.[3] The committee nominated Olin Trivette Binkley, professor of Christian Sociology and Ethics at Southern Seminary. Dr. Binkley was unanimously elected by the board of trustees, but he declined to serve.

The search for Southeastern's first president continued, and at the first annual meeting of the board in February 1951, the search committee brought to the board the recommendation that Sydnor Lorenzo Stealey, professor of Church History at Southern Seminary, be elected president. Dr. Stealey was elected on 15 February 1951. The following quotation from the "Minutes" of the board of trustees is a primary source report on this significant event:

> Perry Crouch brought the report for the Committee to Recommend a president. The report was a recommendation that Dr. S. L. Stealey, professor of Church History in the Southern Baptist Theological Seminary, be elected president. Dr. Crouch stated that the committee was unanimous in making the recommendation. He then read his letter to Dr. Stealey in which it was stated that the president's salary would be $8,000 per year with a house furnished,

traveling expenses when representing the Seminary, and an entertainment fund not to exceed $600 per year. Dr. Crouch also reported that the committee had indicated the willingness of the board of trustees to pay Dr. Stealey's moving expenses, and also its proportionate part of his annuity payments. He then read a telegram from Dr. Stealey concerning his nomination. Motion was made and seconded that the report of the committee be adopted. After free and full discussion and after a period of prayer led by Dr. Hurt, the motion was unanimously passed and Dr. Stealey was elected. Dr. Crouch was then asked to inform Dr. Stealey of the action of the board.[4]

Dr. Stealey accepted the call to the presidency, and on 23 February 1951 he attended a meeting of the executive committee of the board of trustees and spoke briefly of his ideas and ideals for the seminary. He called for the best possible faculty and for a student-faculty ratio to be carefully managed and adjusted by increasing the number of teachers as the size of the student body increased. If this could not be done, he called for a limitation on the size of the student body.

Dr. Stealey stated his desire to see the seminary "emphasize a warm-hearted preaching ministry, leaving any thought of post-graduate work to the future." He further noted the great need for training ministers for the rural churches of the South and expressed the opinion that this was one of the great challenges before the new seminary. These comments were enthusiastically received, and the president-elect then spoke concerning the securing of a faculty. The executive committee passed a motion authorizing Dr. Stealey to say to prospective faculty members that salaries and retirement provisions would be comparable to those of the other seminaries.[5] Sydnor L. Stealey, elected on 15 February 1951 and in attendance at a meeting of the executive committee of the board of trustees eight days later, was already on the job, although his official beginning time would be 1 June 1951! The seminary was moving from a "school on paper" to a real institution.

Sydnor L. Stealey: Man of Destiny

Sydnor Lorenzo Stealey was uniquely qualified to become the first president of Southeastern. His spirit had been touched by God's Spirit. He was a man who had been tested in war, in the hard experiences of life on the plains of Oklahoma, in the rigors of graduate study, in the death of a four-year-old son, in pastorates in four states, in denominational life as a member of the Executive Committee of the Southern Baptist Convention, and in nine years of teaching at the Southern Baptist Theological Seminary.

S. L. Stealey brought to his presidency a keen understanding of Baptists. He had a sharp mind, a love of learning, and exceptional skill as a communicator both in oral and written prose. He sought to incarnate and express "the great commandment," actually the twin imperatives commended by Jesus: "Thou shalt love the Lord thy God with all thy heart, and with all thy soul, and with all thy mind. This is the first and great commandment. And the second is like unto it, Thou shalt love thy neighbor as thyself" (Matt 22:37-39 KJV).

President Stealey was a friendly, democratic kind of individual. He related well to all sorts of persons. He did not appreciate pretense or pomposity. His expressed ideal in the governance of the seminary was stated in his commitment that the president and the faculty work together as "a cooperative society."

The theological acumen and knowledge of history possessed by Stealey—when combined with his practical wisdom—served trustees, faculty, administration, students, and the Southern Baptist Convention quite well when it was necessary to select articles of faith to which all faculty members must subscribe. Article VIII of the seminary's original bylaws, which were adopted 7 December 1950, required a statement. (The bylaws were later amended and expanded, and this article became Article IX.) Stealey recommended, the board accepted, and all who have served on the faculty have publicly subscribed to and signed the Abstract of Principles, the oldest confessional statement originating among Southern Baptists. This statement has also been in use at the Southern Baptist Theological Seminary since 1859.

An administrator's personal characteristics become known to those who work closely with him. Any occupant of the president's office is carefully scrutinized. Among characteristics observed in Stealey were the following: shrewdness, fiscal conservatism, but sometimes a "soft touch" for a student with a good story about his "need" for financial aid! Nevertheless, in the perspective of the passing years, the superb fitness of S. L. Stealey as first president is affirmed, confirmed, and affectionately remembered.

The First Year

The seminary opened to receive the first group of students on 12 September 1951. Eighty-five students enrolled for the first semester with a total enrollment for the 1951–1952 academic session of 102.

Wake Forest College was able to make available a part of one classroom building. Crowded conditions necessarily continued until the college moved to its new campus in Winston-Salem in the summer of 1956. Despite the crowded conditions, the first year was an exciting time for students and faculty members alike. The students who enrolled during the first year came from thirty-three colleges in fourteen states.

The first faculty was composed of President Stealey, who also served as professor of Church History; J. Leo Green, professor of Old Testament; J. B. Hipps, professor of Missions; William C. Strickland, tutor in New Testament; and Marc H. Lovelace, visiting professor of Archaeology. Joseph R. Robinson served as comptroller and also assisted the president in other administrative duties. All teachers of the first faculty were highly qualified persons of proven ability and valuable prior teaching experiences.

J. Leo Green had taught Old Testament and Hebrew at Southern. He was a member of the original board of trustees of Southeastern, representing Florida. He had served First Baptist churches in Pensacola and Gainesville prior to coming to the Southeastern faculty. Both at Southern and at Southeastern, Green was a popular teacher and dynamic preacher. These achievements, along with his Christian commitment and his knowledge of Old Testament languages and literature, were highly acclaimed by students and colleagues throughout his long tenure.

John Burder Hipps had served as a Southern Baptist missionary in China for thirty-six years prior to coming to Southeastern. He had taught and served in administrative positions at the University of Shanghai. He and his wife, Margaret Stroh Hipps, reluctantly left China in September of 1949 as a result of the fall of Shanghai to the Communists earlier that year. Students in Burder Hipps' classes at Southeastern will remember that he had such a storehouse of "China lore" that it was as if he had never left China! Dr. Hipps, who was sixty-seven years of age in 1951, continued to teach at Southeastern through the 1956–1957 session. He was a man who shared a world vision of Christianity with his students and who encouraged his younger colleagues to give attention to the relationship between Christian thought and effective, progressive Christian action.

William C. Strickland came with Dr. Stealey from Louisville. During his graduate work at Southern, Strickland had served as a teaching fellow in Theology. Strickland completed his doctoral work at Louisville in his early years at Southeastern and advanced in rank accordingly. Bill Strickland as a teacher of New Testament and Greek demanded of himself and of his students a continuous dialogue with the New Testament, and he inspired students to work hard in order to understand, to teach, and to preach from the New Testament. Many times he reminded students that a difficult exegetical or hermeneutical matter would be resolved if the students themselves would "yield to study."

Marc H. Lovelace was already established as a teacher in the department of Religion at Wake Forest College when the seminary opened. After serving as a visiting professor during the 1951–1952 session, while retaining his position with the college, Lovelace was elected by Southeastern trustees as associate professor of Archaeology in 1952. From that date Professor Lovelace served very effectively as a full-time teacher in the seminary. He tempered exacting demands of students with a sense of humor and a vivid portrayal of his subject matter. He helped generations of Southeasterners to understand the importance of archaeology, geography, and the history of the canonization of scripture for effective interpretation of the Bible.

In preparation for the first year of operation, the seminary published a brief *Bulletin* as a catalog in 1951. It contains the earliest published statement of purpose of Southeastern. Because of the importance of this early statement, both then and in future years, I am quoting it in its entirety.

> The aim of the seminary is to enable its students to arrive at a full understanding of the origins, content, and history of the Christian faith and of its applicability to the needs of the world. Courses of study which contribute to such an understanding are the core of the curriculum. The needs both at home and abroad will be studied; and the seminary will be always mindful of the immediate needs of its own constituency. Training in the specific skills of the ministry is provided.
>
> To these ends the seminary proposes to maintain a faculty of teachers who are especially qualified by training for such tasks. It proposes also to maintain high standards of achievement in both the intellectual and spiritual spheres.

It is believed that these ideals can be realized in consonance with consecrated hearts, clear heads, established facts, and good English.[6]

Dr. Stealey, faculty, and trustees undertook a Herculean task in opening the seminary in September 1951. President Stealey and Mr. Robinson arrived in June, and three months later the school opened. Two local trustees, Dr. J. Glenn Blackburn, pastor of Wake Forest Baptist Church, and Dr. John W. Kincheloe, Jr., pastor of Hayes Barton Baptist Church in Raleigh, had worked on many of the details that required attention prior to June of 1951. Such was the helpful spirit that was manifested in those beginning months.

There is something intoxicating about a new venture, and, although the first year was unique, the excitement of new beginnings continued. Professor Edward A. McDowell, Jr., in an address in 1970, recalled:

Even before we came [to Southeastern] some of us dreamed of a seminary which, because it was new, would be free of inhibiting traditions and open in spirit and vision to the future. . . . We were conscious that we were laying the foundation of a new seminary and charting the course of an institution that would be free in spirit and loyal to the truth as revealed in Jesus Christ. In all of this Syd Stealey was our fellow worker and inspired leader.[7]

1952–1956: Growth and Development

Five years remained before the college would move and the seminary would be in full and sole possession of the campus. These years found trustees, administration, faculty, and students busily engaged in the educational and professional aspects of the developing school. Simultaneously, plans were being formulated to insure prompt and effective modification of the physical plant in 1956 and the years beyond.

President Stealey gave top priority to the growth of the faculty. Experienced, highly regarded, and top quality theological educators joined the faculty in 1952. Two came from teaching posts at Southern, two from Southwestern, one from a strategic pastorate, and one from Wake Forest College. People across the Southern Baptist Convention territory, and especially those in other seminaries and colleges, expressed amazement, envy, joy, and incredulity at Dr. Stealey's successes. Many began to speak of President Stealey as President Steal - y!

Edward Allison McDowell, Jr., came from Southern after seventeen years of service to become professor of New Testament. Olin Trivette Binkley gave up his eight-year occupancy at Southern to become professor of Christian Sociology and Ethics. Stewart A. Newman and Robert T. Daniel left positions long held at Southwestern to come to the new seminary, Newman as professor of Theology and Philosophy of Religion and Daniel as professor of Old Testament. M. Ray McKay left a prestigious pastorate and a record as a premier preacher when he moved from Second Baptist Church, Little Rock, Arkansas, to become professor of Preaching at Southeastern. Marc H. Lovelace moved from Wake Forest College's department of Religion to teach Archaeology at Southeastern.

While it is undoubtedly true that every faculty appointment is important, it is probably accurate to say that the 1952 additions were the most significant ones during Stealey's tenure as president, especially when viewed from the perspective of advancing the place of the new seminary in the convention and in theological schools across the nation. The February 1952 meeting of the board of trustees was a happy occasion, especially so because of the election of these six men in a unanimous standing vote. The board also elected W. Perry Crouch as chairman, replacing C. C. Warren, who had resigned from the board. Emery B. Denny was elected vice-chairman; J. Glenn Blackburn, secretary; and William L. Wyatt, treasurer.

The enrollment more than doubled the second academic year. Two hundred and thirty students enrolled, representing sixteen states and forty-nine colleges. Many applicants were denied admission due to the lack of space.

Professor Olin T. Binkley spoke at the chapel service for the orientation of new students on 9 September 1952. His message, which dealt with essential elements of the common life of the school, was entitled "Fundamental Emphases." Binkley said the primary purpose of the school was a many-sided and demanding task to prepare men and women for Christian leadership for the present and future generations. To achieve this purpose called for a program of theological education with three fundamental emphases: (1) The seminary is a community of learning. This task requires attention to the serious business of Christian scholarship in which hard work is accompanied by reliance on the Holy Spirit, who will lead learners in the way of truth and empower the community of learners "to think effectively, to preach the gospel of Christ ardently," and to guide persons toward Christian maturity. (2) The seminary is a community of faith. The primary loyalty is to Jesus Christ, "to whom we have responded affirmatively and gratefully." (3) The seminary is a community of action. A close and vital relation is sought between study on the campus and service in the churches. To implement this emphasis a program of supervised field work is anticipated in which students can earn and serve while they learn and, at the same time, make "a genuine contribution to the churches in this area." Binkley closed his message by expressing the hope "that the total program of the school will help to adorn the gospel of Christ and the ethic of righteousness and love which issue out of it."[8]

By the second year the library contained approximately 9,000 volumes. The school employed Edwin C. Osburn as catalogue librarian. Mr. Osburn remained with the seminary until his retirement on 31 July 1967. He accomplished the task of cataloging and, in addition, became librarian and associate professor of Bibliography. Mr. Osburn was one of the inadequately heralded heroes of Southeastern. He was eventually given faculty status.

Attention was given from the earliest days to the acquisition of a good theological library and the integration of the resources of the library into the teaching, research, and study functions of the faculty and students. The school was given valuable books from the libraries of such notables as L. L. Carpenter and J. Clyde Turner. The first sizable gift was the library of William Hersey Davis, an eminent New Testament teacher at Southern Seminary. Following Professor Davis's death, his wife and son gave this excellent collection to Southeastern Seminary.

Three hundred and forty-three students attended Southeastern during its third year, 1953–1954. Seventeen states and forty-nine colleges were represented. Five persons were added to the faculty. Pope A. Duncan left a position in the Religion Department at Stetson University to become associate professor of Church History. Richard K. Young, director of the School of Pastoral Care at North Carolina Baptist Hospital, was elected to serve on a part-time basis as associate professor of Pastoral Care. Garland A. Hendricks of the faculty of Gardner-Webb College was elected to the position of associate professor of Church-Community Development and director of Field Work. John T. Wayland left the position as pastor of the First Baptist Church of North Wilkesboro, North

Carolina, to accept the position of professor of Religious Education. Ben C. Fisher joined the faculty as assistant professor of Religious Education and also began his work as administrative assistant to the president and director of Public Relations.

The persons who joined the faculty in 1953–1954 gave continuity to the classical theological emphases, as in the case of Pope A. Duncan, teacher of General Church History and Baptist History. There appeared, also, some important innovations. Garland A. Hendricks developed and directed throughout his tenure the earliest program of required supervised ministry for all the students in a Southern Baptist seminary. John T. Wayland inaugurated the first three-year degree program in Religious Education in a Southern Baptist seminary. Richard K. Young developed a model program in which the seminary and the School of Pastoral Care of the North Carolina Baptist Hospital collaborated in offering several levels of work in Clinical Pastoral Education. The 1953–1954 session, therefore, witnessed a considerable strengthening of the practical side of theological education.

Southeastern graduated its first class in the spring of 1954. Sixty-three men received the Bachelor of Divinity degree. The first graduate was William Franklin Askins. J. W. Storer, president of the Southern Baptist Convention, and Southeastern Seminary president Stealey were the commencement speakers. The alumni association was formed.

A number of the graduates had expressed interest in pursuing further academic studies. The school, consequently, began to offer the Th.M. degree in 1955. This degree, requiring twenty hours of course work in seminars and special courses, and also research and the writing of a thesis, proved to be a very good educational experience. For some students it served as a way to determine whether or not they should apply to enter a Ph.D. program following completion of the Th.M. work. Through the succeeding years a number of students decided to enter Ph.D. work and were accepted into good programs in first-rate graduate schools in this nation and elsewhere. I have been told by several of these students that the Th.M. served to prepare them for the rigorous Ph.D. work. Other students, some of them quite capable of doing further graduate work, decided to use the Th.M. degree as their terminal degree experience. From the graduation of the first Th.M. class in April 1955, our overall experience with the Southeastern Th.M. degree has been positive.

At a meeting of the board of trustees held in St. Louis, Missouri, on 2 June 1954, Denton R. Coker was elected assistant professor of Religious Education. He came from Southern's faculty and began his teaching in the fall of 1954.

The student enrollment reached 392 in the 1954–1955 session. Others who desired to attend could not be admitted due to limited space. L. J. Morriss, an employee of the Baptist State Convention of North Carolina, was a part-time teacher in religious education. Paul S. Robinson, a music teacher in Wake Forest College, was also employed to teach music in the seminary that session on a part-time and temporary basis. In December 1954 the seminary began to work toward accreditation by becoming an associate member of the American Association of Theological Schools (eventually renamed the Association of Theological Schools).

The 1955–1956 session opened with fourteen full-time and four part-time faculty members. Four hundred and fifty-nine students enrolled. The library had continued to grow, with 20,000 catalogued volumes by this time. The faculty had a very active library committee that met frequently and carefully considered acquisition requests. A small library staff, headed by Librarian Osburn, worked effectively and prodigiously.

Joseph R. Robinson died at his desk on 3 June 1955. He was the first person employed by President Stealey. Robinson dealt with business matters, served as registrar, assisted with various administrative tasks, and on occasion taught classes. He was the first seminary staff person to die and the first to be buried in the Southeastern Seminary cemetery. He gave a full measure of devotion to the school from the pre-opening days in 1951 until he was released from his tasks by death.

In the 1955–1956 session, J. Carroll Trotter, Jr., started teaching Homiletics and Speech, and James E. Tull Theology. B. Elmo Scoggin, a Southern Baptist missionary to Israel, was a visiting professor of Missions. These three colleagues remained with the seminary until they reached retirement, serving with distinction. (Their imprints are noted elsewhere in this volume.)

The administrative staff was enlarged with the employment of Gordon M. Funk as business manager and Fred Sandusky as registrar. Both men came at a time of need for their services, and each of them brought consecrated skills to their tasks. Funk served throughout the remainder of President Stealey's tenure and through a time of transition with President Binkley. Funk resigned to accept another position, and Sandusky continued as registrar until his retirement in 1985.

Fred Sandusky, whose first day of service was 7 March 1955, and whose day of self-chosen retirement was 7 March 1985, worked with three presidents, hundreds of students, and every person who taught during these years. He dealt with students from pre-admission through graduation. He became an "institution" within the institution, and he continues to be held in the affection and esteem of persons whose lives and careers he touched.

The session of 1955–1956 was the last year of joint occupancy of the campus by Wake Forest College and Southeastern Seminary. On 1 July 1956 the seminary came into full possession of its campus. Important and multidimensional tasks demanded immediate attention. An old era ended, and a new one began for two institutions with the relocation of Wake Forest College to its Winston-Salem campus in June 1956.

1956–1960: Living With Growth in Larger Surroundings

The particular reasons that Southeastern came to acquire the campus occupied for 122 years by Wake Forest College can be traced to developments pertaining to the college in the late 1930s and 1940s. Assets of the Bowman Gray Foundation of Winston-Salem were offered to the college in 1939 on the condition of moving the two-year medical school to Winston-Salem and expanding it to a four-year school to be associated with the already present Baptist Hospital. Wake Forest's trustees accepted the offer, and the Bowman Gray School of Medicine opened in Winston-Salem in 1941.

Five years later, in 1946, the Z. Smith Reynolds Foundation offered an annual grant in perpetuity if the college would move to Winston-Salem. Members of the Reynolds family offered, in addition, to give land to the college on which the buildings would be located. Following acceptance by the board of trustees of this arrangement, the Baptist State Convention, in a special session in Greensboro in the summer of 1946, approved the move. After taking a decade to build necessary buildings and to prepare the new campus, Wake Forest College opened in Winston-Salem on 18 June 1956.

The trustees of Wake Forest College sold the facilities of the college in the town of Wake Forest to the Southern Baptist Convention in 1950 for the sum of $1,600,000. This was generally considered to be an excellent acquisition for the price, in view of the evaluation by a recognized firm that placed the value of land and buildings, less depreciation, at more than $3,000,000.

What property did the seminary receive as a result of this purchase? Land acreage of 469.7 acres; nineteen college buildings; an athletic field; a football stadium with a seating capacity of 15,000; all-weather tennis courts; a nine-hole golf course; and ten residences comprised the real estate. The main part of the campus consisted of twenty-five acres enclosed in a plot set within a rock wall. The seminary received funds to pay for the campus, plus funds to repair, remodel, and add new buildings largely through the capital funds appropriations of the Southern Baptist Convention.

The seminary and Wake Forest College lived together on the Wake County campus for five years, 1951–1956. Agreements were worked out for the seminary to pay its share of the operating expenses and to pay student fees based on enrollment, such fees being used to pay for shared services. Early in the joint occupancy, the college entered into an agreement with the seminary promising to vacate the premises and release the property no later than 1 July 1956. This promise was kept. In general it appears that the two institutions lived together harmoniously.

Planning the renovation of the campus had begun early in the seminary's history. The board of trustees had an active buildings and grounds committee and also a long-range planning committee. The latter committee was composed of trustee, administrative, and faculty representatives. The buildings were inspected by construction engineers, and the architectural firm of Six Associates of Asheville, North Carolina, worked on renovation and on plans for new construction. It was estimated that the first phase of the renovation program would cost $1,000,000. A plan was approved by the trustees in 1955 in which the details for the first phase were indicated and a timetable was set up. Much of the renovation was done under the supervision of Frank M. Swett, superintendent of buildings and grounds. New construction, including the cafeteria, was by contractors.

The summer of 1956 was an unusually busy time in Wake Forest. There was a slight delay in the opening of the fall semester, but the autumn of 1956 was a great time as the seminary community settled into the larger quarters in which to live and work. The following paragraph records some of the results of the initial phase of the renovation program:

> In the early summer of 1956 Wake Forest College moved to its new college in Winston-Salem, leaving the seminary in full occupancy of its Wake Forest home. The board of trustees had been engaged in plans for the renovation and remodeling of the campus and its buildings, and during the summer crews were at work everywhere, readying the buildings for use in the fall. A new cafeteria was constructed and was in use in November. Two dormitories were converted to apartment buildings, the chemistry building was turned into a bookstore and student center, and the administration building was remodeled to provide office spaces. Furnishings were bought and placed in classrooms, dormitories, and apartment buildings, and offices. The library, now containing more than 24,000 volumes, continued to occupy its cramped quarters in the Music and Religion Building while the work of demolishing the condemned part of the old library building and of replacing it with a new three-story structure was under way. During the year work was begun on the chapel interior, which had been left by the college as an unfinished auditorium.[9]

Enrollment reached 681 in the 1956–1957 session. One hundred and twelve students graduated. Four new members of the faculty were added. Thomas A. Bland came from William Jewell College's faculty to become assistant professor of Christian Sociology and Ethics. E. Luther Copeland arrived from Seinan Gakuin University in Japan to assume the position of associate professor of Missions. B. Elmo Scoggin left the mission field in Israel to take up duties as associate professor of Old Testament. John E. Steely moved from a faculty position at Southern Baptist College, Walnut Ridge, Arkansas, to the post as assistant professor of Historical Theology. In addition, Thelma Arnote became special instructor in Religious Education. Ben S. Johnson began service as special instructor in Music. William L. Palmer was instructor in Greek, and J. Henry Coffer served as instructor in Religious Education.

The first summer school, a four-week session, was held in the summer of 1957. One hundred and twenty students were enrolled. The seminary also sponsored its first summer conference.

The 1957–1958 session was one of growth and physical expansion. The enrollment reached 714. One hundred and thirty-seven students graduated in January and May commencement exercises. The library renovation was completed, and the holdings—now consisting of 28,000 catalogued volumes—were moved into the spacious new building where enlarged services were provided. The remodeling of the chapel was completed, and the first services held in that beautiful worship center were those of the May commencement. Thelma Arnote became associate professor of Religious Education, the first woman to be elected to the faculty. R. C. Briggs of Union University began his work as professor of New Testament. John W. Eddins, Jr., and Harold H. Oliver were named special instructors, Eddins in Theology and Oliver in New Testament.

In June 1958 Southeastern Seminary was accredited by the American Association of Theological Schools. This accreditation was granted as early as possible in the school's history, a requirement of the AATS being the graduation of three classes before accreditation could be granted. In addition to this requirement, the seminary had been thoroughly and comprehensively examined by a team of eminent theological educators sent to the campus by AATS. Accreditation is an important achievement, a recognition of competency, and a link into a network with other institutions of quality. We rejoiced to have our efforts validated. It should be noted that the level of work at Southeastern was recognized to be of sufficient merit to enable the transfer of credit to outstanding institutions prior to the 1958 granting of accreditation.

Southeastern functioned for several years without a dean. Faculty committees were very active, and the faculty in session approved or disapproved the work of its committees. Every student was assigned a faculty advisor. President Stealey, an experienced academician, and Fred Sandusky, registrar, administered numerous academic matters. By the seventh session it was increasingly evident that the position of dean should be established. One compelling reason, among others, was to provide an opportunity for the president to devote more time to other aspects of administration. Consequently, the board of trustees created the office of dean of the faculty. Professor Olin T. Binkley was named dean of the faculty. Dean Binkley began in this office at the end of the spring semester of 1958 and continued to serve until he became president on 1 August 1963. His service as dean of the faculty was highly acceptable and enhanced the academic community. An appreciative faculty, polled in 1963 on the possibility of Dean Binkley being nominated to become president upon Dr. Stealey's retirement, gave a unanimous endorsement of their colleague, O. T. Binkley.

During the 1958–1959 session, another phase of the campus development program began. In the summer of 1958 construction began on duplex apartment buildings for students, and before the opening of the 1959 session twenty-five buildings had been completed, offering comfortable and reasonably priced housing for fifty student families. A long-standing need had been addressed.

There had also been a desire to have a suitable building to house the child care program. This program was designed to serve in the preparation of ministers in their pastoral and education ministries with children. Of importance, likewise, was the provision of a child care experience for children of seminarians. The seminary was successful in combining funds received from a bequest with gifts from the Baptist Sunday School Board and the Z. Smith Reynolds Foundation to construct the building. Miss Ruby Reid, a Wake Forest resident, left a sum of money in her estate for Southeastern Seminary. This money was a part of the funding for the child care building. In recognition of such support by a citizen of the town, the name chosen for the building was the Ruby Reid Child Care Center.

Enrollment reached 752 in the session of 1958–1959. John W. Eddins, Jr., signed the Abstract of Principles at the beginning of the fall semester as he took up the duties of assistant professor of Theology. The spring meeting of the American Society of Church History was held on the campus in April 1959.

The seminary gave Groves Stadium to the Wake County board of education for use by the Wake Forest High School, a gift applauded in the Wake Forest community.

The death of Professor Robert T. Daniel on 16 May 1959 brought grief and shock to the seminary community and his many other friends. He was the first member of the faculty to die. He was a driven man with great ability as a scholar and teacher of Old Testament. In a struggle with illness, and in acute depression, he took his life the day after commencement.

Emily K. Lansdell gave up the presidency of the Carver School of Missions and Social Work in Louisville, Kentucky, to join Southeastern's faculty in the fall of 1959 as professor of Missions. She was the second woman to be elected to the faculty. George H. Shriver and John Durham served as instructors, Shriver in Church History and Durham in Old Testament. J. D. Sistrunk became associate librarian. The total enrollment in the 1959–1960 session was 779.

Jesse Burton Weatherspoon, following his retirement from the faculty of Southern Seminary, began a tour of duty at Southeastern in the fall of 1959 as visiting professor of Preaching, a position he retained through the 1962–1963 session. A widower for a number of years, he married Professor Emily K. Lansdell in 1962.

A highlight of the fall semester was the dedication of the Reuter organ in the chapel on 1 October 1959. The organ was the gift of Mr. and Mrs. Walter M. Williams of Burlington, North Carolina. Mr. Williams, a devout Baptist layman, was a member of the seminary's board of trustees. Prior to his death on 4 May 1959 he provided funds for the purchase and installation of the organ.

The Last Years of the Stealey Presidency: 1960–1963

The seminary observed the tenth anniversary of its founding during the 1960–1961 session. Enrollment was 736. Max Gray Rogers began his teaching career, coming as instructor of Old Testament.

The trustees gave special recognition to President Stealey by naming the administration building Stealey Hall. The building originally bore the name of Samuel Wait, first president of Wake Forest College. On 16 February 1961 the seminary's trustees voted to change the name to honor the founding president of the school now in possession of the campus. When W. Perry Crouch, trustee chairman, announced the action in a chapel service on 17 February, the news was received with hearty approval. Dr. Stealey made a brief response. He expressed his gratitude for the honor. Then, with a twinkle in his eyes, he said, "Brethren, not many men have the privilege to live in their own tomb. I am grateful for this honor!"

The seminary acquired additional property in 1961 through the purchase of a large residence located at 321 Durham Road. By this time there were larger numbers of women students, and it would be 1965 before the women's dormitory was built. The trustees learned of the availability of Miss Jo Williams' large house and bought it for $55,000. "The Manor Guest House" continues to serve as the seminary's official facility for housing special guests.

There was concern from the first year of the seminary and through all the years that we not become an isolated, insulated community. A program of special lectures, preaching events, and missionary emphases was inaugurated. Eventually there were some endowed lectureships. In the tenth-anniversary year, the chief executive of the Foreign Mission Board, Baker James Cauthen, and Courts Redford of the Home Mission Board gave Missionary Day addresses. Samuel H. Miller, dean of Harvard Divinity School, opened the session with a convocation address. Albert C. Outler, professor of Theology in the Perkins School of Theology of Southern Methodist University, gave a series of lectures, and Clarence Cranford, pastor of Calvary Baptist church, Washington, D. C., preached in a week of special spiritual renewal services.

By 1961 the need for students to have regular access to professionally trained Christian counselors had surfaced with the faculty and members of the seminary's administration. On 16 February 1961, Truman S. Smith, a well-trained and compassionate Christian counselor who was then serving as instructor in Pastoral Counseling and assistant director of Field Work, was elected by the trustees as director of Student Activities and instructor in Pastoral Counseling. He was specifically directed to give attention to all areas of the life and welfare of the student body and of individual students. Mr. Smith performed these responsibilities effectively throughout his tenure in this position.

R. Eugene Owens joined the faculty as assistant professor of Preaching at the beginning of the 1961–1962 session. Harold H. Oliver was elected assistant professor of New Testament and moved forward in the teaching career he began earlier as special instructor. The teaching force was augmented in 1961–1962, as in most years, by several visiting and adjunctive teachers.

The building in which the new seminary had begun its work in 1951 was called the Music-Religion Building by college personnel. On 15 February 1962 the Southeastern board of trustees renamed the building the Scott B. Appleby Building in recognition of Mr. Appleby's generous gifts to the student aid fund.

Dr. S. L. Stealey informed a joint meeting of the executive committee and the instruction committee of the board of trustees on 16 January 1962 that he would be sixty-five years old on 7 March 1962. Because he felt burdened by the heavy demands of the presidency and was concerned that his strength was insufficient, he announced his desire to retire 1 August 1962 or as soon thereafter as was practicable. The trustees present asked the chairman of the board, the chairman of the finance committee, and the chairman of the instruction committee to bring a recommendation on how to proceed in this matter.

In the meeting of the board of trustees on 15 February 1962, Judge Denny brought a recommendation from the group identified above and from consultation with President Stealey and Dean Binkley. Dr. Stealey was asked to continue as president through 31 July 1963. Dean Binkley was asked to take on responsibilities of the president's office in ways mutually agreeable between Stealey and Binkley. Binkley's teaching load would be reduced. This recommendation was adopted, the plan was implemented, and the process of an orderly transition in the seminary administration was begun.[10]

The 1962–1963 session, President Stealey's final year, brought 595 students to enroll. This number represented a decline, but it was a part of the national trend of the 1960s.

President Stealey was honored in a number of ways as he approached retirement. He was named president emeritus; given a year's pay in recognition, in part at least, that he had not received any sabbatical leave time; and provided additional benefits to continue through the year in which he would attain the age of seventy. He was presented a new automobile by trustees and other friends of the seminary. A beautiful laudatory resolution was adopted by the trustees, who also expressed gratitude to Mrs. Jessie Wheeler Stealey, Sydnor's beloved wife.

Dr. Stealey delivered the "Charge" to the graduates at commencement on 3 May 1963. It was vintage Stealey. He spoke of "four things, three things, two things and one person." His wisdom and experience in Baptist life came through in the following statement:

> The second set of three things is the tripod or trilogy of strength for Christian and denominational cooperation. The dynamic words are Missions, Evangelism, Education. . . . Christian statesmen you can never be if you seriously lengthen or shorten any one leg, for the tripod topples and Christian objectives become grotesque forms of ingrown scholasticism or obscurantism or crass selfishness.[11]

"Creative Continuity in Theological Education": Olin T. Binkley

The journey that brought Olin Binkley to succeed S. L. Stealey as president of Southeastern Seminary was marked by significant milestones and some unexpected turns in the roadway.

First, the unexpected turns. Binkley had declined to serve as Southeastern's first president because he concluded that he could not then undertake the burdens of administrative work. Stealey was elected in 1951. He invited Binkley to join the faculty of the new seminary. Binkley came to Southeastern in 1952 to continue his teaching of Ethics and Sociology. In 1958 President Stealey and the faculty asked Dr. Binkley to take up the work of dean of the faculty. Then, in 1963, after the two men had worked closely together in administration, Dr. Binkley succeeded Dr. Stealey as president. Dr. Stealey wrote, "I am very proud that Binkley is succeeding me."

The significant milestones along the way to the presidency are identifiable in the experience of Olin Trivette Binkley. He was born in Iredell County, North Carolina, the son of the Reverend Joseph N. and Minnie Trivette Binkley. Rev. J. N. Binkley spent sixty-one years in the Baptist ministry, over fifty-one of them at the same rural church, Holly Springs, near Harmony. Mrs. Minnie Binkley also had a profound influence on her son's life. The family heritage was a positive Christian influence.

Olin Binkley's personal commitment to Christ has been nurtured by a sense of inner persuasion and an unashamed outward expression of the way of life to be seen in Jesus of Nazareth.

An exceptionally bright mind, combined with diligent work, contributed to a brilliant school career. A magna cum laude graduate with the B.A. degree from Wake Forest College, Binkley excelled as a student at the Southern Baptist Theological Seminary. With the Th.B. from Southern, Olin Binkley went to the Yale Divinity School, from which he received the B.D. degree in 1931. In 1933 he received the Ph.D. degree from Yale University. He is a member of Phi Beta Kappa.

Dr. Binkley and Miss Pauline Eichmann of New Haven, Connecticut, have been husband and wife since 24 August 1933. They have worked together as a cooperative team all of the years they have shared together.

Following a pastorate in New Haven, Connecticut, where he served as associate pastor of the Calvary Baptist Church from 1931 to 1933, the Binkleys came to Chapel Hill, North Carolina. Olin Binkley served as pastor of the Baptist Church of Chapel Hill (now University Baptist Church) from 1933 until 1938. Although he moved away from that community more than fifty-five years ago, his ministry is still remembered there with affirmation and appreciation of his pastoral care and prophetic ministry among students, faculty, and townspeople.

Dr. Binkley has said that he thinks of his "fundamental purpose" in life "primarily in terms of a pastoral and teaching ministry." He has found ways to bring these emphases together in academic settings in which he has worked.

Olin Binkley was a lecturer in sociology at the University of North Carolina in 1937 and 1938. In 1938 he became head of the department of Religion at Wake Forest College, where he remained until 1944. He taught Ethics and Sociology from 1944 to 1952 at the Southern Baptist Theological Seminary. He returned to the town of Wake Forest in 1952, but to a different institution. He joined the Southeastern faculty in 1952 as professor of Christian Sociology and Ethics. He continued to teach during the years he served as dean of the faculty, 1958–1963. As he approached his call to the presidency, he saw the work he would do as "being in harmony with the work as dean," a work he described as "sharing the heavy responsibilities upon the president" and of "assisting the faculty in educational leadership." More milestones passed on the journey!

Binkley was the unanimous choice of trustees and faculty as successor to Stealey. A journalist for the Raleigh *News and Observer* wrote of him, "When young Southeastern Baptist Theological Seminary at Wake Forest marks a milestone August 1 with the installation of its second president, it will come under the direction of a teacher-theologian whose leadership has the virtual universal approbation of the Southern Baptist denomination."

I have heard Dr. Binkley speak on occasion about the peril of being subjected to unreasonable expectations and incompatible demands. He has not made this reference in my presence concerning the tasks of a president. His terms, however, certainly describe what many an administrator experiences. Olin Binkley did not enter the office of president unaware of what he faced. He had to continue to address and seek to resolve serious matters. There was unfinished business to be completed. We will get to these matters soon.

Between the time of his election and his inauguration, Binkley was invited to give the address on theological education to the 1963 meeting of the Southern Baptist Convention in Kansas City. He made a plea for Southern Baptists to love and trust their theological faculties. He spoke as one who had spent years "in unrelenting toil" in classrooms. He spoke to the convention about three characteristics of the essential nature of theological schools: (1) A theological school is a community of learning. He warned against "diluting and damaging" the quality of the work if, "at this convention or elsewhere," the springs of Christian scholarship are quenched. (2) A theological school is a community of faith. The Holy Spirit is our teacher. We must not resist, grieve, or quench the Holy Spirit. (3) A seminary subjects itself to critical and constructive self-examination. Quoting a passage of scripture the President-elect held out hope: ". . . our sufficiency is from God, who has qualified us to be ministers of a new covenant . . ." (2 Cor 3:5-6).

Binkley entered the presidency on 1 August 1963. His inauguration was on Thursday, 17 October 1963. The title of his inaugural address was "Creative Continuity in Theological Education." He pledged creative continuity, including creative continuity between the Stealey administration and the new administration. He thanked Dr. Stealey for his leadership and the solid accomplishments of the first twelve years in Southeastern's history. He declared that "the fundamental purpose of the Southeastern Baptist Theological Seminary is to seek a deeper knowledge of God as revealed in Jesus Christ and to guide the intellectual and spiritual growth of students for the diversified ministries of the churches and the agencies of the denomination." The President then spoke of four essentials of excellence in a theological school: (1) systematic and thorough study; (2) financial resources and their utilization in ways that give priority to the educational aim, both in the annual budget and in long range plans; (3) the sincere worship of God; and (4) indefectible loyalty to Jesus Christ and his way of life. Binkley referred to the generous tenure policy at Southeastern. He then said, "This policy of tenure gives no sanction or protection whatsoever to the betrayal of trust or to disloyalty to Jesus Christ as he is presented to us in the New Testament." He closed with this sentence: "It is our prayer that the men and women who go out from this community of faith and of learning will be courageous prophets of God's redemptive purpose and trustworthy interpreters of His authoritative and life-giving Word."[12]

In the two addresses referred to above, Olin Binkley was giving a confessional statement of the milestones that had marked his own journey with the Lord, and he was also saying that these emphases would be the milestones to mark the way in which he would seek to lead the seminary during his presidency.

On 11 June 1964 President Olin Binkley was elected president of the American Association of Theological Schools. He had worked in various capacities with the association over a period of several years.

The History of "A Complex Issue"

Reference has been made to unfinished business requiring the attention of President Binkley. On 18 February 1965 the board of trustees approved the following statement for release "in an effort to give a true version of a complex issue which has troubled the Southeastern Baptist Theological Seminary."

The statement is the most complete account of what happened between 1960 and 1965 that I have seen:

> In 1960 a problem emerged in the life of the school. The theological dimension of the difficulty was related to the interpretation of the New Testament. Disavowing any desire to interfere with the freedom and tenure of colleagues, some members of the faculty strongly opposed the predominance of one point of view in the interpretation of the New Testament, a point of view associated with the exegetical method and conclusions of Rudolf Bultmann concerning the nature and message of the New Testament. The faculty was divided and theological communication broke down between the groups. After attempts to resolve the problem had failed, and after he had informed the faculty of his intention, President S. L. Stealey appealed to the trustees for help.
>
> The committee on instruction of the board of trustees spent May 15–17, 1961 on the campus and interviewed members of the faculty.
>
> These interviews revealed that interpersonal relations within the faculty had been damaged by earlier conversations regarding trends in New Testament studies and fractured by the decision of a few professors not to discuss theology with their colleagues. The committee made no formal charge against any member of the faculty but it reported concern about faculty morale and the doctrinal presuppositions of certain members of the instructional staff to the board of trustees.

Upon the recommendation of the committee on instruction, the board of trustees in its annual meeting on February 15, 1962 authorized procedures aimed at clarification of issues through consultation, including a process of inquiry and counsel with some members of the faculty. It was agreed that the committee on instruction should complete this assignment by February 18, 1965.

In the search for a constructive solution of the exceptionally complicated problem, the trustees and administration have exercised restraint, forbearance, and fairness. They have made no formal charge of deviation from the Abstract of Principles against any member of the instructional staff and no professor has been requested to resign, nor has any member of the faculty been pressured to do so.

As an alternative to a continuation of his participation in the process of inquiry and counsel authorized by the board of trustees, Dr. R. C. Briggs preferred to resign. On October 19, 1964 he arranged a conference with the president and informed him that he had decided to resign provided satisfactory adjustments could be made. He stated that he preferred to terminate his service at the end of the 1964 fall semester.

After a series of consultations with trustees, including the president of the board and the chairman of the committee on instruction, and after allowing ample time for Dr. Briggs to rethink his decision, the president drafted a statement which included Dr. Briggs' stipulations and which was approved by him on December 15, 1964.

The proposal set forth in this statement provided (1) that Dr. R. C. Briggs be permitted to terminate his membership in the faculty by resignation effective January 2, 1965; (2) that the provision in the policy regarding sabbatical leave that a professor must return to the service of the seminary for at least one year after the completion of a leave or return one-third of the salary paid him during his leave be waived in this instance; and (3) that his salary plus a sum equivalent to what the seminary would have expended during the period involved for his fringe benefits be paid through December 31, 1966.

The proposal was recommended unanimously by the committee on instruction and approved unanimously by the executive committee of the board of trustees, meeting in executive session, on December 17, 1964.

This action of the committees was reported by telephone to the other members of the board and in the conversations by telephone the trustees expressed approval of the proposal adopted by the executive committee.

The decision of the trustees to pay Dr. Briggs' salary through 1966 was based upon several considerations: (1) Dr. Briggs' resignation was conditioned upon the payment of salary through December 31, 1966; (2) he was a full professor with tenure and had no plans for immediate employment; and (3) the trustees and the administration desired to be just and generous.

In harmony with the instruction of the trustees, the administration announced on December 29, 1964 that the resignation of Dr. R. C. Briggs as professor of New Testament had been accepted with regret by the executive committee.

The trustees are profoundly grateful for the devotion and faithful work of the able and dedicated teachers who comprise the faculty and regret the excessive and unwarranted criticisms which have been made of them.

Throughout his career Dr. Olin T. Binkley has placed high value upon academic excellence in the education of ministers. The trustees have unqualified confidence in his personal integrity and professional competence. They will support him and the teachers and students who cooperate with him in the advancement of theological studies at the Southeastern Baptist Theological Seminary.

The administration and trustees from the beginning have observed with utmost care the principle of responsible academic freedom. The requirement regarding the theological covenant outlined in the Abstract of Principles and signed by each member of the faculty is fully compatible with the document on academic freedom and tenure which was adopted as an advisory norm by the American Association of Theological Schools in 1960 and which explicitly states that a theological institution may expect its faculty to subscribe to a confessional or doctrinal standard.

This is a Southern Baptist seminary, established and maintained by the Southern Baptist Convention, and it is the responsibility of the trustees to formulate policies in harmony with the nature and purpose of the school. The faculty and students are encouraged to participate in creative theological inquiry and to make effective use of the resources of this school which is thorough in scholarship, sound in Christian theology, and vitally related to the churches.

Approved and adopted unanimously by the board of trustees of the Southeastern Baptist Theological Seminary, February 18, 1965.

Some Other Significant Events between 1963 and 1974

During these years the following persons came to the faculty: John I Durham, Old Testament; Raymond B. Brown, New Testament; Donald E. Cook, New Testament; Archie L. Nations, New Testament; Robert E. Poerschke, Christian Education; J. Colin Harris, Christian Education; Ellis W. Hollon, Jr., Philosophy of Religion; John W. Carlton, Preaching; Thorwald Lorenzen, New Testament; Richard A. Spencer, New Testament; Ben Johnson, Music (he had come in 1956 as a special instructor in Music); Max Smith, Music (he first was employed in 1959 as artist in residence); George W. Braswell, Jr., Missions; Eugene McLeod, librarian; Donald Moore, Pastoral Care; Robert L. Richardson, Jr., Field Education and D.Min. program director; and James H. Blackmore, A.Div. Studies.

The following persons were brought into the administration: James H. Blackmore, public relations; Wilbur N. Todd, business manager; O. L. Cross, business manager; W. Christian Sizemore, library staff; James R. Moseley, M.D., seminary physician; Jerry Niswonger, development; David Lee, superintendent of buildings and grounds; John I Durham, acting dean and later associate to the president; Eugene McLeod, librarian; and Raymond B. Brown, academic dean.

Among those who served as visiting or adjunctive teachers were: Theodore F. Adams, Preaching; I. N. Patterson, Missions; Walter Ross, Music; Walter Sanders, Counseling; Charles L. Taylor, Old Testament; Roy Porter, Old Testament; Edward Hughes Pruden, History; and Jack Heath, Christian Education.

Persons who retired were: Edward A. McDowell, Jr.; M. Ray McKay; John T. Wayland; Richard K. Young; Frank M. Swett; and E. C. Osburn.

Deaths included: George C. Mackie, M.D.; Sydnor L. Stealey; and J. B. Hipps.

Buildings constructed were: Health Center; Women's Dormitory; Mackie Hall; and additional duplex apartments.

Buildings named were: Olin T. Binkley Chapel; Emery B. Denny Library Building; and Mackie Hall.

President Olin T. Binkley reached his sixty-fifth birthday on 4 August 1973. He announced soon thereafter his intention to retire at the end of the fiscal year. He retired on 31 July 1974.

Olin Binkley gave twenty-two years of his life to Southeastern Seminary, serving as teacher, dean, and president. His careful adherence to orderly and documented administrative procedures brought the school through a major crisis, and he led the institution to the threshold of a new era of unprecedented achievements accomplished during the years of service of his successor, President W. Randall Lolley.

Three Final Thoughts about 1951–1974

(1) We had many excellent trustees. They were persons who loved the school, who nurtured its early and more recent development, who saw trusteeship as a trust, and who respected the principles of shared governance. W. Perry Crouch, Emery B. Denny, Claud B. Bowen, and J. Glenn Blackburn are remembered as persons who served well in the position of

chair of the board. Emery B. Denny, chief justice of the supreme court in North Carolina, was involved as leader and/or supporter of progressive policy-making. His fine legal mind was of great value in the board's work. William L. Wyatt, Sr., was another layman whose skill in financial matters was extremely helpful. Doak Campbell, Phil Elliott, Robert Smart, and A. E. Tibbs brought their valued perspectives as professional educators. C. R. Daley and James O. Duncan possessed valuable insights as editors of Baptist papers. Earl Edington, Ralph Herring, Harold Seever, and Frank R. Campbell were pastors who affirmed the seminary and were of considerable help in its governance.

(2) We were fortunate in the leadership of Presidents Stealey and Binkley.

(3) We enjoyed a great Christian fellowship. This place was never Camelot, however, and we have always lived some distance east of Eden! Our thousands of alumni who are serving the Lord in Christian ministries all over the world are the living history, the epistles of commendation, and the validation of the work of those who served faithfully in the founding and building of Southeastern Baptist Theological Seminary.

Notes

[1]Pope A. Duncan, "Southeastern Baptist Theological Seminary," *Encyclopedia of Southern Baptists*, 4 vols. (Nashville: Broadman Press, 1958) 2: 1239-42.

[2]W. Perry Crouch, "The Beginnings of Southeastern Seminary," no date, 11 pages.

[3]Ibid., 11.

[4]"Trustee Minutes," 15 February 1951, 3.

[5]"Minutes," Trustees' Executive Committee, Robert E. Lee Hotel, Winston-Salem NC, 23 February 1951, 2.

[6]*Southeastern Baptist Theological Seminary Bulletin* (1951) 12.

[7]Edward A. McDowell, Jr., "S. L. Stealey, Southeastern's First President," *Outlook* 19/7 (July-August 1970): 32.

[8]Olin T. Binkley, "Fundamental Emphases," Chapel Talk at Orientation, Southeastern Baptist Theological Seminary, 9 September 1952, *Biblical Recorder*, 4 October 1952, 3.

[9]"A Brief History," Southeastern Baptist Theological Seminary, Founders' Day, 16 February 1961, 11.

[10]"Trustee Minutes," 15 February 1962, 7.

[11]Sydnor L. Stealey, "Charge to the Graduates, May 3, 1963," *Outlook* 13/2 (October 1963): 4.

[12]Copies of Binkley's address to the Southern Baptist Convention and his inaugural address are on file in the Southeastern Baptist Theological Seminary Library.

Chapter 2

Years of Pleasure and Pain: 1974–1988

W. Randall Lolley

I. One Hundred and Twenty Months of Pleasure: 1974–1984

Twenty years separate my two significant arrivals at Southeastern Seminary. In the fall 1954, I arrived as a student; in the fall 1974, I arrived as president. In 1988, when I concluded as president, the seminary was thirty-seven years old, having opened for classes in the fall 1951. I had been on the campus for eighteen of those thirty-seven years.

My student days were illumined by the glow of the founding dream of the seminary—to be a Southern Baptist school of the highest quality within the original territory of the Southern Baptist Convention (SBC). Here amidst the greatest concentration of churches anywhere in the country we would build a community of learning firmly anchored in the Bible, the classical body of divinity, and the liberal arts (that is, the liberating arts).

I arrived in the fall following Southeastern's first commencement. Wake Forest College and the seminary still jointly occupied the main campus in Wake Forest. Facilities were limited, but hopes ran high.

In 1956 the college moved to Winston-Salem. During the academic year 1956–1957 we expanded to occupy the campus. I served that year as president of the student body. Syd Stealey was the president, and Olin Binkley was the dean. Both were my teachers. Not in my wildest dreams could I have believed that I would follow these two as the third president of Southeastern.

My first graduation was 1957 (B.D. degree); my second was 1958 (Th.M. degree). I was more surprised than anyone to be told both times at the commencement exercises that I had achieved a perfect grade-point average. My theological mother had extracted the very best from me. In return, she had given me moorings in biblical, theological, historical, and practical studies that would mark my life forever. Her gifts to me have indelibly flavored my Southeastern presidency and my three pastorates since graduation—First Baptist Church, Winston-Salem; First Baptist Church, Raleigh; and First Baptist Church, Greensboro.

Stewart Newman's admonition came to pass. He told me at the conclusion of my very first visit to the campus, "Lolley, come on up here. We'll treat you so many ways, you'll have to like some of them."

Alma Mater's Call

President Olin T. Binkley announced a year earlier his intention to retire on 31 July 1974. The presidential search committee worked for months before they contacted me in mid-March 1974. Claud Bowen, chairman of the trustees and chairman of the search committee, called to request a very preliminary meeting with me. In early April they invited me to meet again. Lou and I attended despite the fact that we were leaving almost immediately to lead a tour to Europe and the Holy Land.

I encouraged the search committee to hold three meetings while I was overseas and to notify me of the outcome. I asked them to meet with the faculty, the alumni council, and elected leaders of the student body—which they did.

When we reached Jerusalem on our trip overseas, I had a letter awaiting me at our hotel from the newly-elected chairman of trustees, Carl Hudson of Louisiana. Our hotel was the Intercontinental (now The Seven Arches). It sits astride the peak of the Mount of Olives on the road that, in the days of Jesus, led from Bethany across the Mount of Olives through the Golden Gate into the temple area. Separating our hotel from Mount Moriah where the temple stood was the deep gorge of the Kidron.

I opened that letter while standing at a spot near our hotel where the Kidron valley borders a grove of old olive trees that marks the Garden of Gethsemane. As I read the chairman's letter outlining the substance of the three meetings I had suggested, something inside me made a Gethsemane commitment: "Thy will be done."

Upon my return from Israel, I encouraged a meeting with the entire faculty and the board of trustees so that this matter could be dealt with swiftly and conclusively. After considerable dialogue and a warm word from President Binkley as to his own feelings about my succeeding him, I was unanimously elected president by the trustees in mid-May 1974.

I had put out five piles of fleece—encouraged five meetings—and God had wet them every one. So far as I can tell from the human side, three elements entered into my decision to accept the presidency:

—The school was nearing twenty-five years of age. It was time for an alumnus to be president. I was an alumnus who sincerely loved Southeastern.

—I was a pastor who had served First Baptist Church, Winston-Salem, for twelve years; moreover, I had been assured by many on campus and off campus that a pastoral-type president was needed to lead the school at this juncture.

—Southeastern's presidency offered me the best possible opportunity to multiply the impact of my own ministry through the training of other men and women for their ministries.

Following an exciting and exacting month of orientation and transition with President Binkley, I literally ran to work on my first day as president—1 August 1974.

Some Ingredients in the Pleasure

The first decade of my presidency was marked by any number of serendipities. These, coupled with much hard work, yielded ten years of sheer delight.

Shared governance. I came to the presidency committed to a participatory administrative style. We inaugurated a tailored form of Peter Drucker's "management by objectives." Happily, my concepts of shared governance fit very well with the standards of Southeastern's accrediting agencies. In our administration trustees, administration, faculty, students, and alumni all had clear roles.

Trustees. The denomination owned the seminary, and the charter was crystal clear that the ultimate authority for its governance was entrusted to thirty trustees.

Immediately I undertook several strategies to bring the trustees well into the loop of seminary administration. One of the first actions was to revise the by-laws to mandate two meetings of the trustees each year instead of the one annual meeting previously held. Additionally we planned a series of trustee/administration/faculty retreats designed for improving communication and team-building. We developed a fund to send our trustee chairman each year to the September meeting of the SBC executive committee in Nashville.

Since we had no voice whatsoever in who became a trustee, the best hope was to begin working with new trustees upon their election. Ben C. Fisher served as a consultant to produce a first-rate manual for our seminary trustee orientation. We discovered in the process of producing our manual that it was, at that time, the only one available in all Association of Theological Schools (ATS)-accredited seminaries.

The Lily Endowment awarded Southeastern a grant designed to enhance trustee participation in seminary governance. Utilizing funds from that grant, I began a practice continued throughout my presidency. I visited all new trustees within their first year on the board. This opportunity to experience trustees' homes and workplaces gave me rare insight into their lives. We began to operate on the assumption that when trustees came to campus, reinforcements had arrived (an insight shared by Swan Hayworth at one of our early retreats).

Moreover, we brought all new trustees to campus for three days of orientation between their election and their first trustee meeting. They met the people and felt the pulse of the seminary firsthand. We worked very hard together to achieve the goals outlined in a chapter of the trustee manual on "esprit de corps."

Administration. I knew that when it came to administration the buck stopped with the president. Yet I sought throughout to keep a pastoral perspective in my presidency.

We administered the school through an executive council of seven persons. None of these was given the title of vice-president because it seemed a bit out of place in our structure. Additionally there was an administrative council consisting of all administrative officers and a seminary council with equal representation of administrators, faculty, and students.

Through these systems we set annual goals, negotiated their implementation, and evaluated outcomes.

Faculty. I arrived in 1974 to join a faculty that consisted of an interesting mix. There were twenty-four full-time teachers. One-third had been my teachers during my student days. One-third had been my classmates. They had completed their doctorates and returned to the seminary. One-third were persons who had joined the faculty during the time I had been away from the campus.

Since I was so thoroughly convinced of it myself, I had little difficulty convincing my faculty colleagues that I believed the only reason Southeastern had a president was to help teachers to teach and students to learn. From the very beginning I contended for a genuine in-depth partnership in the teaching/learning process. It worked. We became a community of learning.

Southeastern did not offer a Ph.D. or a Th.D. degree. Therefore we could be more intentional in faculty recruitment and prevent the inbreeding that characterizes so many seminaries. As the student body grew and faculty acquisitions were made, we refined a faculty recruitment process that modeled shared governance. The dean administered faculty evaluations, tenure considerations, and sabbatical leave requests in ways that included considerable faculty participation.

Faculty support financially was always on a front burner. We undertook to increase salaries and benefits. At the same time, we developed a faculty endowment program in which every colleague participated annually. Awards were developed to encourage excellence in classroom work.

All classrooms were renovated, and state-of-the-art equipment was acquired. Again, faculty involvement in the planning and purchasing was achieved. Faculty support systems were enhanced, and student work grants were directed toward a network of faculty assistance. Faculty members were encouraged and assisted in their participation in professional societies.

By 1988 the full-time faculty had grown to thirty-four. Our faculty was enriched by outstanding adjunctive teachers. For example, Methodists taught courses in Methodist polity. Jewish rabbis taught courses in Jewish faith and folk, and Roman Catholic priests taught courses in Catholicism since Vatican II.

Students. Students were perceived as full partners in the teaching-learning process. Everything from housing to food service was repeatedly reviewed and improved. We renovated all the dorms, adding air conditioning, and constructed 120 units of married student housing during my presidency. The cafeteria was renovated and food service carefully monitored. The Ledford Student Center was constructed and the Ruby Reid Child Care Center renovated. All the while, we kept a keen eye on student fees, always keeping them exceptionally competitive when compared with those at other Southern Baptist seminaries.

We inaugurated a monthly president's forum in the cafeteria, complete with doughnuts and coffee. The ground rule was that if concerns were important to the seminary community, then they were important enough to bring to the forum. Enormous good will resulted from these monthly exchanges. In them, all of us sought to model the qualities we expected from the persons in the Southeastern family.

The student coordinating council was always one of my favorite campus entities. Having served a year as president of the student body, I knew something of the importance of believing that students mattered to the seminary president. We developed a fund for our student council president to attend the September meeting of the SBC executive committee each year. We fiercely defended the freedom and the responsibility of the student newspaper, *The Enquiry*.

There were 634 students when I arrived in 1974. By 1980–1982, the enrollment peaked at 1246.

Increasingly women students migrated to Southeastern. They were welcomed and their callings celebrated. In the early 1980s a Women's Resource Center was developed and housed at the seminary. Southeastern had the first female student body president among Southern Baptist seminaries.

Non-Southern Baptist students paid more to attend Southeastern, but they were accepted; every effort was made to prepare them for ministry within their various denominations. Freewill Baptists, Pentecostals, and Assembly of God students especially chose Southeastern.

Ethnics were always a minority on campus, but their presence was applauded and their diversity celebrated. Native American and African-American students came in ever enlarging numbers.

Student aid was a priority throughout my presidency. In 1986–1987 for the first time we distributed over a million dollars in aid to our students. From the first we focused on work scholarships rather than grants. Thus there was forged a sense of earning one's aid throughout the campus.

Alumni. At Southeastern the alumni were a cherished and valued resource. My being an alumnus created an immediate rapport with our graduates. Throughout my presidency the alumni gave to the school, sent us students, came to campus for seminars and continuing education events, and served as friendly critics with an eye toward improving any number of programs and services. We kept in touch with the alumni through various means, including the *Outlook*, a campus news magazine published six times a year. The graduates responded overwhelmingly when our faculty undertook to publish *Faith and Mission*, our own scholarly journal.

I presided at the graduation of 4500 Southeasterners. They fanned out across the nation and the world. They were organized into ten state chapters. I visited them regularly, and I met them everywhere I went. With very rare exceptions they loved their school and appreciated its faculty and staff. During the firestorms of 1987–1988, the graduates stood tall and demonstrated a quality of care and support that to this day sends thrills up and down my spine.

Accreditation. Contrary to some popular opinion, accreditation is important for a seminary. Such scrutiny by peers not only helps a school to evaluate its own standards, but it also enhances participation in the wide reaches of academe. Accreditation is crucial in the transfer of credits earned at member schools.

President Olin Binkley served as president of ATS, one of the first Southern Baptists to do so. He and President Stealey led Southeastern to achieve ATS accreditation in record time. When I arrived in 1974, the seminary did not have regional accreditation by Southern Association of Colleges and Schools (SACS). No attempt had ever been made to achieve this additional certification.

In my initial visits with every faculty and staff member I became aware that several colleagues considered SACS accreditation crucial for our future. We undertook to qualify for SACS accreditation and achieved it, without notations, in record time. The comprehensive and massive self-study, 1980–1982, serves as a resource for marking the pulse of the seminary during that period.

Our accreditors always functioned as our colleagues and friends. Several of our faculty and staff served on visitation teams for both ATS and SACS. In my opinion, the accrediting agencies have been both fair and firm in their dealings with Southeastern following the events of 1987–1988.

Long-range planning. I believe firmly in planning and envisioned from the first an overall plan for Southeastern. Actually we propounded two plans—one for the first ten years and another for the rest of the century until the year 2000. In both instances, the plans were firmly anchored in the seminary's statement of purpose. The purpose statement was revised and sharpened by the trustees and faculty in 1980.

The plans embodied a boldness and a freshness. They involved hundreds of persons—including Wake Forest townspeople—in processes of research, imaginative thinking, intelligent compromise, and a sensible ordering of priorities. The plans were flexible enough to allow revision and fine tuning, yet sturdy enough to provide muscle and nerve for all our endeavors. With the plans in hand, we subjected every objective, goal, and action plan to two rigorous tests: (1) Is it consistent with the purpose of the seminary? (2) Does it fit within the plan of the seminary?

One enduring result of the planning process was that every primary document governing the school was assembled into a manual and shared with trustees, administrators, and faculty.

Curriculum design. Our documents provided that all matters pertaining to the curriculum were administered by the dean and that they involved faculty participation to the fullest. I guarded this prerogative as a sacred trust. Part of the reason was that I believed the dean and faculty to be the best resources for curricula development. I felt that in the rhythm between their individual vested interests and their collective interests in their classes and students, we would produce the best possible curriculum design. It worked.

Throughout my presidency the curriculum was reviewed and revised. Three projects deserve special mention:

(1) *The Ministry area.* The M area of the curriculum contained most of the course work in the practical areas of ministerial training—Christian education, evangelism, music, preaching, pastoral leadership, and so forth.

In my inaugural address I tried to shape the vision for a recasting of this entire area so as to complement the biblical, theological, and historical studies curriculum. I called for a rhythm between classical and practical curricula, a blending of information and competency in Christian ministry training.

In time we did expand the practical areas of our training and enriched the preparation of our students through an extensive student field ministries program. Leaders in this program helped our seminary to interface with the churches and assisted our students in placement. Some years ninety-five percent of our graduates had ministry positions consistent with their calling and preparation within six months of their graduation.

(2) *The Associate of Divinity degree program (A.Div.).* Within our student feeder system there were large numbers of persons who had reached age thirty but had little or no formal education beyond high school. Southeastern from the first had a certificate program for such persons called a bit late into ministry.

We undertook to develop for the first time in ATS/SACS–accredited seminaries a program leading to a degree (A.Div.) for these students. A few of those who took this program later transferred all their A.Div. credits into a college, earned an A.B. degree, and returned to Southeastern to work on the M.Div. degree.

(3) *The Doctor of Ministry degree program (D.Min.).* When I arrived, the D.Min. program had been in place at Southeastern for three years.

Frankly, it resembled our own Th.M. degree. Moreover it came perilously close to a "mini-Ph.D."

The goal for the degree was advanced work in both academic and competency training for the practice of ministry. While the Ph.D. was designed for research and teaching, the D.Min. was designed for ministry in the churches.

We got right to work on the design for our D.Min. degree. Working together, we transformed it into one of the strongest and most popular offered anywhere.

The Library. On the very first day of my presidency I spent two hours in a conference going over plans for constructing a new library wing and expanding all library services. Obviously the plan was well underway when I arrived. I gave full support to the project, gladly exerting leadership in this first major construction effort of my administration. Once the building was completed and in service, we undertook an extensive plan of library staff development, materials acquisition, and on-line computer networking. In time, we had full-time library professionals heading acquisitions, circulation, and reference services.

Financial Development. Everything I envisioned for Southeastern seemed to cost more money. Increasingly it became obvious that the usual funding sources, including the Cooperative Program, would not be sufficient for the seminary.

Three years after my arrival we undertook to put in place an institutional development component. Since this was a new venture for Southeastern, and since it would involve a substantial expenditure to develop the office and staff, I sought to meet with administrators, faculty, students, and alumni to explain my rationale and timing for this venture. Amazingly I received virtually unanimous encouragement to proceed with the organization.

An office was established and equipped, a four-person staff employed, a development council enlisted, and the seminary's first-ever capital campaign planned—all in a matter of months. We must have done something right, because in no time we were generating over a million dollars annually in unrestricted revenues. Moreover, our capital campaign over-subscribed its goal by more than two million dollars, and we experienced more than a ninety percent collection rate on pledges during three years.

Campus Development. During my fourteen-year presidency, every building on the seminary campus was renovated, updated, and tooled to fit its function in the life of the school. The one exception was Mackie Hall, and the plans for its renovation into a faculty center were approved by the trustees and put into the vault awaiting completion of funding during my next-to-last meeting with the trustees in 1987.

We parlayed Cooperative Program capital funds; funds from friends, foundations, and alumni; as well as funds generated by our own seminary investments into adequate resources to do all the renovations. Additionally, a comprehensive landscaping and campus lighting plan was adopted to be implemented incrementally over ten years. All projects were completed debt-free, and funds were dedicated in endowments for the maintenance of three major buildings (Adams Hall, Broyhill Hall, and Ledford Student Center).

Binkley Chapel was air-conditioned, and the main organ was renovated and substantially expanded in 1987. Again, these projects incurred no indebtedness.

Wake Forest Community Relations. I was in Wake Forest when the college relocated to Winston-Salem in 1956. I had been a student at Southeastern for two years. I sensed firsthand the frustration, tapering off into anger and despair, of some of the townspeople over the college's departure. After all, since 1834 the town and the college had grown up together in the forest of Wake.

I remained for two more years as a student and watched the vacuum for many persons in Wake Forest worsen. Everything from the churches to the restaurants was affected. Everyone from the mayor to the children was remorseful. Of course it was not the seminary's fault that Wake Forest College moved, but persons by nature nevertheless placed blame—at least emotionally.

Then I left for sixteen years.

Surprisingly, when I returned in 1974, the climate was still clouded, and many Wake Foresters simply could not get over 1956. After all, Southeastern Seminary owned over three hundred acres of "downtown Wake Forest," including the golf course where Arnold Palmer starred as a collegiate golfer. All of it was tax-free.

Lou and I determined that we would give prime time to the community and do what we could to make the town even prouder of the seminary as a neighbor and friend. We joined everything—the Wake Forest Baptist Church, the Rotary Club, the High School Boosters, the local Tree Board, the Chamber of Commerce, the Wake Forest College Birthplace Society, and other entities too numerous to mention. We participated in an incredible array of community functions ranging from the Christmas Parade and Open House to the Fourth of July fireworks extravaganza. We traded with the local merchants, including the Hardee's right downtown where we went almost every morning to chat with the townspeople when we were in Wake Forest.

Additionally, we began a concerted effort to make the seminary a good citizen-neighbor. Rod Byard, assistant to the president, was elected to the town board, a post he held for eight years. The trustees supported our plan to provide services in lieu of taxes. We dedicated some seminary land for a town electrical substation. We gave Wake Forest a new fire truck and supported substantially the local rescue squad. We worked out joint usage agreements for seminary athletic fields and tennis courts. We assisted in the development of security systems and in the recruitment of light industries, and we supported the town's efforts to have the area surrounding the seminary campus designated a National Historic District.

Actually the most popular and pervasive thing we did was to open the seminary cafeteria on New Year's Day to serve the entire community a free lunch consisting of black-eyed peas, hog jowl, greens, cornbread, and iced tea. Hundreds came. The seminary staff, including the president and the faculty, prepared and served the meal. This annual event generated more goodwill than anything we attempted.

In time we felt acceptance, and beyond acceptance we felt genuine inclusion into the Wake Forest community. When everything began to change at the seminary during the late 1980s, townspeople provided some of our most sincere and ardent support.

II. Forty-Eight Months of Pain: 1984–1988

Actually the pain began with the election of Adrian Rogers as president of the Southern Baptist Convention in 1979. Increasingly I found more and more of my time and energy being siphoned off by controversy. My mail and my telephone calls conveyed increasing hostility. I have two lateral files of correspondence from 1979 to 1984, most of it expressing "concerns," "inquiries," "I-have-heard-this" reports, and "I-just-wanted-you-to-know" kinds of information. With rare exceptions I responded to every letter, received or returned every telephone call, and granted every appointment requested by persons who wanted to talk about some facet of the SBC controversy.

Others have chronicled the events throughout the convention and the six seminaries, including Southeastern, quite adequately.[1] My task is to take a look at the final forty-eight months of my presidency and to speak autobiographically of the pain for me and the community of learning I helped to build in the forest of Wake.

The Conservative Evangelical Fellowship (CEF)

During the fall semester 1982, David Wood, a bright, articulate student from Winston-Salem and a graduate of the U.S. Naval Academy, Annapolis, Maryland, asked for an appointment to discuss the organization of a student group on campus. In our conversation he reported that some "conservative students" had been meeting regularly since July and wished to form an official student organization to represent "conservative views" on campus. He suggested that "the conservative viewpoint" on most issues was either omitted or misrepresented in seminary circles.

We discussed the process for formally recognizing student organizations. To receive formal recognition, a group was required to meet seven guidelines, including the enlistment of a faculty advisor, approval by the student council, and endorsement by the executive council of the seminary. Once an organization was formally recognized, it qualified to use seminary facilities, to be listed in seminary publications, and to request funds through appropriate channels from the seminary.

In due course, David Wood submitted a formal request to organize the Conservative Evangelical Fellowship (CEF). The stated purpose was "to meet to provide discussion and presentation of ideas of importance to conservative, evangelical Christians." It was further understood that the purpose of the organization was to provide programs basically by students for students.

In December the student council approved the organization, and on 21 January 1983 the seminary executive council also approved it. Glenn T. Miller, professor of Church History, agreed to be faculty advisor for the CEF.

Throughout the process I supported approval of the organization, all the while knowing the risks for division inherent in such action. My sense of openness and fair play motivated me to give these students their forum.

In February 1983, while the six seminary presidents were together for meetings in Nashville, Tennessee, I learned that similar efforts to organize such student groups were being made on all our campuses. The push had begun during the previous fall on every campus. The timing was simply beyond coincidence.

During the years that followed, the CEF at Southeastern exerted repeated pressure for preferential treatment and permission to sponsor programs far beyond the purview of a student organization. Moreover they frequently beamed their promotion and programs to persons off campus rather than to students.

My files are thick from confrontation after confrontation with CEF leaders. The organization was a controversial, divisive presence on our campus. Repeatedly I got the distinct impression that the CEF leaders were being counseled and funded by persons off campus.

On 11 February 1986, the CEF was put on one-year administrative probation for their clandestine meeting with representatives of the Peace Committee without consultation beforehand with either their faculty advisor or any official of the seminary.

In retrospect, I was wrong to support the formal recognition of such a militant and divisive group of students on our campus.

Seminex II

Humor was mixed into the trauma at Southeastern. One of the most amazing episodes was the hoax of Seminex II.

On Monday, 16 September 1985, I traveled to Nashville, Tennessee, for a meeting of the SBC Executive Committee. No sooner had I left the campus than a delegation arrived there with a document in hand entitled "Seminex II: Southeastern Seminary In Exile." The document was dated 8 July 1985 and was purported to have been written by Southeastern seminary faculty. Russell Kaemmerling, editor of *The Southern Baptist Advocate*, led the group that came to campus, knowing that I would be away. Other visitors included a trustee (Eddie Sellers), a pastor from North Carolina (Robert Tenery), and three former students at Southeastern (Greg DeMarco, Dade Sherman, and David Wood).

They made inquiries about the document with Carson Brisson, registrar/director of admissions, and four faculty members, Glenn Miller, Robert Culpepper, Delos Miles, and Richard Spencer. Concurrently another trustee, Robert Crowley, contacted ATS, one of the seminary's accrediting agencies, and Union Seminary officials in Richmond, Virginia. He discussed with those persons the contents of the six-page document they had received sometime earlier from a student on campus who sent a cover letter explaining that he had found the item labeled "Confidential Memo" among items shelved for filing in a faculty office where he was working while the faculty member was teaching a class. The student, who used a pseudonym in his cover letter, said that he took the memo, copied it, and returned it to its file folder.

The document, written on Southeastern Seminary stationery, elaborated in some detail an alleged plan the faculty had propounded to follow the example of Concordia Seminary of the Lutheran Church, Missouri Synod. When ultra-conservative forces within that denomination gained control over the Synod and its seminary in St. Louis, Missouri, the Concordia faculty resigned *en masse* and established the "Concordia Seminary in Exile" (SEMINEX).

The document brought to the campus by the visitors (investigators?) claimed that the Southeastern faculty members were preparing to resign *en masse*, reorganize themselves, transfer to Richmond, Virginia, and in a matter of weeks resume classes on the campus of Union Theological Seminary, a Presbyterian school in Richmond. It claimed further that all details of the transfer had been approved both by the Southeastern accrediting agencies and by officials at Union Seminary.

It was indeed a remarkable plan on paper.

The next day—Tuesday, 17 September—I was contacted, along with Charles Horton, chairman of trustees, while we were together in meetings, by Russell Kaemmerling, who had traveled to Nashville overnight from Wake Forest. He and an attorney met with me and the trustee chairman for over an hour. He showed us the document and told us that *The Southern Baptist Advocate* had spent approximately $5000 trying to check it out before he broke the story in his paper. These men appeared to believe that it was entirely appropriate for them, along with other trustees, to investigate this matter for weeks before discussing it with me and the trustee chairman. Neither Charles Horton nor I had ever heard of such a plan or seen the document, but I did promise to check it out when I returned to the campus.

The next day, Wednesday 18 September, Dean Morris Ashcraft read the document to the faculty during their regular monthly meeting. They were stunned but also amused by such a preposterous idea and by an investigation of it. The faculty immediately adopted a statement declaring that they did not write the document, nor did they know the origin of it. Furthermore they repudiated "the document, its contents, and its implications." Every faculty member, including those who were absent from the faculty meeting and others who were on sabbatical leave, was contacted, and each name ascribed to the unanimous faculty statement.

Seminex II was a hoax, and an expensive one at that for *The Southern Baptist Advocate*. Yet it had to be taken very seriously, and in the climate of the time it had ominous overtones.

I brought the entire matter to the attention of the seminary trustees during their semi–annual meeting in October. It was discussed thoroughly and dismissed by them as a hoax. To this day we do not know who wrote either the cover letter or the document.

Professors in the Crossfire

One of the most painful parts of the SBC controversy, as it affected the seminary, was the impact that it had on individual professors and on their families. By 1984 my telephone calls and my mail had become the media for constant questions about our teachers and their teachings. One did not have to be paranoid to detect organized efforts at creating suspicions of Southeastern's faculty. We were in a time of cultivated distrust.

One of my telephone logs indicates more than 100 phone calls over a period of slightly more than three months. Our faculty members were under attack. They felt it, and so did their families, when I went to talk with them or wrote a memo to them about some fresh concern that had come to my attention. Yet I was determined to keep them posted on such matters. There was, in my opinion, nothing worse than a colleague being blindsided.

The pressures mounted in our classrooms. One situation illustrates many such episodes. Malcolm Tolbert, professor of New Testament, made some comments in class about political power plays in the Southern Baptist Convention. Less than three hours later he was telephoned by Paige Patterson, at that time a high-profile and vocal critic of the seminary from Dallas, Texas. A student in the class had contacted the critic and reported on Professor Tolbert. The entire climate for teaching and learning was clouded by the controversy.

Perhaps the most chronicled attack on a professor came in 1985 when John I Durham, professor of Old Testament and Hebrew at Southeastern, became embroiled in a controversy over some Sunday School lessons he wrote on Job.

He contracted to write five lessons for adult Bible study quarterlies in the *Life and Work* curriculum. The contract was signed in May 1982. He submitted the materials for editing in April 1984. The first lesson was published for use in the adult Sunday School materials 7 July 1985. It was based on Job 1:1 through 2:10.

Although John Durham had written lessons previously for the Sunday School Board, he attended the writers' conference for this series of lessons. The instructions given to writers for this lesson had two notes at the end of the sheet:

> 1. Briefly explain the function of the heavenly council to which the angels and the Satan belong. (See 1 Kgs 22:19-22; Isa 6:1-3.)
> 2. Briefly explain the meaning of the Hebrew word "satan" and the fact that in the book of Job the word always has the definite article. Literally it is "the Satan." Explain that this development of Satan is not the fully developed New Testament concept.

Dr. Durham submitted the lesson believing that he had been true to the Bible, true to Job, and also true to the instructions of the Sunday School Board editorial staff. Yet the lesson brought numerous letters and phone calls to the Sunday School Board. I also began to receive correspondence and calls at the seminary.

Following this negative reaction to the lesson upon its publication, the Sunday School Board began a review and determined that there had been some mistakes in its editorial handling of Dr. Durham's material. An official spokesman for the board called me and John Durham to apologize for the mistakes and to say that the Sunday School Board took full responsibility for the distortion of the original material. He requested that all of us allow the board to respond to all correspondence and calls related to the lesson.

The board released a statement through Baptist Press 15 July 1985 affirming that several statements in the lesson were the result of errors made in the editing process and were not the fault of the lesson writer. The news release went on to say emphatically that "John I Durham . . . did not write the statements that are errors. These statements were inserted by a temporary editor called to work because of a staff vacancy."

This might have resolved the matter except that at least one Sunday School Board trustee, Robert Tenery, a pastor from North Carolina, began to exert enormous pressure on board leadership to pin the fault on the writer instead of on the temporary editor or on the editorial process. Less than a month later, the Sunday School Board trustees met at Glorieta, New Mexico, and issued another news release through Baptist Press 5 August expressing "regret and concern about errors in a July 7 Sunday School lesson, and urging study of editorial processes and care in selecting writers."

Moreover, the North Carolina trustee wrote all the Southeastern Seminary trustees a letter on 24 September 1985 making statements about Dr. Durham that were unfavorable and untrue. He did this without ever writing or calling me to discuss this entire matter.

At this point Dean Morris Ashcraft and I realized that we must become involved in the controversy along with John Durham. The attack on him was in fact an attack on the seminary and every teacher who would ever write Sunday School lessons for the churches.

We three talked at length. The dean and I asked Dr. Durham for copies of the lesson manuscripts that he had sent to the Sunday School Board more than a year earlier. He provided them, and the dean made a careful comparison of his manuscript and the first printed lesson.

Here are the dean's findings. They focus on two editorial changes. There were others, but these were the important ones:

(1) *Durham wrote,* "Two mistaken impressions have interfered with our understanding of the Book of Job. The first of these is that the 'Satan' mentioned in chapters 1 and 2 is the Devil, Lucifer, Mephistopheles, the Prince of Darkness, Evil personified."

The editor revised, and the printed lesson reads, "Two mistaken impressions have interfered with our understanding of the Book of Job. The first of these is that the 'satan' mentioned in chapters 1 and 2 the devil of the New Testament, evil personified."[2]

(2) *Durham wrote,* "There is here no question of any save God being in charge, and 'the one who accuses' is his loyal servant." He went on to discuss in this paragraph the word in Job, *ha satan* or "the accuser."

The editor inserted a sentence at the beginning of the paragraph that had no resemblance to the rest of the paragraph. It read, "There is in the Old Testament no concept of an empire of evil opposed to God. God was in charge, and 'the one who accuses' was his loyal servant."[3]

The starkness of these two editorial changes apparently startled some readers who saw the statements as a denial of the reality of Satan or evil. Who can say, however, how the readers would have reacted if the statements had gone unrevised? The fact is that people were by now looking for chances to discredit "liberal Southeastern professors" and to destroy trust in the seminary.

Interestingly, the January Bible Study book published by the Convention Press of the Sunday School Board in 1971 and used in thousands of churches presents the same view of Satan in Job as the Durham material outlined. When Ralph Smith wrote that book, *Job: A Study in Providence and Faith,* there was not a climate of cultivated and orchestrated distrust and thus not one howl of protest.

Dean Ashcraft, John Durham, and I compiled a three-page statement on this matter and released it in September 1985 seeking to put the matter in perspective and to prepare our trustees for their discussion of it during their October meeting.

Meanwhile, I went to Nashville and discussed in detail the concerns that had been lodged with the Sunday School Board over this lesson. During the meeting I pledged to call every person who contacted me on the matter, and officials at the board agreed to telephone the fifty–five or so persons who had contacted them. Additionally, we agreed that all matters relating specifically to John Durham would be referred to me and that I would personally pursue the concerns with each one expressing them.

Our trustees reviewed the statement prepared by the president, the dean, and the professor, accepted our explanation of what happened and why, and expressed their confidence in the way we had sought to handle the controversy.

That did not resolve the larger two-fold fallout from this episode, however. The Sunday School Board stopped enlisting Southeastern faculty to write Sunday School lessons, and the Southeastern faculty stopped running the risk of writing curriculum materials for the churches. Both losses have been grave and painful.

The Peace Committee

During the annual meeting of the SBC in Dallas, Texas, 11–13 June 1985, a special committee (later called the Peace Committee) was appointed "to determine the sources" of the SBC controversy, to make "findings and recommendations" so that Southern Baptists might "effect reconciliation. . . ."[4] Twenty-two persons were designated to serve on the committee. Charles G. Fuller of Virginia was elected chairman.

The Peace Committee (PC) by design represented both the old majority and the new majority within the SBC. It included some of the six seminaries' most ardent supporters and outspoken critics.

The PC developed subcommittees to visit all Southern Baptist institutions and agencies and granted these subcommittees wide–ranging powers to investigate them. From the first, those of us at Southeastern regarded these visits as an inappropriate intrusion between our seminary and its trustees responsible for governance. Moreover, we deemed it unwise for us to submit to this inquiry because of its threat to the seminary's integrity and academic freedom. Southern Baptists were weary of the controversy, however, and even our best friends were unwilling for us to question or oppose a "peace" gesture. So we agreed to a visit by the subcommittee assigned to Southeastern Seminary.

Careful negotiations between Chairman Charles Fuller and me yielded a written set of ground rules for the visit. The PC's major purpose, according to the chairman, was "to sensitize agencies to convention concerns, and to solicit their active participation with us in the peace-making process."[5]

The PC was to send four persons—two friendly, two critical of Southeastern. We were to arrange all details of the visit and were to have the president, the dean, and the chairman of trustees as seminary representatives. I desired that the vice-chairman of our trustees be added to make the numbers equal. Chairman Fuller objected, however, advising me that the rules for the visit had been rigidly set for all seminaries.

Shortly before the visit, the president of the Southeastern student body inquired whether he might arrange for the student council to meet with the subcommittee while they were at Southeastern. I denied his request, explaining the chairman's specific ground rules.

Jim Henry of Florida was chairman of the subcommittee visiting Southeastern on 5 February 1986. He and I corresponded sufficiently to determine the materials that he desired from us, the agenda, and the general process for the discussions on our campus. He and the other three members were to be guests with my wife and me at our home for dinner on 4 February. As it turned out, only Jim Henry arrived in time for dinner. Another member came to our house in time for dessert. The two left early to return to the Plantation Inn, as the chairman explained, to go over details for the meeting the next day.

No mention was made to me that a meeting had also been planned later that evening at the motel between the subcommittee and students belonging to the CEF. This disclosure seriously damaged the meeting on 5 February, since I had tried carefully to abide by the established guidelines and the subcommittee had breached them flagrantly. I felt betrayed.

Perhaps the best way for me to describe the matter is to quote from my written report on the PC visit to the Southeastern trustees 10 March 1986. I advised the trustees of the secret night meeting and quoted from my letter to Jim Henry written six days after the subcommittee visit:

The only thing which marred the visit of the subcommittee to Southeastern Seminary was the rather grave misunderstanding regarding the meeting with students on Tuesday evening. Beyond anything that you and I can do there are many disappointed, even angry, persons on this campus who feel that some of us simply mismanaged the information regarding that meeting as well as the willingness of the subcommittee within the guidelines to which we had agreed to meet with persons other than the president, the dean, and the chairman of the Board of Trustees.[6]

Further, I notified the trustees in my report:

Since both the nature and the number of the concerns shared by the sub-committee were influenced by a meeting held with a Southeastern Seminary student organization on February 4, the evening before the meeting with the president, the dean, and the trustee chairman, some mention of that meeting must be made in the report. Two members of the subcommittee met almost four hours (a third member left after the first hour and one half) with approximately fifteen persons representing the Conservative Evangelical Fellowship, a student organization which had been formally recognized on campus for the past two and one half years.

The meeting was arranged without any communication with either the organization's faculty advisor or the president of the seminary. The problem created by this meeting lies not with the meeting itself but with the procedure for arranging it without the knowledge of the seminary president, who was functioning as the official host, according to the guidelines for the sub-committee visit. Other student groups, including the Student Council, had been advised by the seminary president weeks before that while the subcommittee was on the official visit to the seminary, they were to meet *only* with the president, the dean, and the chairman of the trustees.

The meeting on the night before was brought to the attention of the seminary president by Dr. Robert Cuttino, a subcommittee member, when he was leaving at 11:00 A.M., February 5, to catch a private plane to conduct a funeral for a member of the congregation he serves. The matter was discussed during the afternoon session with the three remaining members of the subcommittee, all of whom attended at least part of the meeting with the students/graduates of the seminary and members of the CEF.[7]

The official meeting of the seven persons representing the PC and the seminary was held in Broyhill Hall and lasted from 8:00 A.M. until 6:00 P.M. The meeting was taped and the tapes sealed by decree of the PC for ten years. Minutes were taken in the morning by Robert Cuttino of South Carolina and in the afternoon by William Poe of North Carolina. Mr. Poe had a fever and showed extraordinary stamina by staying for the entire meeting. From the beginning the discussions were candid, as we sought to respond to every question and deal with every issue, major and minor.

Perhaps an excerpt from my report 10 March 1986 to the trustees on the meeting will best summarize what transpired:

> The subcommittee shared twenty-seven (27) specific, written concerns. Seven (7) of the concerns were accepted although they were anonymous. The other twenty (20) concerns came from seven (7) persons, five (5) who are presently student members of the Conservative Evangelical Fellowship (CEF), and two (2) who are recent seminary graduates and members of the CEF. These concerns involved a total of fifteen (15) seminary faculty members, one (1) visiting teacher, and one (1) retired Southeastern Seminary teacher.[8]

The concerns dealt with students' perceptions of faculty members' lectures on the nature of the Bible, specific interpretations of Scripture, and other doctrinal questions. It is stretching the point to call these "convention concerns" as the PC chairman had suggested in the guidelines. For the most part, the concerns originated with one small, vocal, militant group of students in the clandestine meeting the night before our official meeting.

Moreover, one student at that meeting had borrowed another student's class notebook under false pretenses and registered concerns from the notes that were not at all concerns of the author. That student was later disciplined under guidelines of the Southeastern student code of ethics.

I personally conveyed in writing every concern to the seventeen faculty members involved, requesting that they write appropriate explanations, responses, or interpretations. All did so, and I compiled them in my report to the subcommittee and to the trustees.

Some of the concerns were legitimate and substantive. Some were misunderstandings of what the teachers had actually said. Some were trivial and worded so vaguely that the professors had to guess at the meaning. For example, one student was concerned because a professor "endorsed women in leadership." The concern did not mention ordination by a congregation or a call to ministry. Another student expressed concern that a professor "supported the views of liberation theology," with no further specifics.

Still the dean and I studied every response to every concern, concluding that the concerns might be legitimate as concerns, but that there had been no matter presented to indicate that any member of the faculty at Southeastern Seminary was teaching contrary to the Abstract of Principles.

I heard nothing further from either the PC or the subcommittee until 5 August 1986. On that date Jim Henry, subcommittee chairman, wrote me advising that the subcommittee had reviewed my report forwarded to them in March and that "in some places there needed to be some clarification."[9]

Again I went personally to the eleven persons involved and asked them to give "further clarification" on the items requested by the subcommittee. Again all responded. I sent a written report to Jim Henry on 18 September 1986. Along with my second report, I submitted an urgent appeal:

> Please submit to me *just as soon as possible* a copy of your report to the SBC Peace Committee. I have gone to the teachers involved twice already requesting responses. None of us, neither myself nor the faculty members, have heard a word from you, the subcommittee, or the Peace Committee regarding the substance of our report submitted 12 March 1986.
>
> Of course, the media has carried information to the effect that three SBC seminaries are now released from further investigation by the Peace Committee. So far as Southeastern Seminary goes, we are perilously near to the greatest of all ironies—being held hostage, without information, response, or charges, in of all things, a process seeking peace. I am sure that you and your colleagues can understand with what gravity I view, on behalf of the seminary, this extraordinary situation.[10]

Finally the PC presented its full report to the Southern Baptist Convention in St. Louis, Missouri, 16 June 1987. I voted against the report. It marked for me an intrusion into the legitimate role of trustees of the seminary, and, what is worse, it recommended that trustees "determine the theological positions of the seminaries' administrators and faculty members."[11] This latter recommendation potentially bypassed the function of our signatures on our Abstract of Principles and opened the floodgate for all sorts of "witch-hunts."

The Glorieta Statement. Prior to the formulation of the PC's report to the SBC in June 1987, there was a flurry of activity focusing on the seminaries. Friends on the PC brought reports to the seminary presidents that the committee was virtually deadlocked on how to proceed in their deliberations toward formulation of a report. After almost two years, matters had come down to where we all knew they were at the beginning—the seminaries were the focal point of the controversy.

Our friends on the PC urged a meeting of the seminary presidents with the officers of the PC and asked us to provide any information whatsoever that might become an initiative by the presidents to contribute to the peace process. We held this meeting on 18–19 September 1986 in Atlanta, Georgia.

The presidents agreed on a statement with the officers attesting a high view of Scripture and a sensitivity to the concern for "fairness" or "balance" (parity was the concept) in our faculty and other appointments. We committed ourselves to address these two issues in a report for the PC by the time of the prayer retreat called by the PC at Glorieta Baptist Conference Center near Santa Fe, New Mexico, 20–22 October 1986.

In preparation for that engagement, the six presidents met in New Mexico a day earlier. We worked all day and into the evening on what has become known as the "Glorieta Statement." We knew from the outset that such an endeavor was fraught with grave risks of misunderstanding both by the PC and by Southern Baptists generally. After all, it would be a unilateral statement of our convictions and intentions without the advantage of discussions with our trustees, faculties, or anyone else on our campuses. Yet we thought the chance toward peace was worth the risk.

We perceived our statement as a final effort to reach out to the new majority controlling the SBC. We discussed and debated every point in our statement. We intended it to touch on the crucial points blocking the peace process as these points had been communicated to us by the PC officers a month earlier in Atlanta.

At the prayer retreat Milton Ferguson, then chairman of the Presidents' Council, presented our statement. It covered our high view of Scripture:

> We believe that the Bible is fully inspired; it is "God-breathed" (2 Tim 3:16), utterly unique. No other book or collection of books can justify that claim. The sixty-six books of the Bible are not errant in any area of reality. We hold to their infallible power and binding authority.[12]

The statement went on to commit the presidents to the resolution of the problems in the SBC and to full partnership in the peace process.

Specifically we committed to working on increased adherence to confessional statements, balanced presentations in our classrooms, respect for all persons despite their beliefs, fairness in faculty and other appointments, and practical renewal for our seminary communities through fostering a spirit of evangelism and missions on our campuses.

Additionally we scheduled at the seminaries' expense three national conferences for all Southern Baptists—a Conference on Biblical Inerrancy (1987), a Conference on Biblical Interpretation (1988), and a Conference on Biblical Imperatives (1989).

An entire afternoon and part of an evening were given at the prayer retreat to discussion of the presidents' statement. It became crystal clear that we had attempted to move as far as possible toward the new majority without capitulation. We had come as close as we could come toward affirming our high view of Scripture without actually adopting their language of "inerrancy."

I sought to make my position clear about the nature of the Bible. While I did not intend to adopt either the tenets or the language of "the inerrantists," I did attest to my complete confidence in the Bible ("the sixty-six books" we have) and expressed my disbelief that a single author deliberately wrote an error with a design to deceive in any area of reality.

The next morning at breakfast, I joined Cecil Sherman of Texas, one of the most ardent supporters of the seminaries on the PC. He told me with tears in his eyes that in spite of our efforts to the contrary, our statement "sold the store" to the new majority. I was shocked and saddened later that day when he resigned as a member of the PC expressing that, for at least himself, the peace process was doomed. I soon reached the same conclusion in the aftermath of the "Glorieta Statement." It communicated to no one. It offended almost everyone, both friend and foe, in the controversy.

I returned to Wake Forest and called meetings of the entire seminary community to explain the statement, its content, and its intent. No one responded positively. My friends saw it much as Cecil Sherman did. My critics soon charged, as I sought to explain the meaning of the language for me, that I had "backtracked" from the Glorieta Statement. I learned painfully that there was a sentiment that whenever a seminary president made any gesture toward peace, he did so with his fingers crossed.

Although I tried to carry through on the unilateral commitments I made at Glorieta in my "Plan of Action" presented to the trustees in

March 1987, the fallout from the "Glorieta Statement" did not contribute to the elusive search for peace. That fact both saddened and motivated me in subsequent months as the firestorm mounted for Southeastern.

The Crucial Year 1987

Seven intertwined events from February to November 1987 brought about my resignation as president. Of course, I approached these events weary from controversy and frustrated at my inability to function effectively in any authentic peacemaking endeavor. Altogether these events steeled my conviction that the new majority since 1979 in the SBC and, as of June 1987, on the board of trustees at Southeastern Seminary really did have an alien vision for our denomination and for my *alma mater*.

Trustee Instruction Committee, 21 February 1987. This meeting was called to interview two persons recommended for election to the faculty after months of careful work according to the faculty appointment procedure. The dean and I brought our recommendations to the trustee instruction committee after unanimous concurrence by the area faculty (in this case, M-area and T-area) and the entire faculty. Generally these meetings had been pleasant occasions for exchange, dialogue, and mutual sharing on matters relating to the seminary, the candidates' experience and commitment, and wider issues of theological education.

This meeting was different. For one thing, one of the candidates was female. Elizabeth Barnes was recommended as assistant professor of Theology. She was a graduate of Meredith College, Southeastern Seminary, and Duke University with a recently earned Ph.D. She was a trustee at Meredith College, Raleigh, North Carolina, and had already taught at Southeastern for three years as an adjunctive teacher.

The interrogation of both candidates was intense. All five members of the instruction committee engaged in the questioning. The Chicago Statement on Inerrancy (December 1978) was introduced into the dialogue along with another non-Southern Baptist confession of faith, while the Southeastern Seminary Abstract of Principles was scarcely touched on at all. This for me constituted an infringement of our faculty appointment process. It introduced perspectives and documents foreign to the established documents of the seminary as criteria for faculty selection. These trustees sought precipitously to narrow the doctrinal gate through which prospective faculty had to pass. The candidates were pressed to subscribe to extreme literalistic views of the Bible and were chided for being insensitive to the "conservative resurgence" in the SBC and for refusing to adopt the language of "inerrancy."

Nevertheless, the committee on instruction voted unanimously to recommend Roy D. DeBrand as professor of Homiletics, and by a 4–1 vote to recommend Elizabeth Barnes to the faculty. I notified both candidates of the decision and communicated to the trustees that the recommendation would be on the agenda of the March trustee meeting.

Trustee Meeting, 9–10 March 1987. Two key items marked this meeting of the trustees. One was the report of the instruction committee, and the other was debate and decision on my proposed "Plan of Action."

The meeting in which the report of the instruction committee was considered was tense. The tension heightened when it came to light that at least two members of the committee worked toward changing the committee's recommendation of Dr. Barnes, holding meetings for that purpose on the evening of 9 March and early morning of 10 March. One trustee, Frank Jordan of California, reported intense efforts to intimidate him to change his vote.

Dr. DeBrand was elected by the trustees 25–2. Dr. Barnes was elected after lengthy debate 14–13.

On the first evening of the trustee meeting, I presented my "Plan of Action." I had propounded the plan in large measure to keep the unilateral commitments I had made in the "Glorieta Statement." The faculty and staff had reviewed it. The plan pledged fair and responsible action when faculty members were "charged" with deviation from the Abstract of Principles. It addressed and promised balance in the selection of faculty, chapel speakers, and lecturers on campus. It also pledged that the seminary community would "emphasize and exemplify afresh the distinctive doctrines of our Baptist heritage."[13] The trustees slightly revised and endorsed the Plan of Action. I believed that the trustees, administration, and faculty had responded adequately to the concerns of the Peace Committee and that we had a plan for charting our future.

At the SBC meeting in June 1987 for the first time a new majority were elected trustees at Southeastern Seminary. When these trustees met the following October, they ignored the Plan of Action completely and set out on an abrupt new course for the seminary. Their actions convinced me that I would not be able to negotiate a mutual vision with the new majority trustees. In my view, their alien vision would increasingly prevail. In that vision they desired not parity but complete control.

Southeastern Faculty Organizes AAUP Chapter. For some months prior to 1987, faculty members had discussed among themselves and with me their exploration of the possibility of establishing on campus a chapter of the American Association of University Professors (AAUP). No Southern Baptist seminary and few Southern Baptist-connected colleges had such a chapter.

The national organization had worked for over seventy years within the academic community to promote the interests of higher education in this country. It consisted of college, university, and graduate school faculty members committed to upholding high professional and ethical standards and to preserving academic freedom.

I sensed a growing threat to academic freedom by the SBC new majority, and I frankly felt that my administration could not assure protection of freedom much longer in light of some trustees' stated intentions and actions. Working with our former trustees we had assured the tenure of every elected member of the faculty except the newly-elected assistant professor of Theology, Elizabeth Barnes.

On 30 April 1987 twenty-five members of the Southeastern faculty established a local chapter of AAUP. I attended the organizational meeting and gave my support to the effort.

Officers of the chapter sought legal counsel, met regularly to discuss issues and to adopt strategies, talked frequently with the press, and made their views public. The AAUP chapter welded the faculty into a genuine unity, improved morale, and provided much-needed pressure on the more radical trustees.

Of course, the AAUP chapter provoked the ire of the new trustee majority, who regarded it as a "union." The strategy of the new trustees was, as much as possible, to ignore the chapter. This became increasingly difficult, because by the October meeting of the trustees every full-time elected teaching faculty had joined the AAUP, and by December the chapter had raised over $10,000—$8,000 of which came from the membership.

Rumors came to me that administrators of other SBC seminaries did not approve of the Southeastern faculty having an AAUP chapter and did not want chapters on their campuses. None of my other president colleagues ever discussed the matter with me.

One of the most eventful outcomes of the firestorm that struck our campus occurred on 18 June 1988, when in Washington, DC, the national AAUP awarded the Beatrice G. Konheim Award to the Southeastern chapter and the Alexander Meiklejohn Award to me. These awards, in defense of academic freedom, had never before gone to a theological seminary chapter or to a seminary president.

President's Convocation Address, 25 August 1987. I always brought the message during the fall convocation. In 1987 I determined to open our thirty-seventh year by speaking to several issues giving rise to the mounting anxiety I detected on our campus. I was careful to relate my remarks to the vision communicated in the Plan of Action endorsed by seminary constituents and trustees earlier in March. I titled the address "Quo Vadis, Southeastern Seminary?" Issues I sought to address included adherence to the original dream of our school, a defense of academic freedom, the use of contemporary tools in biblical scholarship, affirmation of women in ministry (including their ordination by churches), and adherence to Southeastern's tradition of ecumenical involvement.

I indicated as strongly as I could that I was ready to administer a school like the school I had known since 1954 but that I could not support or administer the kind of seminary that would result if the new majority had its way. My address drew severe criticism from new majority trustees and SBC leaders. I received many calls and letters asserting that I had "thrown down the gauntlet." Students, alumni, faculty, and staff enthusiastically acclaimed the vision I sought to shape for our school. But from that moment on, I realized that the polarization was unalterably set.

New Trustee Orientation, 7–8 September 1987. For years we had brought all our new trustees elected during the SBC annual meeting in June to the campus before their first trustee meeting in October. Trustee officers joined us in Wake Forest for a time of orientation and team building. Our meetings had been pleasant and constructive.

This meeting in September 1987 was different. The new trustees arrived in Wake Forest with an agenda of their own. They constituted for the first time a new majority on the Southeastern board. These trustees elected in St. Louis had little interest in learning about the seminary or about its governing documents. They showed minor concern over matters of heritage and precedent. Their questions indicated their intention to control, especially at such crucial junctures as faculty appointments and student recruitment. They indicated that only inerrantists should be added to the faculty and that only males should be prepared for pastoral ministry. Furthermore, there was the hint that Southeastern's Abstract of Principles had best be revised in light of the Peace Committee Report.

I knew when these new trustees left campus that a real "gauntlet" had been thrown down.

Trustee Meeting, 12–14 October 1987. This was the first trustee meeting for the new majority at Southeastern. Five trustees attended their first meeting. The new majority of trustees caucused without the other trustees' knowledge in Raleigh on the night of Monday, 12 October 1987. There they set their agenda. It consisted of five actions, none of which had been previously discussed with me or other trustees. While I was not completely surprised by the actions, taken in combination they brought to a climax my growing sense that no mutual vision was possible involving me and my new "bosses."

The actions were:

(1) The trustees elected Robert Crowley, a pastor from Maryland, as chairman by a 15–13 vote, thus replacing Jesse Chapman, a surgeon from North Carolina, after only one year as chairman and denying him the customary second term. Robert Crowley had been a vocal member of the trustee instruction committee. He was a graduate of Bob Jones University, an independent Baptist school in Greenville, South Carolina.

(2) The trustees elected James DeLoach as vice-chairman by a vote of 17–11. He was an associate pastor from Texas and also a graduate of Bob Jones University. All other trustee officers were also elected from the new majority. The takeover of the trustees was complete.

(3) The trustees approved by a margin of 16–12 a substitute motion, brought by two trustees attending their first meeting, to replace all the recommendations of the nominating committee, thus giving the new majority control over every trustee working committee. Cecil Rhodes of North Carolina, the new trustee bringing the substitute motion, acknowledged that his list had been compiled in a meeting the night before.

(4) The trustees revised the procedures for electing faculty members and appointing temporary teachers. Heretofore, documents outlining these procedures had been jointly agreed to by trustees, administration, and faculty. They constituted a time-tested hallmark of my participatory decision-making. They modeled shared governance at its best.

Under procedures in effect prior to this action, the following steps were taken to elect new faculty: (a) declaration of a vacancy by the president and preparation of a position description by the area faculty; (b) solicitation by the dean of recommendations and applications; (c) designation of candidates by the area faculty; (d) following appropriate preliminary contacts by the president, a presidential selection of one candidate to visit the campus; (e) interviews with the candidate by the area faculty, student representatives, the faculty as a whole, and the instruction committee of the trustees; (f) the recommendation of the candidate by the president through the instruction committee to the board of trustees; (g) election of the candidate by the whole board of trustees.

The unilateral trustee action on 13 October 1987 changed the procedures as follows: The president, rather than the area faculty, (a) selects candidates for a faculty position; (b) must confer with the trustee instruction committee in the selection of candidates; (c) recommends to the instruction committee his choice of a candidate, and that person is presented to the trustee executive committee before being acted on by the whole board of trustees.

This revised procedure reduced, if not fully eliminated, the roles of the dean and the faculty in the procedure. It allowed the trustees to get exactly whom they wanted using the office of the president to accomplish that end. For me, it took the faculty election process out of the hands of those who knew the most about the teaching needs at the school and placed it in the hands of those who knew the least. I strenuously objected to these changes, pointing out that they undermined the participatory nature of my administration.

Heedlessly, the new majority also hammered through a revised procedure for making temporary faculty appointments. Previously, the procedure as specified in the *Southeastern Administrative Manual* read: "Temporary appointments to the instructional staff are made by the President and the Dean of the Faculty following appropriate consultation with the area Faculty."[14] The trustees unilaterally changed this procedure to read: "Temporary appointments to the instructional staff may be made by the President with approval of the Instruction Committee of the Board of Trustees."[15]

Again the revised procedure strengthened the complete control of an administrative process by empowering the trustees to use the office of the president for their ends. It was inimical to academic freedom mainly because it removed the dean and the faculty from the process and left them with no effective voice in the selection of their new teaching colleagues. This constituted, in the worst possible way, both an attitude and an action contrary to shared governance and was precisely the reason Southeastern Seminary almost immediately began to have problems with our accrediting agencies.

(5) By a vote of 14–10 the trustees entered an executive session with me, the president. For me personally, as nothing else, this put the entire agenda of the new majority in perspective.

I vehemently opposed the closed session and reminded the trustees that only once before had we gone into executive session—to clear some personnel matters early in my administration (1975). I remember to this day my sadness as the meeting room was cleared of over 100 persons, including members of the press.

The executive session lasted from 3:25 p.m. until 4:25 p.m. There are no public minutes of the session, but I kept thorough written and mental notes. James DeLoach, newly-elected vice–chairman of trustees, a classmate of mine at Southeastern and a person whom I had long considered a friend, had been previously designated spokesman during the closed session. In fact, few other trustees said much. He spoke for the new majority. The other trustees had not been given any clue about the meeting and thus had nothing prepared to say.

James DeLoach took almost the entire hour, referring often to his written notes. He started by expressing his "love" for me and commending my thirteen years as Southeastern's longest-serving president.

After that, he "took me to the woodshed," holding me responsible for everything from my convocation address to several statements made in the media by Southeastern-connected people regarding the SBC controversy. He wondered why I supported the ordination of women and disclaimed the "conservative resurgence." He suggested that conservative students, like those in the CEF, had been treated less than fairly.

Then he outlined the vision of the new majority of trustees for the seminary, including adding only inerrantists to the faculty and staff. Not one time did he ever mention changing presidents, or suggest that I should resign or be fired. Instead, he did a more diabolical thing in my opinion. He made it clear that the trustees intended for me to become the agent for implementing their alien vision, no matter how much it contradicted my own. They would surround me with policies that in good conscience I could not administer.

When DeLoach finished, a few others spoke. I was given a chance to respond, a chance I passed up, telling the trustees only that I had ears and could hear, and that I had taken careful notes. The fact is, I knew that from this time forward I was beset by the worst irony of all—I could not trust the trustees.

By this time the hundred or so people outside had surrounded the building where we were meeting, and they were singing songs. One new trustee suggested that we open the doors, ending the executive session with me in the middle of the room kneeling and all the trustees standing around me with their hands on my head.

That made me mad, and I vigorously protested such a charade. One of my friends in the room said, "You have done our president enough damage today. Do not add insult to injury."

They opened the doors, and the people returned. The meeting came to a swift end.

Decisions to resign. Turmoil marked the campus after the trustees went home. Ironically, I was distracted over the following weekend. My father had been in a nursing home near Marion, North Carolina, for over a year. Word came from my brother that his doctors had decided to amputate

Dad's right leg due to continued poor circulation. I went to western North Carolina to be with my family and to sign papers for the amputation. During that time I talked with those who knew me best—my wife, my two daughters, and my brother. There by the bedside of my father, I recalled something he had told me. "Son," he often said, "remember that once you have been nailed to a cross, nothing much can hurt you anymore."

Strangely, I felt peace—if not in the SBC, then in me.

Early the next week I talked with several persons on campus—the dean, administrative colleagues, faculty colleagues, and students. I phoned some alumni. Not one of them gave me any real counsel, but they all gave me real support.

Months earlier I had committed to preach a series of three sermons in chapel the week following the trustee meeting. The chapel committee and student council had promoted the period as a time for spiritual renewal.

On Thursday, 22 October 1987, I preached on the text Matthew 26:36-46—Jesus in Gethsemane. At the conclusion of the sermon, I announced my intention to resign the presidency. Strangely, preparation for that sermon and for that moment stirred memories of my own "Gethsemane commitment" in coming to the presidency early in 1974.

Earlier that week Dean Morris Ashcraft had written a letter of resignation as dean of the faculty, stating that he was unwilling to carry out the takeover agenda of the new majority trustees.

Before chapel on Thursday, I had told absolutely no one, including my own family, that I intended to resign. I did, however, make a mid-morning call to Robert Crowley, trustee chairman, at his church office in Rockville, Maryland, to advise him of my decision and to request that he meet with me and three others to plan the transition. I was not at all surprised to learn that Paige Patterson and Paul Pressler, two architects of the SBC controversy, were with him just then at his church for a "Bible conference."

Following my decision to resign, four other colleagues announced their intentions to resign their administrative posts. These included John Rich, seminary attorney; Robert Spinks, assistant to the president: financial development; Jerry Niswonger, assistant to the president: student development; and Rod Byard, assistant to the president: communications. These persons, along with the dean of the faculty, constituted the core of my administration. Only two persons on the executive council remained at the seminary.

Called Trustee Meeting, 17 November 1987

Robert Crowley and I agreed to invite James DeLoach, vice-chairman of trustees, and the two immediate past chairmen of trustees still on the board, Jesse Chapman of North Carolina and Lee Beaver of Missouri, to meet and discuss the transition at the seminary. Our meeting took place at the Plantation Inn, Raleigh, on 3 November 1987.

We agreed unanimously to make eleven recommendations at a called meeting of the trustees on 17 November. The recommendations included plans to accept "with regret" my resignation and those of the dean and four administrators. Our tenure would extend to the end of the academic year, 31 July 1988, or end earlier if a new president were elected. I agreed to a transition procedure consistent with the wishes of my successor and accepted a generous transition financial provision. I also agreed to continue paying premiums on two life insurance policies with the seminary as named beneficiary.

The called meeting of the trustees convened at the Plantation Inn on the morning of 17 November 1987 with considerable numbers of interested persons and the media present. Prior to the meeting, there was a caucus of the new majority trustees, urged by some North Carolina trustees among them, who were angry with me about my nomination of Leon Smith to be president of the Baptist State Convention of North Carolina a week earlier in Winston-Salem. They pushed for my resignation to become effective on 1 January 1988. Their caucus caused the meeting to be delayed.

When word of the caucus reached me I advised James DeLoach that this move undermined an agreement I had with the small unofficial transition group and that the caucus' precipitous action would disrupt the seminary. Furthermore, if he persisted on this course, I would state that I was no longer resigning but was being fired from the presidency.

A further caucus apparently yielded the opinion that firing me was too great a public relations price to pay. The new majority trustees dropped their plan and accepted my resignation and those of the five other administrators on terms previously negotiated.

Later that day, a press conference was held on campus. Chairman Robert Crowley, Dean Morris Ashcraft, and I made statements to the press and an auditorium filled with interested persons, including many trustees. Dean Ashcraft and I explained why we had resigned. For me, in a word, the reason was vision. The trustees and I shared a different vision for Southeastern. Our differences ranged from matters of governance, through theology and ecclesiology, to management and leadership styles.

Trustee Meeting, 14–15 March 1988

This was my final meeting with the trustees. I knew as early as January 1988 that there would be a new president elected at this trustee meeting. Robert Crowley had come to the campus for a meeting of the persons formulating a profile for the new president. While there, he came by my office to make one final attempt to persuade me to vacate the presidency immediately and to let Paul Fletcher, assistant to the president: business affairs, take the responsibilities of the office. After a painful exchange I knew that he detected my resolve to stay by the agreement negotiated with the trustees in November. He left that day determined to have a new president by March.

Dr. Lewis Drummond, Billy Graham Professor of Evangelism at Southern Baptist Theological Seminary, Louisville, Kentucky, was elected Southeastern's fourth president on 14 March 1988. It was decided that he would assume office in two weeks, 1 April 1988. The trustees requested that I work with him as he desired during the time from my vacating the office until the date of my resignation on 31 July. As it turned out, the time the two of us spent together was limited to one breakfast that he invited me to attend with him. For two hours we discussed just about everything except Southeastern Seminary.

Upon invitation of the trustees, I presided at graduation exercises in May and July. On 30 July 1988 we vacated the president's house in Wake Forest and moved to Raleigh, where on 1 July I had become pastor of the First Baptist Church.

"The Southeastern Mistake"

Following the precipitous events in 1987 at the seminary, talk circulated, especially on some of the other SBC seminary campuses, about "the Southeastern mistake." This analysis argued that we had handed over the school to the new majority without a fight.

In my opinion, all such analysts were wrong. Early in 1988 I visited personally every member of the faculty and staff at Southeastern. Many times since 1987 I have talked with the persons who weathered the firestorm on our campus. Not one Southeasterner with whom I have talked believes that we made a mistake.

We struggled gallantly together so long as there seemed to be any chance to prevail and preserve our collective vision for the seminary. When the alien vision of the new majority gained ascendancy we decided to resign rather than to capitulate—to go with our principles rather than with our positions. There was no chance to negotiate a mutual vision with the new majority. Their agenda was set against it.

To this day I believe we did the right thing, the Baptist thing, the Christian thing in resigning. In doing so we all affirmed together that here in one time and at one place free-conscience Baptists said "*No*" to militant, New Right fundamentalism.

I am proud to have been a part of that time and place and people!

Notes

[1]See, for example, Morris Ashcraft, "Southeastern Seminary in Crisis, 1986–1987," *Faith and Mission* 6/1 (Fall 1988): 47–61; Grady C. Cothen, *What Happened to the Southern Baptist Convention? A Memoir of the Controversy* (Macon GA: Smyth & Helwys Publishing, Inc., 1993); Robison James, ed., *The Takeover in the Southern Baptist Convention* (Decatur GA: SBC Today, 1989).

[2]"Accepting Both Good and Bad," *Adult Life and Work Curriculum* (7 July 1985): 7–8.

[3]Ibid., 8.

[4]"Proceedings," *Annual of the Southern Baptist Convention*, Dallas TX, 11 June 1985 (Nashville: Executive Committee, SBC, 1985) 64.

[5]Charles Fuller letter to Randall Lolley, January 1986.

[6]Randall Lolley letter to Jim Henry, 11 February 1986.

[7]Randall Lolley, "Peace Committee Visit," Report to Board of Trustees, Wake Forest NC, 10 March 1986.

[8]Ibid.

[9]Jim Henry letter to Randall Lolley, 5 August 1986.

[10]Randall Lolley letter to Jim Henry, 18 September 1986.

[11]SBC Peace Committee Report, "Recommendation 5," *Annual of the Southern Baptist Convention*, St. Louis MO, 16 June 1987 (Nashville: Executive Committee, SBC, 1987) 241.

[12]SBC Seminary Presidents, "Glorieta Statement," Glorieta NM, 20 October 1986.

[13]Randall Lolley, "Plan of Action," Report presented to Board of Trustees, Wake Forest NC, 9 March 1987.

[14]*Administrative Manual* (Wake Forest NC, 1981) 24.

[15]"Trustee Minutes," 14 October 1987, 1.

——————— Chapter 3 ———————

The Educational Vision
of Southeastern Seminary

Morris Ashcraft

It was a practical need to those on the Committee on Theological Education of the Southern Baptist Convention. The whole southeastern part of the United States, which was the location of one-third of the SBC churches, had no Baptist seminary. Those selected to establish the school accepted the challenge of the practical need, but they added to that effort a dream. They dreamed of an excellent seminary faithful to its Baptist tradition and contemporary task but also participating in and contributing to the whole church.

In the Founders' Day Address on 10 March 1981, Professor James E. Tull, who had shared the dream as a faculty member for twenty-six years, stated the dream most clearly:

> I remember that the founders and others among the earliest teachers used to refer to what they called the "Southeastern dream." I was intrigued by the term, and curious about it. Although I never heard it precisely defined, I discovered that it referred not particularly to any institutional or pedagogical innovation, but rather to a spirit and an aim that my colleagues hoped would be embodied in the seminary's life.
>
> In those beginning days there was a climate of excitement on this campus as students, administration, staff, and faculty took up the launching of a dynamic new school and accepted the challenge of a new opportunity. There was a rare feeling of comradeship among those who participated in the new venture. . . .
>
> There was here something of the spirit that goes with a pioneer endeavor. Because the school was new, there was a feeling that it did not have to be bound unduly by old ways and old styles. It was felt that the materials of life here were malleable and flexible, capable of being shaped in the mold of all that was best of our past, but also by the needs and challenges of a new time. The curriculum and institutional organization were traditional, for the most part,

but many persons hoped that this would be a place where we could break out of our chronic denominational isolationism. While maintaining a loyal commitment to Southern Baptists, it was thought that we would join to a greater degree than ever before the larger Christian family. Some believed that, while holding firmly to our distinctive denominational beliefs, we would feel no separation or estrangement from other Christian scholars, because we belonged to a world fraternity of learning and to the universal brotherhood of Christ that transcended all our differences.

There was a hope that here, in a geographical area that was characterized by some cultural pluralism, we might address more effectively Christian insight and compassion to great ethical issues of our time, like those of race, war, and the vast depersonalizing influences of a mass industrial society.[1]

The Launching of Southeastern Seminary

The Origin of SEBTS

For several years numerous churchmen had worked to locate a Baptist seminary in the Southeast. The Committee on Theological Education of the SBC, after three years of study, recommended the founding of two new seminaries, Golden Gate Seminary on the west coast and Southeastern Seminary in Wake Forest, North Carolina. The SBC voted to do this on 10 May 1950 and spelled out the mission of the school for the Articles of Incorporation:

> The objects and purposes for which this corporation is formed are: to establish, maintain, and operate schools and institutions of learning for the educational and missionary training of Christian workers, for all kinds and character of Christian service, and to confer degrees; having full authority to do all things necessary to put into execution the purposes for which this corporation is created.[2]

The SBC then elected a board of trustees that chose the first president and began the necessary steps toward building an accredited seminary. In connection with establishing the school and getting a charter, the trustees approved the primary documents, two of which were a Statement of Purpose and the Articles of Faith. These are two of the most important documents in the life of a seminary and deserve special attention.

Statement of Purpose

The Statement of Purpose is an institutional document produced and revised by the several areas of the seminary, but always subject to final approval by the trustees, and reported to the Convention. The Statement of Purpose guides in electing faculty, planning all courses, and conferring degrees. It serves as the standard of all educational evaluations, particularly in institutional self-studies for accreditation reviews, and for all curriculum reviews. It serves as the standard by which all departments of the seminary plan and do their work: financial planning, renovation and construction of buildings, library resources, and public relations.

The first Statement of Purpose was revised before the second year of the school's life and appeared essentially in the same form until 1992. The Statement appears in every annual *Bulletin* of the seminary (see appendix).

Articles of Faith

The first board of trustees adopted as the Articles of Faith the statement that had served as the doctrinal norm of Southern Seminary since 1859. That statement, the Abstract of Principles, had been written by Basil Manly, Jr. of the first faculty. The Southern Baptist Convention did not adopt a confession of faith until 1925. The Articles of Faith appear in every *Bulletin* of SEBTS and Southern Baptist Theological Seminary.[3]

Article IX of Southeastern Seminary By-Laws states:

> All members of the Faculty shall be required to subscribe to the Articles of Faith, or Beliefs, as adopted by the Board of Trustees, and to sign these Articles publicly at the opening of the session in which they enter upon their duties. The Articles of Faith shall only be amended after prior action by the Southern Baptist Convention, and this article shall not be altered or amended except with such consent.[4]

The ceremony of signing the Articles is a meaningful occasion to both the professor and the witnesses. It signifies that the professor's faith is in harmony with this statement and that he or she will teach in accordance with and not contrary to that statement.

The administrators and faculty members who founded the school and those who joined later believed that the SBC founders wanted Southeastern Seminary, in addition to meeting the immediate needs of the churches in the Southeast, to be "a progressive seminary" serving "as a center for research, writing, and teaching related to Baptist life and the larger Christian community."[5]

Autonomy and Accountability

In keeping with the Baptist convictions that had prevailed since the origin of Baptists, the belief in soul liberty and local autonomy, the Southern Baptist Convention allowed Southeastern, as the other seminaries, a great deal of freedom. Those entrusted with founding and directing the seminary, the trustees, chose the Articles of Faith and approved the Statement of Purpose. These were reported to and approved by the convention.

The trustees and presidents reported regularly to the SBC. The president and faculty were always accountable to the trustees; the president, in constant communication with the trustees, made a formal "President's Report to the Trustees" at each semi-annual meeting; once a year the faculty submitted a formal "Faculty Report to the Trustees" that discussed any curricular changes, faculty matters, and the like. Recommendations for all faculty additions followed a trustee-approved procedure that included supporting documents assuring the competence of the proposed faculty member and his or her agreement with the Articles of Faith. The public signing of the document was a form of accountability and sacred pledge of faithfulness. Faculty members were accountable at all times to the president. They presented all course proposals to faculty for revision and approval. All curricular reviews were submitted to the trustees. Once every ten years the entire seminary underwent an "Institutional Self-Study" that finally resulted in a bound volume of reports measuring institutional achievement and plans judged by the Statement of Purpose. The volume was approved by the trustees and submitted to the Association of

Theological Schools and the Southern Association of Colleges and Schools.

One Seminary Among Six

Southern Seminary in Louisville had begun operation in 1859; Southwestern Seminary in Fort Worth had become an SBC seminary in 1925. The New Orleans Seminary, which had previously been the Baptist Bible Institute, became an SBC seminary in 1946.

When the SBC established Southeastern and Golden Gate (Golden Gate had existed previously under other sponsorship) in 1950, Southern Baptists already had three seminaries that served as models for the new institutions. In 1957, the SBC authorized Midwestern Seminary for Kansas City, Missouri, which opened in 1958. It is amazing that the convention established three seminaries in one decade, four seminaries in eleven years.

Most of us associated with Southeastern Seminary at any time during those first thirty-six years believe Southeastern was special and distinctive. In all fairness, however, all six of them were special. A general similarity existed among them: they belonged to and accounted to the same supporting group; their administrators and professors had come from the same Baptist families and churches and had been fellow students and colleagues in Baptist colleges and seminaries; their graduates worked as fellow pastors and missionaries all over the world; their presidents met twice annually to coordinate their work to assure their faithfulness to the overall task; their faculties met on occasion for serious discussions; their transcripts were transferable; and their faculties were often shared in exchanges.

While these general similarities prevailed, there were differences. Southern and Southeastern Seminaries were guided by the Articles of Faith, while the other four had adopted the Baptist Faith and Message approved by the SBC in 1925 and revised in 1963. This diversity was considered very appropriate by Baptists prior to the controversy of the last fifteen years. The Baptist Faith and Message, both 1925 and 1963, acknowledges and encourages this diversity.[6]

Unfair generalizations that stated that one seminary was "liberal" and another was "conservative" were sometimes heard. There was diversity within all six faculties, but none was "liberal" in the theological meaning of that term. I was on the faculties of Southern and Midwestern prior to going to Southeastern. I have great respect for all six of the seminaries and their faculties during the period of my evaluation and, while maintaining a distinctiveness for Southeastern, do not intend in any way to lessen respect for the other five, which earned and maintained their full accreditation and reputations and made their contributions.

The Winds of Change

Many powerful forces that changed both the convention and the churches were at work on the Southern Baptist scene after World War II. These forces arose from two factors: (1) We were in our period of greatest growth and expansion accompanied by a strong centralizing force and a narrowing exclusivism. (2) We were in a setting in which other major religious denominations were moving toward more cooperation or inclusiveness.

To use the phrase of W. C. Fields, the period from 1949–1979 was the "Golden Age" of Southern Baptists.[7] We expanded into all states; our funding instrument, the Cooperative Program, grew incredibly; we established many new churches; our mission boards expanded; we founded four seminaries in a span of eleven years. The Southern Baptist Convention—with one funding program that undergirded state and local as well as SBC causes, one publishing house, and six seminaries that provided tuition-free theological education to almost all of our ministerial students—became much more centralized at the top than any other Baptist group.

The rapid expansion was interpreted as God's favor and bred an arrogance out of which convention leaders and spokesmen boasted that we were right and the other denominations were being rejected by God. Many of our efforts advanced by such methods and rationales led to a denominational exclusivism and isolation.

Baptists have never been free of exclusivism; perhaps our origin in a time of persecution by other religious groups was a factor. The greatest boost, however, toward our exclusivistic attitude came from the Landmark Movement, which began in Tennessee in the 1850s.[8] The Landmark claim that only Baptist churches are "true" churches could hardly be more exclusive. That claim led to the notion that only Baptist-ordained ministers were authoritative, that only Baptist baptism and Lord's Supper were valid, and the like.

The new state conventions in the West and Northwest had had an influx of Baptists from the states of heaviest Landmark influence: Tennessee, Arkansas, Texas, Oklahoma, parts of Kentucky, Louisiana, and others. From the beginning, the element of exclusivism was obvious. Many people call this conservatism. It *was* conservative, but exclusivism is somewhat different.

The Landmark exclusivism deeply changed the entire Southern Baptist Convention. One direct result was the Whitsitt Controversy at Southern Seminary.[9] Professor and President W. H. Whitsitt had published an article showing historical evidence to support the fact that early Baptists had recovered believers' baptism by immersion in 1641. The resultant storm, Landmark-in-SBC-inspired, forced his departure, even though practically all Baptist church historians agree that he was correct.

The exclusivistic Landmark influence is also obvious elsewhere. Southern Seminary Professor and President E. Y. Mullins published his systematic theology, *The Christian Religion In Its Doctrinal Expression*, without a chapter on The Church, even though he believed in it.[10] The 1925 Baptist confession—The Baptist Faith and Message—included an Article XII, "A Gospel Church," but no reference to The Church. Prior to the 1925 statement, denominational publications had circulated widely the New Hampshire Confession of Faith of 1833 in church manuals. This confession spoke only "Of a Gospel Church." The Landmark view of only local churches prevailed so that the revision of the BFAM in 1963 was stiffly opposed when the SBC voted to add to Article VI, "The Church," the statement, "The New Testament speaks also of the church as the body of Christ which includes all of the redeemed of all the ages."[11]

In 1951 Southeastern Seminary was launched in a turbulent sea of contrary winds. The region in which it was located had not yet been overcome by the trend toward denominational exclusivism that was growing elsewhere and destined to spread. The seminary founders believed in a wholesome denominational loyalty that encouraged participation in and contribution to the whole Church. This sentiment shows in the primary documents and was reaffirmed in institutional self-studies as late as 1981. That report stated in the "Critique of the Statement of Purpose" that the first members of the board of trustees and faculty understood this larger purpose.[12]

A trend toward inclusiveness was at work in American Christianity. The Ecumenical Movement was an inspiration to most of the mainline American denominations. It, too, was a powerful force. Many Southern Baptists joined on the local level with more cooperation and an attitude of inclusiveness. The SBC refused to send representatives to the historic World Council of Churches meetings, but many Southern Baptist leaders were in Amsterdam, Evanston, and New Delhi as more than interested observers. Southern and American Baptists, separated in 1845, had for a time cooperated in a regional seminary in Kansas City, Kansas. Central Seminary had trustees, faculty, and students from both conventions. An SBC decision, however, in the mid-1950s to support no institutions whose trustees the SBC did not elect ended that relationship and almost destroyed Central Seminary. In 1957 the SBC voted to locate a new seminary in Kansas City, Missouri.

An effort was made to secure closer ties with other Baptist groups in the North American Baptist Fellowship. The Southern and American Conventions both scheduled their meetings in Atlantic City in 1964. Leaders such as Dale Moody and Carlyle Marney had hoped that this Fellowship would help heal the breach and move the SBC into a more inclusive and cooperative stance. A banquet had been planned as a celebration occasion. I recall, however, that actions in the SBC during the day changed that meeting into a somber realization that no such relationship was then possible.

Southeastern Seminary was launched in the context of a growing denominational exclusivistic isolationism among a people, many of whom still believed in and worked for a more cooperative relationship with other Christian groups. The founders of Southeastern Seminary and those who joined later were of this more inclusive outlook. The seminary followed this course for its first thirty-six years. The strong political force that declared in 1979 its intent to control exploited both the centralization of the SBC at the top and the exclusivism that reached its peak in the drastic changes approved by the SBC when it adopted the Peace Committee Report in 1987. The openness and inclusiveness in the spirit, style, and primary documents of Southeastern Seminary (and I think Southern Seminary, as well, if not all SBC seminaries) were condemned in that vote by messengers, many, if not most, of whom did not know fully the intentions and implications of the action.

Southeastern's Educational Course, 1951–1987

Southeastern's curriculum and degree requirements were quite traditional and not only representative of the other five SBC seminaries but also similar to those of other denominational seminaries and divinity schools.

The faculty areas were Bible (B area), History (H area), Theology (T area), and Ministry (M area). Missions was in the H area. Pastoral Care, Preaching, Education, Evangelism, and other courses were in the M area. Some positions, such as Historical Theology, overlapped two areas.

The seminary degree requirements spelled out core courses or required or foundational studies to insist that all students studied certain necessary areas. The school always sought to provide adequately so that students, through elective work, could tailor their own courses of study with faculty consultation.

Just recently, Dr. Olin T. Binkley, first dean and second president, told me that from the beginning, "We determined that Southeastern would be deeply rooted in the Christian faith, thorough in scholarship, and would maintain a vital relationship to the churches."[13]

It would take chapters to deal with the various course descriptions and degree requirements. These are published in the annual *Bulletin*. It appears to me that the educational vision of SEBTS can best be understood by looking at its Statement of Purpose, which guided the course and degree planning and was the standard by which the faculty judged its own academic work and by which its curriculum reviews and self-studies for accreditation reviews were evaluated.

The Statement of Purpose

The first seminary *Bulletin*, while stating the primary purpose and aim, reads: "The Seminary will always be conscious of its responsibility to help furnish a leadership for its own denomination and for the whole Christian movement."[14] That Statement was revised in the second year.

With minor revisions in subsequent years, it remained in the same form throughout the period under review, 1951–1987 (see Appendix).

The Seminary: What It Is

In the 1973–1974 catalog a brief paragraph defined the Seminary as "a community of learning, deeply rooted in the Christian faith, thorough in scholarship, and vitally related to the churches."[15] As a result of discussions in the annual ten-year accreditation review, seminary faculty and administration wanted to stress the personal nature of the seminary community, its purpose as a school, its commitment to Christian faith, and its vital relation to the churches.

The Primary Purpose

Over the years under consideration, the seminary always indicated that the seminary's "primary purpose is to prepare men and women for Christian leadership in various ministries." The emphasis was always on persons and their ministries. The courses included many of the so-called "content" courses accomplished in the library and classroom. Many required actual ministry for weeks in a ministry setting in this country or abroad. Professors led these *practica* in hands-on ministry. One course involved archaeological research through scholarship-funded travel in Bible lands, and another course involved an eight-week participation in an archaeolgical excavation under the direction of a Southeastern professor. Southeastern early offered Field Work guidance and by the 1970s had a staff of qualified supervisors in ministry and a comprehensive program of supervision in ministry for all students.

Theological Education Prerequisite to Ministry

The founders believed and stated in their Statement of Purpose, "Vital to all these areas of service [ministries listed in the paragraph above] is an understanding of the origins, content, and history of the Christian faith and its contemporary relevance. Courses of study directed toward such

an understanding constitute the curriculum and are regarded as basic."
Baptist polity does not allow for a denomination-wide requirement for a
seminary education prior to ordination. Many Baptist ministers have not
had such an education. Southeastern Seminary founders believed that
such an education was prerequisite for effective ministry, and while it
may be obtained outside a formal theological school, it usually happens
in a seminary setting.

Responsibility and Accountability

A Statement of Purpose must indicate the institution's responsibility and
to whom it is accountable. Though the seminary kept itself reminded of
the responsibility and accountability to the SBC, it had a policy, often
reaffirmed, of openness to students of all denominations: "While the
seminary is conscious of its responsibility to the Southern Baptist Convention, its facilities are open on an equal basis to students of all
denominations. It is the aim of the seminary to help produce a leadership
for the whole Christian movement." The seminary also cherished the
hope of providing leadership for the Christian movement beyond the
Southern Baptist Convention. This openness and inclusiveness influenced
the spirit on the campus.

Many denominations were represented by invited lecturers and
visiting professors in numerous areas, not only in missions. One of our
most popular visiting professors was Anglican Bishop Stephen Neill, who
had years of service in India. We had a course on contemporary Jewish
Studies taught by visiting Jewish scholars. A visiting Roman Catholic
scholar taught our students a course on Roman Catholic Thought since
Vatican II. Our faculty thought that our students who became missionaries in settings with Roman Catholics ought to know the truth rather
than thinking prejudicially because of Roman Catholic beliefs and practices dating from medieval times. The Roman Catholic bishop was
welcomed on this campus to speak with our students. Southeastern had
approximately forty United Methodist students during the early and mid-
1980s. The seminary offered courses on Methodist Polity, Doctrine, and
History that were taught by visiting Methodist scholars so that these students would be prepared for their ordination. These various contacts with
the church beyond SBC life were planned from the beginning in keeping

with our purpose. They contributed to our own campus life, to our students, and hopefully to many beyond our walls.

The main part of the Southeastern campus is surrounded by a low stone wall that was inherited from Wake Forest College. The wall has fallen into disrepair and has been undergoing considerable and much-needed rebuilding during the last couple of years. As I observed the craftmanship with admiration, I could not avoid the sad awareness that the school noted for openness and inclusiveness in the past is now building a wall in a world with walls coming down.

Educational Resources

Southern Baptists richly supported the seminary through its Cooperative Program throughout the period. The seminary pledged to invest those resources in maintaining "a God-called faculty," "adequate physical facilities," and "an excellent library."

During the administration of President Lolley, the seminary developed a faculty growth plan to determine how best to invest these resources in a permanent faculty. The seminary also developed a faculty of "part-time" contract teachers who were specialists in areas such as counseling, music, childhood education, and denominational work. Other part-time teachers taught courses in the biblical, historical, and theological areas. The editor of the Baptist state newspaper taught religious journalism.

The library was a special concern from the first administration and received adequate funding to accumulate a magnificent collection of learning resources.

Objectives

In the Statement of Purpose, *Bulletin* of 1951–1952, the seminary listed six objectives or emphases that undergirded the seminary program.

Objective One: Thorough Knowledge of the Bible. A "thorough knowledge of the Bible" was the first objective. This priority was reaffirmed every time the Statement of Purpose was reviewed. The number of faculty members and courses offered in the B area shows the prominence of biblical study. The requirements for various degrees indicate the priority of biblical study.

Objective Two: A Wholesome and Intelligent Evangelism. The negative implication is present that our founders believed that some of our evangelistic endeavors were neither wholesome nor intelligent. The positive intent, therefore, was to teach and encourage a knowledge and practice of evangelism that was both. Evangelism was in the M area and was adequately staffed by competent people. Southeastern Professor Delos Miles was the outstanding Southern Baptist writer in this area, but the faculty counted on the B-area and the T-area professors to stress a "wholesome" evangelism also.

Objective Three: A Challenging Vision of the World-Wide Mission of Christianity. From the beginning of the school, Southeastern faculty included professors of missions and scheduled missionary scholars on furlough to teach missions. Apartments were also provided for such resident missionaries. A special endowment brought missionary teachers in home missions. Regular missionary days built a missions spirit on campus by presenting outstanding missionaries and missiologists to the seminary and surrounding community.

Objective Four: Christian Commitment. The early statements of purpose called for a "prevailing spiritual dynamic in the lives of students and faculty." The later revision called it "an unqualified commitment to God as revealed in our Lord Jesus Christ."[16] The admissions procedures sought to enroll only persons with a strong sense of calling and deep commitment to the Christian ministry. A graduate of the 1950s spoke movingly to me of the chapel messages of President Stealey in which he read from the Christian devotional classics and of the wholesome spiritual atmosphere on campus.

Objective Five: The Mission of the Local Church. The original state-ment, "A sense of the significance of the local church—urban and rural," was revised in the 1981 Statement to "a sense of the mission of the local church in every social context." The seminary kept the local church in the foreground of interest. Courses focused on both urban and rural churches and their ministry. Most students were already involved in a local church ministry. Most professors and staff members were regularly serving as interim ministers in those churches. The seminary's interest in all of Christianity and churches beyond the Baptist border enhanced our appreciation of the local congregation within the SBC.

Objective Six: Academic Excellence. The original statement, "A consecrated scholarship for providing genuine Christian leadership," was shortened in 1971 to "a commitment to academic excellence in the con-text of an open admissions policy." The open admissions policy advised prospective students of the nature of this campus.

While the records of all institutions will reflect some version of this quest for excellence, it was a genuine goal at Southeastern. This empha-sis appeared in its criteria for faculty selection, granting of tenure, and promoting faculty members.

The seminary records show that all of the faculty members had at least one earned doctorate. The seminary tried to plan against "in-breeding" in the faculty. While we wanted all faculty members to have one degree either from a Baptist university or seminary, we sought fac-ulty members with graduate degrees from non-Baptist schools as well. The *Bulletin* of 1978–1979 pointed out that the forty-nine members of the teaching staff held 178 degrees from fifty-eight different universities, colleges, and seminaries.

The seminary could not afford, nor would class needs justify, a fac-ulty member in every discipline. Fortunately, such specialists were in the immediate vicinity and—as adjunctive or visiting professors—brought their expertise in childhood education, counseling, journalism, music, and other disciplines to enhance greatly the academic excellence of South-eastern.

The sabbatic leave program provided for faculty to be away for post-doctoral studies after every six years of teaching. These study leaves enriched the academic life of the seminary and allowed professors to publish an incredibly large number of works. In 1984 alone, they published seven books and sixty journal articles.[17]

The Vision Reviewed

The Statement of Purpose

The full Statement of Purpose of the second year of the seminary remained essentially the same until the major revision that appeared in the 1992–1993 *Bulletin*. The original purpose discussed previously may be summarized quickly.

The founders of the seminary and those who guided and taught here believed that it was an institution for learning. The seminary was to be characterized by deep rootage in Christian faith and by a vital relationship to the churches. It was to prepare men and women for all the various Christian ministries. The seminary could do its task only if its students learned the historical as well as the theological content of the faith.

The seminary was always conscious of its responsibility to Southern Baptists, both the convention and the churches, but also of its responsibility for, and in a sense to, the whole Christian movement. This inclusiveness was a vital part of the atmosphere on campus in which teaching and learning took place.

The specific objectives of the seminary always insisted on (1) a thorough knowledge of the Bible, (2) a wholesome and intelligent evangelism, (3) a challenging vision of the world-wide mission of Christianity, (4) an unqualified commitment to God as revealed in our Lord Jesus Christ, (5) a sense of the mission of the local church in every social context, and (6) a commitment to academic excellence in the context of an open admissions policy.

The Articles of Faith

The seminary was careful to stay within its doctrinal guidelines as stated in the Articles of Faith. Prospective faculty members were questioned on these. New faculty members pledged by signing the document in a solemn and public ceremony that they believed these Articles and would teach in accordance with and not contrary to them.

The Vision Beyond These Minimums

Official documents, such as legal documents, tend to state only minimal requirements. Seminaries seek to pursue excellence far beyond these minimal limits.

Southeastern always had a strong inclusiveness that reached beyond denominational borders to participate in the life of the whole church and to seek to make a contribution thereto. This inclusiveness permeated the atmosphere of the campus and in my judgment enhanced our denominational loyalty and value.

Dr. Lolley encouraged a complete openness on campus. Meetings, including trustee meetings, were open. The President's Forum permitted discussion of any questions that did not specifically focus on individuals. Classes were cheerful, characterized by an attitude of trust in which controversial subjects could be dealt with seriously. Disagreement did not intimidate. Trustee visits were cheerful and disclosed that they shared the dream.

During the 1980s a visiting university professor, who had previously been a seminary professor in another Southern Baptist seminary, spent a semester teaching at Southeastern. He commented on one occasion that he had found on this campus an attitude of openness and inclusiveness that seemed to him to be the ideal of what a seminary ought to be. The Southeastern vision was one of its greatest resources.

The Vision Replaced

The Southeastern vision did not fade nor die; it was killed. I will not discuss in detail the changes in the Southern Baptist Convention that began in 1979. Numerous publications have done this quite adequately.[18] Instead I will mention only the actions that clarify the replacement of Southeastern's educational vision.

In the early and mid-1980s a small group of students aggressively opposed some faculty members in class and reported to the inerrantist leaders of the SBC. These incidents introduced an element of distrust that disturbed the classroom setting and hampered learning. It damaged the on-campus spirit.

In 1986 trustees introduced the inerrancy issue into the questioning of faculty nominees. They sought to judge such candidates by statements on inerrancy from other schools and in one case used the Chicago Statement on Inerrancy. They did not even recognize that the Southeastern Articles of Faith stated our doctrinal norm on Scripture as follows: "The Scriptures of the Old and New Testaments were given by inspiration of God, and are the only sufficient, certain and authoritative rule of all saving knowledge, faith and obedience."[19] There was no basis for inerrancy in that document—no hint of it.

SBC Approval of the Peace (sic) Committee Report

In 1985 the SBC appointed a special committee, which later became known as the Peace Committee. This Peace Committee had so-called moderate members but was dominated by leaders of the inerrantist group. The committee's recommendation was presented to the SBC in June 1987. Regrettably, it was not published in advance. In fact, many messengers got copies late in the day, leaving little time for study before the vote. Time was inadequate for discussion.

This convention action accomplished a number of significant changes for Southern Baptists, some of which I think were not recognized by the majority of those present and voting: (1) The Peace Committee Report as adopted established inerrancy as the official view of inspiration of scripture for those in Baptist seminaries and other denominational institutions. (2) It authorized the trustees of the various instititions to "determine the theological positions of the seminary administrators and faculty members"[20] and to select future persons only if they reflected these beliefs. (3) Without overtly admitting it, the action officially revised the Baptist Faith and Message by interpreting its Article I on scripture as teaching that view of inerrancy. (4) The action rejected the Articles of Faith of Southeastern Seminary (and Southern, too) by imposing the inerrancy interpretation upon seminaries. Since that date, trustees have left no doubt that they intend to enforce that view on the seminaries, and they have convention approval for so doing. The sequence was Southeastern, Southern, and Midwestern.

The Articles of Faith

The Southeastern *Bulletin* continues to print the Articles of Faith without notation. It also prints the Baptist Faith and Message without notation. Preceding the Articles of Faith in the *Bulletin*, however, the new Statement of Purpose focuses on (1) spiritual development, (2) theological studies, and (3) practical preparation (see Appendix). The introductory paragraph identifies the seminary as "an institution of higher learning established and supported by the Southern Baptist Convention in order to 'contend earnestly for the faith which was once and for all delivered to the saints.' " The key sentence appears in Section II, Theological Studies: "The Seminary is committed to the complete veracity, inerrancy, and infallibility of the Bible as an essential foundation for effective Christian ministry and service."[21]

When the new trustees were making the changes, they studiously avoided revising or replacing the Articles of Faith. The contention of the takeover group had been that they were faithful to the doctrinal documents and stance and that we "moderates" had departed. Therefore, they did not want to change the official doctrinal statement, but rather changed the doctrinal stance of the school by changing the Statement of Purpose.

The New Statement of Purpose

According to the new Statement, "Southeastern Baptist Theological Seminary is an institution of higher learning established and supported by the Southern Baptist Convention in order to 'contend earnestly for the faith which was once and for all delivered to the saints.' "[22] The Statement refers neither to inclusiveness or to recognition of a relationship beyond Baptists, as did all former Statements.

The Southern Baptist trend toward exclusiveness reached its peak in St. Louis with the approval of the Peace Committee report. Theological education was a primary concern of that committee and the most obvious and immediate casualty. The long-range adverse effects, however, may be more serious than the end of a few educational instititions and the transfer of seminary control to those with a different purpose.

Hopefully, the dream may rise again. The SBC, however, has rejected the openness and inclusiveness stated in previous statements of purpose of the seminary. It has adopted a closed and exclusivistic attitude. The trustees of Southeastern Seminary, however much they may have worked for the SBC change, were carrying out the mandate of the convention.

When I came to Southeastern Seminary late in my ministry at age fifty-eight, I found the best of the Baptist tradition in both the seminary and in the churches. The seminary was firmly committed to Southern Baptists and sought to excel in training their ministers. The seminary was also open and inclusive. The campus itself looked and felt like a school. The physical characteristics helped create an atmosphere of learning. The steps on the stairways were grooved by the feet of generations of students and teachers from both the college and seminary. Southeastern had long been an excellent school and was on the verge of being a "great" seminary. That has changed. A rigid exclusivism is now apparent.

In 1963 the Southern Baptist Convention revised its confession of faith. Several minor changes were made. Two major revisions were passed. To Article I, The Scriptures, these words were added for clarification: "The criterion by which the Bible is to be interpreted is Jesus Christ."[23] If taken seriously, this was an important change. The 1925 Baptist Faith and Message made no mention of the universal church, only local churches. The 1963 revision added a short paragraph in Article VI, The Church, that reads, "The New Testament speaks also of the church as the body of Christ which includes all of the redeemed of all the ages."[24] These two changes indicate that in 1963, Southern Baptists were open enough to acknowledge Jesus Christ as Lord of scripture and to include at least a reference to The Church, "the redeemed of all the ages."

Southeastern Seminary was in that tradition of openness and inclusiveness and cherished its relationship to the larger community of Christians.

The SBC action on the Peace Committee report in 1987 placed the inerrancy theory "about the Bible" above the Bible itself. Our Confession of Faith indicates that our criterion for interpreting the Bible is Jesus Christ. Recommendation 5 of the Peace Committee report changed that criterion. It is now the inerrancy theory of inspiration made rigid by literalistic interpretations used as illustrations. A careful reading of Recommendation 5 shows that the trustees of the seminaries are to guard seminary faculties by choosing faculty and staff members "who clearly reflect such dominant convictions and beliefs held by Southern Baptists at large."[25] In other words, Jesus Christ is no longer the criterion for interpreting the Bible; the Bible itself is no longer the supreme norm; rather, the majority opinion of Southern Baptists is.

The educational vision of Southeastern was to be faithful to the best tradition of Southern Baptists while participating meaningfully in the life of the whole church. It was a dream to excel. While we may blame the "fundamentalists" who set out to take control of the Southern Baptist Convention and succeeded, Southern Baptists cannot escape the responsibility. Southern Baptists approved a special committee and then approved the Peace Committee Report that authorized these changes.

In the name of inerrancy, we have made the greatest error of our history.

Notes

[1] James E. Tull, "Southeastern Seminary—Whence? What? Whither?" Founders' Day Address delivered in Southeastern Seminary Chapel, 10 March 1981. Unpublished, located in seminary archives.

[2] *Annual of the Southern Baptist Convention*, 1950 (Nashville: Executive Committee, SBC, 1950) 415.

[3] Regrettably, William L. Lumpkin did not include the "Abstract of Principles" in his Baptist Confessions of Faith. This was actually the first confession of faith to be adopted by any Southern Baptist body. It can be found in any catalog of Southern Baptist Theological Seminary or Southeastern Baptist Theological Seminary.

[4] By-Laws of the Southeastern Baptist Theological Seminary, Inc., adopted 7 December 1950. This statement is included in all seminary catalogs, along with the Articles of Faith.

[5] "Critique of the Statement of Purpose," Section 1.1 of *Self-Study Report, 1981, Southeastern Baptist Theological Seminary, Wake Forest, North Carolina*, 1.

[6] "The Baptist Faith and Message," adopted 9 May 1963, expressed great freedom of Baptists to use, revise, and adopt other confessions of faith and "not to be used to hamper freedom of thought or investigation in other realms of life." See paragraph (5) in the preamble.

[7] For a thorough review of this expansion and its effects, see H. Leon McBeth, *The Baptist Heritage* (Nashville: Broadman Press, 1987), chapter 15.

[8]W. Morgan Patterson, "Landmarkism," *Encyclopedia of Southern Baptists*, 4 vols. (Nashville: Broadman Press, 1958) 2:757; "The Landmark Movement," H. Leon McBeth, *The Baptist Heritage*, 447–61.

[9]Gaines S. Dobbins, "Whitsitt, William Heth," *Encyclopedia of Southern Baptists*, 2:1496.

[10]Edgar Young Mullins, *The Christian Religion In Its Doctrinal Expression* (Nashville: Broadman Press, 1917).

[11]"The Baptist Faith and Message," Article VI, The Church.

[12]*Self-Study Report, 1981*. See note 5.

[13]In November 1993 Dr. Olin T. Binkley spoke to the author about the early years at Southeastern. Dr. Binkley is now in the Hillside Nursing Home of Wake Forest.

[14]See Appendix.

[15]*Southeastern Seminary Bulletin* (1973–1974).

[16]*Southeastern Seminary Bulletin* (1981–1982) 5.

[17]Southeastern Baptist Theological Seminary Report of the Faculty to the Board of Trustees, 11–12 March 1985, 10f.

[18]Robison James, ed., *The Takeover in the Southern Baptist Convention: A Brief History* (Decatur GA: SBC Today, 1989); Nancy Tatom Ammerman, *Baptist Battles* (New Brunswick NJ and London: Rutgers University Press, 1990); Grady C. Cothen, *What Happened to the Southern Baptist Convention?* (Macon GA: Smyth & Helwys Publishing, 1993).

[19]The "Articles of Faith" of Southeastern Baptist Seminary adopted in the beginning of the school in 1950 have remained unchanged "officially." This confession of faith was the official Articles of Faith of Southern Seminary in Louisville since 1859 and was adopted by Southeastern Seminary without revision. The quotation above is the full statement on the inspiration of the Bible. To my knowledge, Southeastern Seminary trustees never voted any change of the doctrinal statement. If they did so, it would not have been valid until the SBC approved it. The fact is, however, the trustees have been operating by a different doctrinal norm since 1987. This is corroborated by the revised Statement of Purpose.

[20]See Appendixes.

[21]*Southeastern Seminary Bulletin* (1992–1993) 2.

[22]Ibid.

[23]"The Baptist Faith and Message" is available in the *Annual of the Southern Baptist Convention*, 1963, and in tract form. See note 6.

[24]Ibid., Article VI.

[25]See Appendixes.

Chapter 4

The Faculty's Response to Fundamentalist Control

Richard L. Hester

At three o'clock in the afternoon of 22 October 1987 the faculty of Southeastern Baptist Theological Seminary stood on the worn granite steps of Broyhill Hall before a group of television and newspaper reporters. We were responding to the announcement that morning by Randall Lolley that he was resigning as president of the school. He was vacating the office in protest of the new policies of a fundamentalist majority of the board of trustees. He announced that Morris Ashcraft, dean of the faculty, was resigning with him.

It was a brilliant fall day, and a gathering of students, seminary staff, and townspeople surrounded about ten media people. As president of the Southeastern Chapter of the American Association of University Professors (AAUP), I was the faculty spokesperson. I read from a text that had been drafted by the faculty during the two hours preceding the press conference. I said that we were grieved by the loss of our two leaders, that we supported their resignations as courageous moral acts, and that we were united in our opposition to the political fundamentalism that had driven them from their posts.

What we were doing was a drama that once before had been played out on this same stage. Broyhill Hall, in front of which we now stood, had been built in the last century as Lea Laboratory, the first science building in North Carolina, and stood on the north side of what had been the Wake Forest College campus. It now housed the "Great Room" where seminary faculty and trustee meetings convened. In 1905 William Louis Poteat, a professor of biology, became president of Wake Forest College. He taught biology in Lea Laboratory. In 1919 he came under attack by fundamentalists for teaching evolution. These attacks helped spark the anti-evolution movement in the South that the Scopes Trial has made famous.

Poteat went to the annual meeting of the North Carolina Baptist Convention in 1922 under heavy fire from fundamentalists. He delivered an address at the convention that was not a defense of his teaching of evolution but a declaration of his conviction that Christian education can occur only in an environment where the freedom of inquiry is protected. He said that faith had nothing to fear from science and warned that it would be unforgivable to "fear that the Spirit of truth will not guide us into all the truth." He appealed to his hearers: "Welcome Truth. . . . And do not stop to calculate the adjustment and revision her fresh coming will necessitate." The following morning Poteat was given a resounding vote of confidence by the convention.[1]

As we stood on the steps of William Louis Poteat's laboratory in October 1987 our lives were linked with his. Sixty-eight years after he had fought for academic freedom our faculty was doing the same thing.

What follows is an account of the faculty's organization to respond to the takeover of the school by the fundamentalists who controlled the Southern Baptist Convention (SBC). This account does not detail the creative and often heroic actions by seminary students who organized "Students for Academic Freedom" and waged their own campaign to protect academic freedom and to support the faculty and the outgoing administration. It does not describe the moral courage of those seminary administrators who refused to capitulate to fundamentalist demands. This is the faculty's story as I saw it during the years of 1987–1989 from my vantage point as the first president of the Southeastern Seminary chapter of the AAUP.

Two Early Jolts of Reality

Fundamentalists had secured the election of their candidate for president at every Southern Baptist Convention meeting since 1979. Although these presidents, through the SBC committee on committees, had systematically placed fundamentalists on Southeastern's board and on the boards of all other convention agencies, our faculty found it difficult to believe they could gain control of our school. Two events, however, jolted the faculty into full awareness that we were about to experience an unprecedented takeover of the school by persons who had no regard for our theological heritage or traditions of participatory governance.

At the SBC meeting in June 1985 a "Peace Committee" was established with the ostensible purpose of bringing about reconciliation between moderates and fundamentalists in the convention. This committee, however, became an instrument of fundamentalist coercion of convention agencies. On 4–5 February 1986 a subcommittee of the Peace Committee visited the Southeastern campus. The subcommittee confronted the president, dean, and chair of the trustees on 5 February with twenty-seven "concerns" about statements allegedly made or positions allegedly taken by members of the faculty in class and in writing. Most of these concerns were the product of an off-the-record meeting the night before of three members of the committee and students belonging to the Conservative Evangelical Fellowship—a fundamentalist group that, with encouragement from SBC leaders, had appointed itself a watchdog of orthodoxy on the campus. Representative concerns were that particular faculty members advocated the ordination of women, did not hold to an inerrant view of scripture, supported the views of liberation theology, did not believe in a substitutionary view of the atonement, and were intolerant of views that differed from their own. Members of the subcommittee took these complaints as charges of faculty misconduct and pursued them as such.

President Lolley asked the fifteen faculty involved to reply to these concerns. In August the subcommittee requested further clarification of some of the replies, and further responses were given. The president urgently asked for a response from the Peace Committee, saying that this situation was "perilously near to the greatest of all ironies—being held hostage, without information, responses, or charges, in of all things, a process seeking peace." He never received a response.[2]

A second jolt of reality came to the faculty a year later on 20–21 February 1987 when prospective faculty members Roy DeBrand and Elizabeth Barnes were interviewed by the instruction committee of the board of trustees. In these interviews trustees James DeLoach and Robert Crowley interrogated the nominees to determine their stand on the issue of the inerrancy of scripture. DeLoach invoked the Chicago Statement on Biblical Inerrancy as his standard for judging the two candidates, despite the fact that this document had no recognized status at Southeastern.[3] The Chicago Statement holds "inerrancy" to mean that "Scripture is without error or fault in all its teaching, no less in what it states about God's acts in creation, about events of world history, and about its own literary origins under God, than in its witness to God's saving grace in individual lives." This view of the Bible is utterly contrary to the historical-critical approach to the Scripture that had been the norm since Southeastern's founding in 1950, and nothing in the school's Articles of Faith, statement of purpose, or other documents supported such a view.

These two events made clear to the faculty that although the seminary's Articles of Faith—to which all faculty members subscribed—did not support an inerrant view of the Bible, nonetheless a norm of inerrancy would be imposed by a new fundamentalist trustee majority. It also became apparent that the fundamentalist trustees would ignore or abrogate established policies or procedures in order to force their ideology on the faculty.

Establishing an Independent Faculty Organization

The governance of the seminary made no provision for a separate organization of the faculty, such as a faculty senate. The chair of the faculty was the president of the seminary. The faculty could convene only under his direction. The faculty began to see that it needed some means of organizing and expressing itself other than through the school's administration. This avenue of separation was not chosen because of our opposition to President Randall Lolley but because of our need to exercise some freedom from the institutional structures of the school.

On 9 March 1987, a group of Southeastern faculty gathered to talk with Jeff Butts, President of the North Carolina Conference of the AAUP, about organizing an AAUP chapter. The American Association of University Professors was established in January 1915 with John Dewey among its founding leaders. At its first national meeting it established the Committee on Academic Freedom and Academic Tenure, committing itself to the protection of the academic profession from attempts to curb academic inquiry.[4]

The AAUP would enable the Southeastern faculty to organize itself for collective action and give it a set of guiding principles in its defense of academic freedom. On 21 April twelve faculty and one administrator gathered to decide whether to proceed with the formal organization of a chapter. In my remarks to the group I contended that we should form an AAUP chapter in order (1) to shift responsibility for our future from the seminary administration and onto our own shoulders as faculty; (2) to promote our emotional well-being by moving us out of a passive and into an active stance; (3) to identify ourselves as an entity separate from the institution itself—a group of scholars who are assuming prophetic responsibility for interpreting theologically the crisis in the SBC and in our society, the crisis of a movement toward authoritarian religion and totalitarian politics; (4) to call to collective action the other five SBC seminary faculties; and (5) to invest ourselves in a life-giving process and faith venture that could move us beyond a narrow preoccupation with institutional survival.

On 30 April 1987, five months before the fall meeting of the board of trustees, following a regular faculty meeting, members of the faculty established an AAUP chapter. The following officers were elected: myself as president; Max Rogers, vice-president; Michael Hawn, secretary; Thomas Bland, treasurer; and John Eddins, Thomas Graves, and Alan Neely as executive committee members-at-large. The AAUP commitment to academic freedom resonated with the historic Baptist tenet of the freedom of conscience. If we were true to our own history as Baptists, we would resist the effort by fundamentalists to force their ideology on us; the AAUP gave us a means to do so. We sought and received the support of Randall Lolley in the establishment of the chapter, and he sat in as an observer at this meeting. His support was an important factor in the new chapter's success. His opposition would have kept some faculty from joining and could have given the chapter two adversaries instead of one.

Building a Consensus

Having organized the AAUP chapter, we then embarked upon the most challenging phase of our work—forging a consensus as a faculty about how we would relate to the new fundamentalist trustee majority. We were entering into a course of direct confrontation and opposition to the leadership of the Southern Baptist Convention, and no other group of convention employees had ventured to do this.[5] Having served all their lives as loyal servants of the denomination, some faculty at first understandably resisted the idea of an adversarial relationship that participation in the AAUP would mean. Nonetheless, by October every faculty member had joined the chapter.

In typical scholarly fashion we took up the challenge of clarifying our position by trying to hammer out a theological position paper. The chapter executive committee drafted a "Working List of Affirmations" to put to the entire chapter on 8 June 1987. It met stiff resistance and was withdrawn from consideration, and from June until October the chapter struggled painfully to establish our collective position. Our work together as a chapter during this time was more intense and difficult than any encounter we had with the fundamentalist trustees or administration.

In early October the chapter finally reached a consensus that was to carry it through the next four years of conflict with the fundamentalist seminary board and administration. That consensus was stated in the following "Procedural Guidelines" agreed to on 2 October 1987:

> The chapter holds to and authorizes the chapter president to express, when necessary, through the president of the seminary or directly to the chair of the board, if this becomes necessary, that the following items are non-negotiable. We as a faculty are properly accountable on doctrinal matters to the guidance of the seminary Articles of Faith, which we have signed, and to the established procedures of the seminary. Therefore:
>
> (1) Chapter members will not approve, give verbal assent to, or sign additional confessional statements.
>
> (2) Chapter members will not individually or collectively submit to any verbal or written interrogation of our beliefs, of the content of our teaching, or of the content of our writing or research apart from current, established procedures.
>
> (3) Chapter members will not consent to directives that are contrary to the present established policies and documents of the Seminary.
>
> On any other matters asked or demanded by the board of trustees, chapter members will respond through the chapter president only after due consultation as a chapter and with our attorneys.

The chapter agreed to one other important procedure, that the chapter president be the only person authorized to speak on behalf of the membership as a whole.

The terms arrived at on 2 October were different from the earlier attempt to prepare a definitive theological document. A change in strategy emerged as we agreed to make decisions by consensus and determined that we would not by a majority vote attempt to override significant dissenting opinion. By working with a consensus model, giving full voice to differing opinions and not trying prematurely to bring closure to our effort, we were building community and mutual trust. Faculty members were taking strong but not inflexible positions, and former faculty adversaries found themselves working together toward a common goal. The guidelines we agreed to on 2 October expressed a confidence in the historical traditions and policies of the school, a commitment to protect any single faculty member from attack, a collective sense of discipline to act as a group, and a trust in the community we were developing in the face of our adversaries.

A Strategy for Confrontation

By late June other developments were helping us determine a strategy for our encounter with the fundamentalist trustees in October. The first of these developments was the chapter's employment of Wade Smith of Tharington, Smith, and Hargrove of Raleigh to be the chapter's attorney. Smith was a Baptist layperson who was well known as a tough, successful trial attorney. He was deeply committed to our cause. Chapter leaders met through the summer with Smith, his partner Wade Hargrove, and a new attorney with the firm, Mark Holt. In October Holt would be present with the AAUP chapter leadership at all the meetings of the board and in constant contact with Smith. Smith knew that the media would play a major role in the impending conflict, and he helped us develop a strategy for relating to media persons. Second, he encouraged us to take the long look. "Decide how you want this story to read ten years from now," he said, "no matter what the outcome." From that vantage point, he asked, "What would you want to have done? What things would you want to have stood for? How would you want your struggle to be remembered?" He encouraged us to take the high road in the controversy—being clear about our values, never overstating our case, and never personally attacking our enemy.

Another development that aided the movement to consensus was the chapter's commitment to raise funds to underwrite a forceful effort, including, if necessary, going to court. In June we initiated a campaign to raise $10,000 by the end of the year. We exceeded that goal by $7,000, and by the time we had been in existence a year we had raised

$35,000, over $11,000 of which came from chapter members. By raising this money we said to ourselves and to others that we faced a crisis and that we did not intend to deal with it from a position of weakness.

A third development that promoted consensus was the employment of a media consultant. By early September Wade Smith helped us to see that we would need the press to help us because our case for academic freedom was more than likely going to be tried not in a law court but in the court of public opinion. He recommended we explore the possibility of a contract with the Crumpler Agency, a small public relations firm, to assist us in telling our story to the public. On 22 September the chapter unanimously approved a contract with Lou Anne Crumpler to be our media consultant.

The fall trustee meeting was on the near horizon, less than a month away. Crumpler advised us to prepare for this meeting by taking the initiative with the media. She recommended that with her help we prepare a press package and send it to media we wanted to reach. We prepared a list of 130 media who we felt would be interested in our story. On 5 October we mailed a press package to these newspapers and television stations. This press package was our most effective attempt to tell our story. In the following months we had extensive communication with media persons, but nothing we did compared with the impact of our October press package, which contained the following:

(1) It led with a cover memorandum and a brief news release that said that the faculty had organized an AAUP chapter to defend academic freedom that was being threatened by a new fundamentalist majority on the board of trustees. The release also stated that we had hired the firm of Tharington, Smith, and Hargrove to serve as our legal counsel.

(2) An opinion/editorial piece entitled "The Political New Right Prepares to Take Over a Southern Baptist Seminary" followed. In this article I described the school's tradition of academic freedom and outlined the political program of New Right fundamentalism: (a) to involve the Southern Baptist Convention (SBC) directly in national politics [At that time the SBC Public Affairs Committee, chaired by Sam Currin of North Carolina, was advocating the senate confirmation of Judge Robert Bork to the Supreme Court.]; (b) to interfere in the internal affairs of other nations in order to bring about "democratic" reform; (c) to aggressively attack "secular humanism" in educational institutions; (d) to bring about legislation that would provide tuition tax credits for parents to send

their children to private religious schools; (e) to secure constitutional amendments to outlaw abortion and to require prayer in public schools; (f) to see that women in the denomination were confined to subordinate roles and restricted from ordained Christian ministry; and (g) to mandate that all SBC agencies affirm an "inerrant" view of the Bible.

The editorial also held that the faculty was conservative—"committed to conserving long-established values in our school, denomination, and society: openness and diversity in the search for truth, inclusiveness of minorities and women in the ordained ministry, and prophetic criticism of all views political or religious that claim to represent absolute truth." We concluded that "if the long tradition of responsible academic freedom is lost at this school . . . then it will be lost elsewhere. Other seminaries will be swept under by the New Right current."

(3) The next item in the package was a chronology, starting with the 1979 beginnings of the New Right movement that were supported by Charles Stanley and Adrian Rogers. The document then chronicled the takeover of the SBC by New Right fundamentalism and continued with recent events at Southeastern Seminary.

(4) A listing of the officers of the executive committee of the Southeastern Seminary chapter of the AAUP followed, and next to it was a listing of the thirty members of the board of trustees.

(5) The package included an article on academic freedom from the *Southern Baptist Encyclopedia*, written by Penrose St. Amant.

(6) Finally, the package contained reprints of lead articles from the October 1987 issue of *SBC Today* that reported on the SBC Public Affairs Committee's endorsement of U.S. Supreme Court nominee Robert Bork and provided evidence of strong connections between the political New Right and the elected leadership of the SBC. The concluding article was the full text of Randall Lolley's fall convocation address "Quo Vadis, Southeastern?" that described the seminary as "*a free conscience, free church, free country* way of doing theological education." He affirmed as hallmarks of the school a freedom of inquiry balanced with responsibility, the use of modern tools of biblical interpretation, servanthood, the ordination of women, and ecumenical cooperation.

This press package went out on Monday and arrived at its 130 destinations on Wednesday and Thursday. The response astonished us. By noon on Thursday the president of the seminary, the chair and other members of the board, and I received a steady flow of calls from the media. I stayed on the telephone from Thursday noon until the weekend answering media inquiries. At various points in the next six months the Southeastern story was covered by the Associated Press, the *Atlanta Constitution*, Baptist Press, the *Biblical Recorder*, CBS News, the *Charlotte Observer, Christian Century, Christianity Today*, the *Chronicle of Higher Education*, the *Fort Worth Star-Telegram*, the *Greensboro News and Record*, the *Houston Chronicle*, the *Louisville Courier-Journal*, the *Miami Herald*, the *Nashville Banner*, the *New York Times, Newsweek*, North Carolina News Network, the *Raleigh Independent*, the *Raleigh News and Observer*, the *Raleigh Times*, the *Richmond Times-Dispatch*, the *St. Louis Post-Dispatch*, the *St. Petersburg Times, SBC Today*, the Triangle *Spectator*, United Press International, the *Virginian Pilot and the Ledger-Star*, the *Waco Tribune-Herald*, the *Wake Weekly*, the *Washington Post*, the *Winston-Salem Journal*, WDNC Radio, WBTV TV, WGST Radio, WPTF TV, WRAL TV, WTVD TV, and WUNC TV. These are the media that we know carried our stories. Others carried stories without direct contact with us. As a result of the chapter's contacts with the media, every session of the trustee meeting was covered by more than one North Carolina television station.

The Takeover

The trustees convened on 13 October. Persons committed to a political fundamentalist agenda took over the board for the first time in the school's thirty-seven year history, overturning the slate of nominees presented by the board's nominating committee and placing themselves in all key decision-making positions.

Nine days after the fundamentalist majority took control of the board of trustees, President Lolley resigned. He formally tendered his resignation on 17 November. He offered to remain until 31 July 1988, in order to provide an orderly transition. The trustees hastened to replace him by 1 April, making a presidential change in less than 20 weeks, a process requiring a year or more at most institutions of higher education. Lolley was succeeded by a fundamentalist president who had no experience in academic administration.

Lolley's resignation left the faculty without any mediating administrator between us and the board and the president they had chosen without faculty participation, Lewis Drummond. By the time Drummond took office, however, the faculty had a year's experience as an AAUP chapter. This organization provided a way to make collective responses to the board and to the new president. Without it, we would have been in demoralized disarray.

Bearing Witness

By the time the trustees had met and Lolley had resigned, the truth began fully to sink in on us that the fundamentalists had control of the school and that that fact would not be reversed any time soon. We had to decide what our mission was under these circumstances. At the first organizational meeting of the AAUP chapter the previous April, Delos Miles had said that our work was "to bear witness" to what we believed and to what was happening at our school. His observation became a watchword for us—"to bear witness."

The mission of bearing witness as a group gave us a measure of freedom from preoccupation with gaining control of our opponent, and it helped free us from the fear of their threats. We had seen the pattern of threat and intimidation at work in our sister SBC seminaries. The fundamentalists would single out a faculty member whose views they opposed, separate him or her from the rest of the faculty, and use tactics of intimidation to keep other faculty members from speaking out in protest. This worked with unorganized faculties. It didn't work with us. The fundamentalist trustees and administration never succeeded in singling out for "silencing" a member of our faculty from the rest of the faculty. It was clear to them from the time they took control that we spoke with one voice. They knew that if they attempted to coerce one of us they would have to deal with all of us and that we were prepared to defend ourselves.

As we attempted to bear our witness, we were helped immeasurably by the national AAUP organization. We maintained close contact with the national association staff through Jordan Kurland, the associate general secretary. On 23 February 1988 the national AAUP made a grant of $3,500 "to assist the [Southeastern] chapter in meeting its 1988 expenses in defense of academic freedom." On 18 June 1988 at its annual meeting in Washington, D.C., the association honored President Randall Lolley with the seventeenth Alexander Meiklejohn Award for Academic Freedom. This award is presented to an American college or university administrator or trustee, or to a board of trustees as a group, in recognition of an outstanding contribution to academic freedom. Previous recipients included President Clark Kerr and the board of regents of the University of California (1964), Reverend Theodore M. Hesburgh, C.S.C., president of the University of Notre Dame (1970), and the board of trustees of Wake Forest University (1978). The award had last been made in 1984. At that same meeting the association presented to the Southeastern Seminary AAUP chapter the Beatrice G. Konheim Award for outstanding chapter achievement and an additional grant of $1,000.

Actions against the Faculty

In the fundamentalist takeover of Southeastern Seminary of 1987–1988, numerous actions caused setbacks to the role of the faculty in the leadership of the academic program and eroded academic freedom. Three of these actions merit specific attention.

The first action of the new fundamentalist majority of the board was to impose a new process for faculty appointments. Historically, the faculty in the area of the curriculum where a vacancy existed was responsible for making a list of candidates from which the president would select one or more persons to interview. The faculty, along with students and the instruction committee of the board, had a role in evaluating the qualifications and competence of the candidates whom the president brought for an interview. The appointment was made by recommendation of the president to the instruction committee of the board on the basis of his careful review of these evaluations. The trustees first entered these proceedings at the point of the evaluation of candidates chosen by the president as serious faculty prospects. In the new procedure the trustees inserted themselves at the beginning of the search process with the selection of candidates. The faculty members, those most qualified to make a judgment on prospective faculty competence, were given virtually no voice in new appointments. Moreover, the trustees took over the role of clearing even temporary faculty appointments.

The purpose of this change was clear to everyone and expressed unambiguously by Robert Crowley, the chair of the board, who said: "We will hire new faculty who believe that the Bible is without error. We're now able to review people under consideration [as new faculty]; that's brand new and our most significant action."[6] He made clear that the new appointment process was the board's primary agenda: "The one agenda [of the board] is that we will be electing faculty members who agree with the literal interpretation of the Bible."[7]

The earliest direct attack on academic freedom occurred when the instruction committee of the trustees denied adjunctive faculty reappointments to Janice Siler and M. Mahan Siler, Jr., who had taught on annual appointment as part-time faculty for six years and who had been recommended for reappointment by the area faculty, the acting dean, and the president. The instruction committee gave no reasons to the board for this intervention and no reasons were stated publicly. The minutes of a 4 October 1988 conference telephone call of the instruction committee revealed their concern with Mahan Siler's views on homosexuality. Siler had publicly supported proposed legislation outlawing discrimination against homosexuals and had publicly opposed the Southern Baptist Convention's condemnation of homosexuals. His church had been the host for a conference on homosexuality. Janice Siler was apparently considered unfit by the instruction committee because of her husband's views.[8] According to the AAUP censure report, in this decision against the Silers the trustees "acted in violation of the academic freedom to which they were entitled under the 1940 *Statement of Principles on Academic Freedom and Tenure.*"[9]

Another action of the board and the new president that disregarded the faculty's role in the governance of the institution was the selection of a vice-president for academic affairs and dean of the faculty. President Drummond agreed to conduct a search for this person by means of a search committee made up of four faculty representatives, one from each faculty area, with himself as chair—following the precedent of Randall Lolley in this matter. He agreed with the committee on a procedure for the search in which the faculty members on the committee would have a voice in the selection of candidates. He subverted the process, however, by refusing to close the list of candidates, thus leaving open his option to put on the list and then select whomever he wished. When it became clear that his choice for the post was professor L. Russ Bush of Southwestern Baptist Theological Seminary, the faculty members of the search committee made a careful evaluation of his suitability. They reported to the president their opposition to him as unqualified for failing to meet six of the eight criteria for dean set forth in the seminary's administrative manual. After failing to call a meeting of the committee for ten weeks, the president announced his choice of Bush by memorandum on 20 January 1989. The entire faculty had gone on record on 16 November 1988 opposing this nomination; on 1 February 1989 they voted again, unanimously, against the appointment. Russ Bush was appointed, nonetheless. Subsequently, Drummond made clear in a letter to the trustees that he wanted funds to employ a sufficient number of new faculty to establish "a conservative majority . . . as soon as possible."[10]

Central Issues

These events were the focus of an investigation of the school by the national AAUP Committee A on Academic Freedom and Tenure. That investigation led to a censure of the school by the association at its meeting in June 1989. The school remains on the AAUP censure list.

Imbedded in these events are several issues that were of utmost concern for the faculty and deserve careful note. First is the casualty of theological education, the purpose for which the school exists. The fundamentalist administration and trustees showed no interest in the educational process. Their only concern appeared to be that faculty and students adhere to a view of biblical inerrancy and a cluster of other fundamentalist and New Right doctrines. The competence of a professor to teach meant nothing, and the competence of a dean to give creative direction to the academic program was irrelevant. As the school came more firmly under fundamentalist control, it became increasingly difficult for the faculty to carry out the educational mission of the school.

Second, at issue between the fundamentalists and our faculty was an understanding of how truth claims are made. Our view was that if we take the reality of sin seriously, we then must assume that even the most informed and well-intended efforts to discern the truth are blurred by it. All our knowing is provisional and in need of continual revision, not only because that knowing is always partial but also because it is inevitably distorted by sin. In the academic arena our truth claims, therefore, must always be open to testing by differing views. To hold to our beliefs in such a provisional way is an act of faith in which we trust not ourselves but God as the final source of truth. This conviction lay at the center of the faculty's commitment to academic freedom and its rejection of the totalistic claims of the fundamentalist trustees and administration.

Third, the faculty differed with the fundamentalists over the moral issue of covenants. We were committed to covenants in which persons made promises to abide by agreed upon processes in the affairs of the school. We trusted these processes, flawed though they inevitably were, to produce responsible decisions and actions and to assure fair consideration of the views of all parties to the decision. The fundamentalists with whom we dealt would not keep such covenants. They were intent on a certain outcome and were willing to bend or subvert agreed-upon covenants in order to achieve that end. Always the end achieved justified the means of getting there. The methods followed in selecting faculty and a new vice-president for academic affairs and the refusal to reappoint the Silers as adjunctive faculty all bear the marks of significant broken covenants.

Fourth, we disagreed with the fundamentalists over the nature of the Bible and its interpretation. They saw the Bible as a set of inerrant propositions embodying God's revelation. We viewed the Bible as a set of human documents in which persons bore witness to their experience of God. We believed that these biblical witnesses were always limited in their vision by finitude and sin. We believed the biblical testimony was imbedded in a culture and world view different from our own and that it was a challenging task and an act of faith to bring the ancient text to life in the present context. The fundamentalists saw no historical gap between the text in its original setting and its contemporary meaning. One example of the consequences of ignoring the work of hermeneutical interpretation is their understanding of certain issues of gender and sexuality. Because they do not build a hermeneutical bridge between the text in its ancient context and its current setting, they oppose the ordination of women, they can see no problem in the views of God shaped by a patriarchal society, and they fail to understand the difference between homosexual acts addressed in the Bible and homosexuality as a gender orientation—a concept that was foreign to the biblical writers.

Finally, this controversy has caused great suffering and has challenged us to learn from it. What have we learned? "*Access into life,*" writes Walter Brueggemann, "*is mostly through the resistant door of pain.* That door is kept closed by idolatry (of a god who does not suffer) and by ideology (of a system that never fails)."[11] He contends that Israel's praise in the Psalms was rooted in the pain of Israel's suffering. Her praise became empty when it was taken over by the monarchy and used as a litany of support for the established system. Worship then became an expression of a comfortable ideology. Praise is also emptied of meaning when the suffering of oppression gets disconnected from the celebration of liberation. When this occurs, the expression of liberation is emptied of the lively account of the liberation experience and turns into the praise of a god removed from suffering and incapable of redemptive action. The language of liberation may be used, but the words have lost their moorings in human suffering.[12]

The Southeastern Seminary faculty, all white and all male except for one, was not held captive by fundamentalism. We fought that attack off with some success. Our captivity lies in our status as a part of the most privileged and economically secure class of people in the world. Our bondage, as the bondage of many Southern Baptists in this controversy, has been in our resistance to risk our privileges of status and income in order to say a firm "No!" to the excesses of the political fundamentalists who now control the denomination. It would be false to say that in our taking a stand against the fundamentalist majority of the school's trustees we have been liberated from our bondage to privilege and security. It would be more accurate to say we *understand* our bondage more profoundly and more painfully than was possible before we came under fundamentalist attack.

New Right fundamentalism is a place to hide from the suffering of humankind, but one can also hide from the pain of a suffering world within the walls of a mainline Protestant seminary. We, too, are able to put our energies into efforts that insulate us from suffering. We complain about our work load and fight the wars of curriculum and the distribution of required hours without seeing our highly protected and insulated lifestyle. We are fettered by our lifestyle of economic and status security more than we want to admit.

What moves a seminary professor out of the safety of established privilege and into the combat zone of human pain? Such movement typically occurs when we experience the suffering as an insider. We are radicalized, energized by the root issues of the human predicament, only when we are shoved into the arena of suffering ourselves. Conversely, once radicalized, we can become complacent when, in our search for greater stability and security, we find a place of relative comfort. This was true of Israel, who converted the psalms of deliverance into psalms of praise for the establishment,[13] and this can be true of us.

As peculiar as it sounds and as difficult as it is to say, we owe thanks to the political fundamentalists who now control the Southern Baptist Convention and Southeastern Seminary. They have shaken the foundations of our security and privilege. They have threatened our world view—jolting us into understanding of what it means to be excluded from power, to be regarded as second-class citizens, and to be deprived of a voice in our own future. They have pushed us to at least begin to identify with the majority of humankind who live out their lives as strangers to adequate resources, to privilege and security, and to the protection of fundamental human rights.

One Final Question

In his *Laboratory and Pulpit: The Relation of Biology to the Preacher and His Message*, William Louis Poteat described the painful transition he saw going on "in the conservative South" at the turn of the century. "Our old habits of body, mind, spirit are at once our comfort and our safety," he wrote. "To break their protecting shell for a new one is not only painful, it exposes us . . . to thronging perils." Yet, he remarked, these passages are necessary if we are to move from a limited to a larger life.[14] Such is the final question this controversy has put before us as a faculty. Did it defeat us, or did it enlarge us? We carry with us the wounds of the conflict. Where those wounds have broken our protecting shell our lives have been enlarged by the experience. I believe that the seeds of this enlargement were planted in the spiritual community that formed among the faculty as the Southeastern storm gathered on the horizon and finally swept down upon us.

Notes

[1]Suzanne Cameron Linder, *William Louis Poteat: Prophet of Progress* (Chapel Hill NC: University of North Carolina Press, 1966) 124–25.

[2]Robert K. Webb and Leslie H. Peek, "Academic Freedom and Tenure: Southeastern Baptist Theological Seminary (North Carolina) *Academe* 75/3 (May-June 1989): 36-37.

This report, based on a twenty-seven page request for investigation by the Southeastern AAUP chapter and on direct investigation by Webb and Peek.

[3]Ibid., 37.

[4]Ibid., 8.

[5]With one exception, no other group of employees at an SBC agency has to this date engaged in organized opposition to the fundamentalist takeover of the denomination. The action of Alvin C. Shackleford, director of Baptist Press, and Dan Martin, news editor of Baptist Press, is the notable exception. Placed under increasing pressure by the fundamentalist-controlled executive committee of the SBC to report only what would be pleasing to that group, Shackleford and Martin continued their practice of responsible, objective journalism. On 13 June 1990 the officers of the SBC executive committee instructed the president of the executive committee, Harold Bennett, to tell Shackleford and Martin to resign. He was to admonish them to keep silent about the events leading to their termination. If they kept silent they were promised salary and benefits for up to six months. They refused to heed this threat and published a forthright report of the events on 2 July. On 17 July Shackleford and Martin were fired without cause.

[6]*New York Times*, 19 October 1987.

[7]*Greensboro News and Record*, 23 October 1987.

[8]Webb and Peek, "Academic Freedom and Tenure: Southeastern," 40.

[9]Ibid., 45.

[10]Richard L. Hester, "AAUP Censures Southeastern Seminary," *Christian Century* 106/24 (16–23 August 1989): 743.

[11]Walter Brueggemann, *Israel's Praise: Doxology against Idolatry and Ideology* (Philadelphia: Fortress Press, 1988) 133.

[12]Ibid., chaps. 3 and 4.

[13]Ibid.

[14]William Louis Poteat, *Laboratory and Pulpit: The Relation of Biology to the Preacher and His Message* (Philadelphia: Griffith and Rowland Press, 1901) 11–12; cited by Linder, *Poteat*, 72.

Chapter 5

"Our Message Be the Gospel Plain": The Teaching of the Bible and Biblical Languages at Southeastern Baptist Theological Seminary, 1950–1988[1]

Donald E. Cook

The teaching of the Bible at Southeastern Seminary sprang from the deepest sources of faith, so much so that in times of dizzying elation when the school was at its zenith or in times of heart-rending divisions, when strident criticisms rang out, devotion to imparting a "sound knowledge of the Bible"[2] never wavered in any quarter. Methods may have been questioned, but the end was never in doubt. Indeed, the quality and intensity of that devotion sustains the Southeastern dream[3] until the present moment and is the impetus for my attempting to write these words of memory, appreciation, and affection.

I have chosen to write this essay in two parts. In the first, I shall remember those who taught me the Bible and biblical languages at Southeastern. If the reader really wishes to understand what happened within the rock wall during the early days of the school, he or she must sit in the classroom and experience the teaching of the Word. Admittedly, my memories are not objective, but they are based upon the reality of my experience. They are true. In the second part, I shall recount the work of the biblical faculty as I remember it as a member of that group from 1965 to 1994 and as I have observed it based upon research in the pertinent faculty, trustee, and seminary documents and publications.

A Student's Memory

I arrived on the Southeastern campus in the fall of 1953 to be inducted into an academic fellowship presided over by persons whose enthusiasm for learning and patience in teaching transformed academic toil into an adventure of the mind and spirit. They were men of God energized by grace and truth.

Ed McDowell taught me to think and feel in Greek. Through his eyes I began to see the thoughts of Paul and of the evangelists come to expression in that marvelous language. He planted the seed that matured into critical literary and historical study of the scripture. His introduction to Revelation began what has become a life-long quest on my part. He researched the love of God and became a living expression of the concept.

Bill Strickland possessed and communicated an austere passion for integrity in exegesis that remains foundational in my thinking. He taught me the meaning of "friendly toil,"[4] exampling reverence and persistence in addressing the text. He caused me to look at Mark as a statement of faith.

Marc Lovelace made me "dig," and I loved it. Even as I pen these lines I experience again the excitement of his archaeology lectures and the piercing insight that he brought to the interpretation of scripture. Professor Lovelace caused the facts of history to come alive. He made of those ancient stones a context for responsible and intelligent under-standing of the past and thus a basis for meaning in the present. Dr. Lovelace raised with me for the first time the question of the inspiration of scripture and encouraged me to answer the question for myself.

R. T. Daniel gave me the book of Psalms. He taught me the toil and joy of Hebrew exegesis. I can still hear his laughter as he encouraged us to think through the data of a text and make sense of it.

Elmo Scoggin taught me that Jesus was a Jew and therewith gave me a completely new context for understanding my Lord. Under his tutelage I came to appreciate Judaism as a living faith. Professor Scoggin's know-ledge of Hebrew was almost as great as his love for the language. His enthusiasm for all things Jewish was awesome. He introduced me to the Dead Sea Scrolls.

Leo Green personified the prophets. His classes were adventures in which teaching became preaching, where exposition became an art form.

Professor Green demonstrated that the Old Testament is part of the Christian Bible and, when properly understood, proclaims the gospel.

A Brief Recounting

A Dream Come True

Early on, the seminary boasted that it had begun with an outstanding faculty.[5] The first "Core Curriculum" included eighteen hours in the biblical area; although Greek and Hebrew were not required, they were strongly recommended.[6] Leo Green was the first professor of Hebrew and Old Testament interpretation and soon became a concerned spokesman for the needs of students.[7] W. C. Strickland, instructor in New Testament Interpretation, also taught Greek. Marc Lovelace, a member of the Wake Forest College faculty, served as visiting professor of Archeology.

For the second year, 1952–1953, six more teachers were elected, three of whom were in the biblical area. Edward A. McDowell, Jr., was elected professor of New Testament interpretation; Robert T. Daniel, professor of Old Testament interpretation; and Marc H. Lovelace, associate professor of Archaeology. President Sydnor L. Stealey enthusiastically described all six as "outstanding in his field of study."[8] During the second year the library grew to over 6500 volumes, and the 249 students enrolled were urged to take full advantage of the collection, which included 1000 volumes from the library of W. Hersey Davis.[9]

The vigor and optimism of the fledgling scholarly community can be observed in a series of quotations taken from letters written by the newly elected faculty members and addressed to Ralph Herring, chair of the faculty committee of the trustees. The faculty dreamed great dreams, as evidenced by the following statements: "I look upon the call that has come from Southeastern as perhaps the greatest challenge of my life" (E. A. McDowell, Jr.). "I feel that there is a spirit in the Southeastern Seminary which will carry it through all of the difficulties in this period of its beginning" (R. T. Daniel). "There is no question in my mind but that God has led us thus far in our work" (Marc Lovelace).[10]

These were not lightly held dreams. The faculty backed up their dreams with their lives. In a recent letter, Marc Lovelace reflects upon the beginnings of Southeastern after more than forty years:

> I would like to think that we "early-bird" faculty were reasonably united in our purpose to provide a quality theological education, encouraging our students to be honest with the Bible and to see its spiritual and theological heart through eyes of faith, and to learn how to love God with their minds.[11]

This 1993 reminiscence is substantiated by a number of pieces from the pens of early biblical faculty that appeared in the *Bulletin*. In the January 1953 issue, Professor Strickland reviewed A. M. Hunter's *Interpreting the New Testament*, saying, among other things, that it was "a clear presentation of the main currents of New Testament scholarship." Professor Lovelace evaluated Jack Finegan's *Light from the Ancient Past* as "an excellent connected account of the archaeological background of the Hebrew-Christian religion." Professor Green found Norman Snaith's *The Distinctive Ideas of the Old Testament* to be "a scholarly study."[12] The September 1954 issue contained two brief exegeses (Rom 8:28; 3:25) by Professor McDowell that reflect pastoral concern, judicious scholarship, and clarity of presentation.[13] Professor Strickland's "The Proclaimed Word of God" in the February 1955 issue is a model of precision and passion. It reads in part, "When in the New Testament reference is made to the preaching of the gospel, it is always to the preaching of which Jesus Christ is the content."[14]

The author of an article in the January 1959 *Outlook* reported that Elmo Scoggin would assist Robert L. Lindsey, Southern Baptist Missionary to Israel, in translating the New Testament into modern Hebrew. Professor Scoggin served as visiting professor of Missions in 1955–1956 and became associate professor of Old Testament in 1956. Scoggin's coming brought Hebrew as a living language to Southeastern Seminary.

A picture on the same page of the *Outlook* shows Harry Oliver and R. C. Briggs viewing two rare sixteenth century English Bibles that had been presented to the seminary.[15] Professor Briggs joined the faculty in 1957 as professor of New Testament, and Professor Oliver came that same year as special instructor in New Testament. Their presence on the teaching staff added breadth and depth to the New Testament offerings. The 1958–1959 catalog announced the following as among the new courses to be taught by Professor Briggs: The Hellenistic Background of

Christianity, New Testament Eschatology, Advanced Greek Grammar, and History and the Gospels. Professor Oliver would offer The Jewish Background of Christianity, Acts and Primitive Christianity, and Introduction to Textual Criticism.[16]

Robert T. Daniel died in the spring of 1959. In the fall of that year John I Durham, a Southeastern alumnus, was asked to serve as instructor of Old Testament. Durham later received a D.Phil. from Oxford and returned to the faculty of Southeastern in 1963. In 1960 Max G. Rogers, who was completing work on a Ph.D. at Columbia, came as instructor of Old Testament. (He received his degree in 1964.) In spite of the loss of Professor Daniel, the coming of these two young scholars invigorated the teaching of the Old Testament.

As he surveyed the first ten years of the school's life, Ben Fisher captured in his editorial in the *Outlook* some of the old exuberance of Dr. Stealey:

> The finest achievement of the past decade has been the growth of our faculty and administrative staff. . . . They hold degrees from leading colleges, seminaries, and universities. They are teachers by choice.[17]

The Dream under Stress

But all was not well. Problems that centered around the teaching of the New Testament began as early as 1960. Concerns focused on teaching methodology and theological presuppositions. Three members of the New Testament faculty were said to be teaching a kind of liberalism associated with Rudolf Bultmann.[18] Critics of the school roused themselves to action—sometimes with knowledge, sometimes without. The faculty and student body were divided, each side claiming the high ground of academic freedom and theological integrity. Faculty morale plummeted, and the work of educating ministers suffered, yet classes continued and efforts to restore harmony were made. The leadership of President Stealey was the brightest light and clearest voice in this troubled time. In a series of statements dated 12 December 1960, 27 January 1961, and 7 April 1961, he called the faculty to its educational work with candor and love.[19] His efforts at peacemaking were stirring. Dr. Stealey's analysis of the situation and his suggested solutions to the problems have been vindicated with the passage of time, although in the short term he appeared to fail.

The ultimate handling of the matter by the trustees was not Dr. Stealey's wish, but to the extent that the process toward solution showed restraint and concern for all persons involved, the spirit of Sydnor Stealey prevailed.[20] In seeking reconciliation, President Olin T. Binkley was Dr. Stealey's worthy successor. No formal charges were ever brought against any teacher. When resignations seemed inevitable, the terms were generous and without rancor.[21] The resignations of Professor Briggs (1965), Professor Oliver (1965), and Professor Strickland (1966) were grievous losses to Southeastern Seminary,[22] but the school was not lost. The dream had come under stress, and many suffered, yet the dream persisted and the school would rebuild.[23]

Rebuilding the Dream

Even as the struggle eventuated in the resignations noted above, the school slowly turned toward its educational task. In his inaugural address (17 October 1963), President Binkley projected a future for the scholarly study of the Bible at Southeastern:

> The fundamental purpose of the Southeastern Baptist Theological Seminary is to seek a deeper knowledge of God as revealed in Jesus Christ. . . . We invite students to immerse their minds in the primary documents of the historic Christian faith. We require them to use sound principles of research, to study the Bible intelligently. . . .[24]

Changes were occurring within the faculty as well. Edward A. McDowell retired in the spring of 1964. Marc H. Lovelace resigned in 1968.

On 13 February 1964, Raymond B. Brown of Southern Baptist Theological Seminary was elected professor of New Testament interpretation. Brown, holding the B.D. and S.T.M. degrees from Yale as well as the Th.D. from Southern, brought drama and enthusiasm to his classroom at Southeastern. At the same time, John I Durham, who served as visiting professor of Old Testament in 1963–1964, was elected assistant professor of Old Testament interpretation. Fresh from his work at Oxford, Durham challenged students in Hebrew and English studies. In 1965, Donald E.

Cook, a Southeastern alumnus (B.D., Th.M) and Duke graduate (Ph.D.), was elected assistant professor of New Testament. Cook's major interests were in the Gospels and Revelation. Archie L. Nations, a Vanderbilt Ph.D., was visiting professor of New Testament in 1966–1967 and was elected associate professor of New Testament interpretation in 1967. An expert in Coptic literature, Professor Nations brought scholarly precision to the classroom and study.

It should, therefore, come as no surprise that pride in the faculty surfaced again in the publications of the school.[25] During the latter half of the 1960s, the biblical area *gladly* taught.[26] Their work, however, extended far beyond the classroom. The following examples are limited in the extreme: Max G. Rogers studied in Europe on sabbatic leave in 1966–1967. Leo Green published *God Reigns*, expository studies based on Isaiah, in 1968. Elmo Scoggin was on an archaeological dig in Israel during 1968–1969.

There was, however, a small but significant cloud on the horizon. The minutes of the trustees contain a letter from Porter Routh (8 July 1969) advising the trustees of an action of the 1969 session of the Southern Baptist Convention calling for compliance with the 1963 Baptist Faith and Message Statement.[27] This was a portent of major events to come.

The 1970s became a fruitful time for biblical study at Southeastern as well as a season of loss and reflection. Thorwald Lorenzen (Dr.Theol., Zurich) joined the faculty as visiting professor of New Testament in 1971. Although his tenure was relatively brief (1971–1974), Professor Lorenzen's contribution to Southeastern was great. He personified the best of European scholarship, combining critical acumen and profound personal faith. Richard A. Spencer, a Southeastern alumnus who would receive his Ph.D. from Emory in 1976, came as assistant professor of New Testament Interpretation in 1974. Professor Spencer's skills in literary studies aroused new interest in that discipline. Ben F. Philbeck, also a Southeastern alumnus, joined the faculty as professor of Hebrew and Old Testament in 1979, as did Malcolm Tolbert, who became professor of New Testament. Philbeck, who studied Archaeology and Semitic languages with W. F. Albright at Johns Hopkins University, received the Ph.D. from Southern Seminary. Tolbert, holding a Th.D. from New Orleans Seminary, came with special expertise in the Gospels and Pauline letters. Both men had a record of extensive publication in their respective fields.

A sampling of the writing of the biblical faculty during the 1970s indicates that the activities in the classroom were undergirded by research, reflection, and production. In 1970 Max Rogers translated R. Smend's *Yahweh War and Tribal Confederation,* and John Durham edited *Proclamation and Presence.* Donald Cook wrote "The Interpretation of 1 John 1-5" for the *Review and Expositor* (Fall). Also Ray Brown published "First Corinthians" in volume ten of the *Broadman Bible Commentary.* In 1971, John Durham's "Psalms" was published in volume four of the *Broadman,* and Leo Green provided "Jeremiah" in volume six. Ray Brown and Donald Cook contributed articles to volume three of the *Encyclopedia of Southern Baptists.* In 1972, Thorwald Lorenzen published *Der Lieblingsjünger im Johannesevangelium,* and Elmo Scoggin wrote "Micah" in volume seven of the *Broadman.* Archie Nations translated the first part of M. Doi's *Search for Meaning through Interfaith Dialogue* in 1976. In 1977 the first volume of *Southeastern Studies,* edited by John Durham, was published.

An era in the teaching of the Bible at Southeastern came to a close with the death of one senior professor and the retirement of another. Ray Brown, who had become Distinguished Professor of New Testament Interpretation, died unexpectedly on 16 December 1977. Leo Green retired as Distinguished Professor of Old Testament Interpretation on 31 July 1978.

The Dream Attacked

The passage to the 1980s proved difficult for Southeastern Seminary. The question of the inerrancy of scripture became more and more acute. Yet the challenges of friend and foe to the school in general and to the teaching of the Bible in particular were not without their positive features. As in the 1960s, the school rose to her task.[28]

From 1979–1983, countless questionnaires from churches and associations arrived in teachers' mailboxes, purportedly to ascertain the orthodoxy of the faculty. President W. Randall Lolley stood resolutely with the faculty in their ordeal, often answering the queries himself.[29]

The seminary attempted to address concerns about the Bible and the teaching of the Bible at Southeastern by holding a conference on biblical authority (29–30 January 1980). President Lolley, Herschel Hobbs, and

Donald Cook were the featured speakers. Cook asserted that inspired scripture ought to be interpreted critically and devotionally within the context of faith.[30]

On 4–5 February 1986, a subcommittee from the Peace Committee visited Southeastern with twenty-seven "concerns" about fifteen faculty members, one visiting teacher, and one retired professor.[31] Eight of these persons taught in the biblical area. Each responded with clarity and courage. Again President Lolley stood with the faculty and declared "there has been no matter presented to indicate that any member of the faculty at Southeastern Seminary is teaching contrary to the Abstract of Principles."[32] It was disconcerting, however, to learn that a majority of the "concerns" were lodged by seven persons, five of whom were then enrolled at Southeastern and two of whom were Southeastern graduates. All seven had connections with a student organization called the Conservative Evangelical Fellowship.[33]

Amazingly, in these beginnings of troubles Samuel E. Balentine, a Southeastern alumnus holding a D. Phil. from Oxford, accepted election to the faculty as assistant professor of Hebrew and Old Testament (1983). Professor Balentine immediately became a colleague in work, joy, and sorrow.

Evidence of a profound faculty collegiality may be seen in the efforts of the elected biblical faculty in 1988 to secure a more certain place for John Keating Wiles, who had received a two-year appointment as assistant professor of Old Testament in 1987.[34] Although these efforts were initially successful, they failed ultimately.

The 1980s were years of separation and sadness for the biblical faculty. In 1984 Elmo Scoggin retired as professor of Hebrew and Old Testament, although he continued to teach on an appointive basis for a while. In 1987 John Durham, professor of Hebrew and Old Testament, took early retirement. Finally, although it extends beyond the 1988 definition of this essay, it must be noted that 1989 witnessed the retirements of Malcolm Tolbert and Archie Nations, professors of New Testament, and lamentably the death of Ben Philbeck, professor of Hebrew and Old Testament.

In spite of criticism, the biblical faculty continued to be productive in writing, often addressing the issues of the controversy. Articles published in *Faith and Mission* demonstrate this fact. In the spring of 1984 Donald Cook argued in an exegetical article on 2 Timothy 3:14-17 that the author assumed the inspiration of scripture rather than seeking to prove or defend it.[35] During the fall of that same year Ben Philbeck used historical analysis to hear a "word" from the prophet Jeremiah in the words of the text.[36] Two years later, Richard Spencer wrote perceptively that "The Bible is a non-negotiable informer for faith, ministry, and Christian living. . . . The Bible underlies all aspects of ministry."[37] In the fall of 1988, Malcolm Tolbert, sensitive to his subject matter (Mark 8:27-35) and aware of those who would read his work, wrote: "Theological inquiry is not the enemy of faith; rather, it is essential to genuine faith. . . . The God of truth has nothing to fear from an honest search for truth."[38] One can almost hear the founders of the school say "Amen"!

A Postscript

Because of the limitation of space, the main focus of this essay is limited to members of the biblical faculty who signed the Abstract. This note seeks to recognize several persons and groups not included due to that limitation.

Through his many translations, John Steely, professor of Historical Theology (1956–1986), encouraged and challenged both faculty and students in the study of the Bible. James Blackmore, emeritus professor of A.Div. Studies, shared wise counsel concerning the Bible with many students in the associate degree program. Visiting and adjunctive faculty, too numerous to mention, gave freely of time and talent. Visiting lecturers and chapel speakers brought the worlds of scholarship and of the church to Southeastern and enriched our lives almost daily.

Notes

[1]E. A. McDowell, Jr., "The Seminary Hymn," 1954.

[2]This phrase or one very similar occurs in SEBTS statements of purpose almost from the beginning of the school. *Southeastern Baptist Theological Seminary Bulletin* (1952) 16.

[3]Claud B. Bowen uses this term in a Founders' Day address, "A Dream Come True," 12 February 1959, 1.

[4]McDowell, "Seminary Hymn."

[5]*Bulletin* 1/3 (May 1952): 3. [Editor's note: In the early years of the seminary, in addition to the catalog—which throughout *Servant Songs* is referred to as the

Southeastern Baptist Theological Seminary Bulletin with the appropriate year(s) and page —there was another publication titled the *Southeastern Seminary Bulletin*. This publication was a precursor of the *Outlook*, which apparently was first published in June 1956 and designated volume 5, number 3. Like the *Outlook* that succeeded it, the *Bulletin* provided periodic reports about seminary life and events. It also anticipated *Southeastern Studies* and *Faith and Mission* in that occasionally it contained scholarly material such as book reviews and exegeses. The *Bulletin* was first published in May 1952, when for some reason it was designated volume 1, number 3. It appeared from time to time through February 1956 (2/6). In the notes for this essay, the *Bulletin* is always cited by volume, number, date, and page.]

[6]*Southeastern Baptist Theological Bulletin* (1952) 36–39.

[7]"Faculty Minutes," 30 October 1951.

[8]*Bulletin* 1/3 (May 1952): 3.

[9]*Bulletin* 2/1 (January 1953): 8.

[10]Bowen, "Dream," 8.

[11]Letter to the writer, 16 October 1993. Permission to quote secured.

[12]*Bulletin* 2/1 (January 1953): 8.

[13]*Bulletin* 2/4 (September 1954): 11.

[14]*Bulletin* 2/5 (February 1955): 4.

[15]*Outlook* 8/2 (January 1959): 8.

[16]*Southeastern Baptist Theological Seminary Bulletin* (1958) 45– 49.

[17]Ben C. Fisher, Editorial, *Outlook* 10/5 (August 1961): 3.

[18]Chauncey Daley, "Daley Observations," *Western Recorder*, 28 January 1965, 4–5.

[19]*Faculty Document Book I*, 49–52. "Trustee Minutes," dates cited.

[20]That Dr. Stealey saw the larger implications of the Southeastern problem is evidenced by questions that he raised in reference to the Ralph Elliott controversy. See "President's Paragraphs," *Outlook* 12/2 (November-December 1962): 2–4.

[21]"Trustee Minutes," 18 February 1965.

[22]Roy Martin, "Baptist Group," *Raleigh Times*, 16 February 1965, 1.

[23]The fears of some that at this point serious theological research and teaching at Southeastern were over have proven unfounded. "Resignation Reveals Protest at Southeastern," *Western Recorder*, 14 January 1965, 10. "Seminary Professor Resigns," *Durham Morning Herald*, 30 December 1964, 1.

[24]*Outlook* 13/3 (December 1963): 7.

[25]*Outlook* 16/2 (November-December 1966): 8.

[26]Note President Binkley's reference to Chaucer's phrase in *Outlook* 16/5 (March-April 1967): 2.

[27]"Trustee Minutes," 12 March 1970.

[28]W. Randall Lolley, "Impressions," *Outlook* 29/5 (March-April 1980): 2. "SEBTS students voice support for faculty and administration," *Wake Weekly*, 29 November 1984, 5.

[29]Copies of several of these questionnaires (dated 20 April 1975, 10 May 1979, 8 June 1979, and 3 May 1983) are in the possession of this writer, as well as a memo from President Lolley (9 May 1983) indicating his response to the questionnaire of 3 May 1983.

[30]Donald E. Cook, "The Interpretation of Scripture," in "Addresses," Conference on Biblical Authority, Southeastern Baptist Theological Seminary (29–30 January 1980): 9–11.

[31]W. Randall Lolley, "A Report to the Board of Trustees," 10 March 1986, 5. The best summary of the situation is to be found in Morris Ashcraft, "Southeastern Seminary in Crisis: 1986–87," *Faith and Mission* 6/1 (Fall 1988): 47–61.

[32]Lolley, "Report," 3.

[33]Ibid., 5.

[34]Letter from Richard A. Spencer to President Lewis A. Drummond on behalf of the biblical faculty, 28 October 1988.

[35]Donald E. Cook, "Scripture and Inspiration," *Faith and Mission* 1/2 (Spring 1984): 56–61.

[36]Ben F. Philbeck, "Prophetic Word or Editorial Words?" *Faith and Mission* 2/1 (Fall 1984): 56–62.

[37]Richard A. Spencer, "The Role of Biblical Study in Preparation for Ministry," *Faith and Mission* 3/2 (Spring 1986): 13.

[38]Malcolm O. Tolbert, "Elements in a Mature Faith," *Faith and Mission* 6/1 (Fall 1988): 71.

Chapter 6

Historians and Heritage: Church History at Southeastern Seminary

Fred A. Grissom

The teaching of church history has always been an important part of the life of Southeastern Seminary, and those who have taught it have been a talented and colorful group. Required courses have changed several times, the number of required hours has fluctuated, some innovative approaches have been tried, and several faculty members have left an indelible mark. One particular item of interest in recent years is the addition of Baptist History and Heritage as a required course.

From the founding of Southeastern until 1993, church history and missions were part of the same area of the curriculum.[1] In the early years the area was called "Historical Interpretation of Christianity," and the courses were designated with the initials "IC." Beginning in 1968 single letter area designations were used, and church history and missions became the "H" area. In 1985, the H area was expanded by the inclusion of evangelism. In 1993, the H area passed out of existence with the shifting of missions and evangelism, together with preaching, into a new "P" (Proclamation) area. Church history is now part of the "T" area.

Foundations: Sydnor Stealey and Pope Duncan

Twelve courses, all of which were required for graduation, were listed in Southeastern's first catalog, issued in July 1951. Among those courses were two church history courses. IC 71, "Survey of Church History," covered the period from A.D. 100 through the Reformation, with a "brief introduction to the Modern Period." IC 72, "History of the Baptists," not only covered the history of the denomination but also included a comparison of Baptists "with early and medieval dissenting groups, and with modern denominations."[2]

By 1952 the curriculum was greatly expanded, with elective courses and elaborately defined areas. The IC area included two fields, "History of Christianity" and "The World Mission of Christianity." Each field had several "divisions." The history field included not only church history but also specifically historical theology, the history of ethics, the history of missions, and the history of preaching.[3] No courses were listed in these other divisions, however. A history of missions course was included, but it was included in the world mission field. The detailed schema was dropped after only two years, perhaps because it did not fit reality.

The 1952 curriculum contained a fifty-eight semester hour core. Six of those hours were IC 101 and 102, two courses titled "General Church History." The core for Baptist students, however, was actually sixty hours, because the catalog includes the following prescription: "Each Baptist Student will be required to take a course in Baptist History before Graduation."[4] This statement does not appear in the 1953 catalog, nor does the Baptist History course description indicate that the course was required. From 1953 until 1985, no Baptist history course was required at Southeastern.

During Southeastern's first two years, President Sydnor Stealey served as the church history professor. He came to Southeastern from Southern Seminary in Louisville, where he had taught church history for about ten years. After the first few years at Southeastern, he no longer taught any basic church history courses, but he did continue to offer courses in Christian Classics.

Pope Duncan joined the Southeastern faculty in 1953. Duncan was a native of Kentucky, a graduate of the University of Georgia and Southern Seminary, and had taught at Mercer and Stetson. While he was at Southern he served as Stealey's fellow. When the load of being both president and full-time professor became too much, Stealey asked his former student to consider coming to Southeastern. Duncan was excited about coming to a new school and was happy to be part of its formative years. He believes that Southeastern made an important contribution to theological education in those early years, with as fine a B.D. program as existed anywhere: "It was an ideal place to teach. We didn't make much money, but it was exciting."[5]

Duncan's main academic emphases were Baptist history and study of the Reformation. His dissertation was on the history of Baptist thought in the seventeenth century. In teaching Baptist history, he adopted an innovative technique. He would assign a topic to three different students and ask them to do as exhaustive research as they could in the time allowed. Their assignment then was to distill that research into what they could get on one page, as if they were writing an encyclopedia article on the subject. Each student would have one of these assignments approximately every two weeks. The presentation of their findings constituted most of the course. At the end of the semester, Duncan chose the best of the presentations, put them together in a booklet, and distributed them to the members of the class. He believes that Stealey's talent for saying what needed to be said in a minimum of words influenced the adoption of this approach.

Duncan was also instrumental in one of the most innovative experiments tried at Southeastern. In 1957 the church history and missions core courses were combined to create what some have referred to as the "big course." At Stetson, Duncan had worked with others in developing a more comprehensive course. He liked the concept and suggested that the IC area pool its resources and develop a course that integrated various aspects of their discipline. Another source of inspiration for the idea was W. J. McGlothlin's *A Guide to the Study of Church History*, which also took a comprehensive approach.

The result was the creation of IC 101, 102, 103, and 104—a four-semester sequence of three-hour courses taught jointly by several professors. The courses were all titled "History of Christianity," with period designations for each one. The course description in the 1957 catalog is as follows:

> A survey of the historical development of the Christian movement, in its political, philosophical, and general cultural setting. The missionary expansion of the church, its institutional development, and its theological expressions are studied in context.[6]

The course was designed to combine the strengths and emphases of three Southeastern faculty members, with Luther Copeland dealing with missionary expansion, Pope Duncan with the institutional development, and John Steely with the theological expression. These three taught the course together several times, but others, notably Emily Lansdell and George Shriver, also joined in the effort.

The hope was that the teachers would work as a team. The format called for the teachers to take turns leading the class. Too often, however, there was not much coordination. As all who have tried it have discovered, these teachers found that team-teaching required more effort than individual teaching. The courses required a massive commitment of the resources of the IC area. Also, the magnitude of the four-semester sequence and the size of the classes created problems for other professors, who found it advisable to consider the scheduling of tests in the big course when making out their schedules. Apparently in an effort to deal with some of the difficulties, the four three-hour courses became three four-hour courses in 1960.

Duncan was on sabbatical leave from 1960–1961. When he returned, he found Southeastern a changed place, one racked by tension and discord. In his words, "Everything went downhill after that." He did not want to participate in the Bultmannian fray, but he found that the existing atmosphere made remaining neutral impossible. Duncan left Southeastern after the fall 1963 semester. Over the next three decades, he had a distinguished career as an administrator, serving as president of South Georgia College, of Georgia Southern University, and of Stetson University, where he is now Chancellor.

Transitions: George Shriver

One of Pope Duncan's students was George Shriver. He came to Southeastern as a student at the same time Duncan came as a professor. After completing his B. D. at Southeastern, he began work on his Ph.D. at Duke and completed the degree in 1961. While working on his doctorate, Shriver served as an instructor at Southeastern. He became an assistant professor in 1961 and an associate professor in 1965.

As his senior colleague, Duncan tried to help Shriver along in the beginning stages of his teaching career. He thought that teaching the basic church history course for the certificate (later A.Div.) students—those who did not have baccalaureate degrees—would ease Shriver's path. The result was not as Duncan hoped, however. Like most young teachers, Shriver was zealous and had high expectations. After the first test, Shriver came to Duncan full of frustration and disappointment: "My students didn't learn anything. I'm a failure as a teacher."[7] His subsequent career belies that erroneous judgment.

Shriver's emphases complemented Duncan's well. He focused on courses in American Christianity and, after Stealey's death, the courses in Christian Classics and Biography. Shriver was interested in studying American religion in its cultural context and changed the titles of IC 205 and 206, both of which had been called "Denominations and Sects in America," to "Varieties of Religion in American Life and Culture" and "Indigenous American Religious Groups," with concomitant changes in the course descriptions.[8]

Shriver remembers his days at Southeastern with fondness, reflecting on the high level of freedom and responsibility he had there. He does recall one discordant note in the prevailing tone of academic freedom. In February 1965, the trustees were considering Shriver's sabbatical proposal. One trustee noted that the proposal pertained to the Ecumenical Institute and expressed concern about anything that was called "ecumenical." He began to question Shriver about the suspicious implications of the proposal, but he prefaced his questions with extended remarks about himself and his church. He talked until the time for discussion expired, and Shriver did not have to address the questions.[9] George Shriver remained at Southeastern until 1973. Since that time he has been a professor of history at Georgia Southern University.

The comprehensive church history and missions courses were discontinued in 1963. In their place students were required to take three separate four-hour courses: "General Church History," "Christian Missions," and one of four new church history courses—"The Early Church," "The Medieval Church," "The Reformation," or "The Modern Church." Thus, the area requirement was still twelve hours. The shift created the highly unusual phenomenon of large classes in medieval church history. Over the next few years, this course, and the other "electives" as well, averaged almost fifty students per semester.

A more general revision of the curriculum occurred during the 1967–1968 school year. The occasion for the revision was the change in degree nomenclature from B.D. to M.Div. The old area designations were dropped in favor of the letters B, H, T, and M. The same course numbers were retained, however. Three interdisciplinary courses, labeled BHTM and totaling ten hours, were added to the curriculum; "Orientation to Theological Education" and "Christianity and the Contemporary World" were to be taken in a student's first year, and "Senior Synthesis" was to be taken at the end of the degree program. Even with these additions, the core curriculum was reduced by eight hours. Two of those hours came from the H-area requirement. The sequence of four-hour designated electives was dropped and the directed elective requirement was reduced to two hours.

The 1967 revision was only a temporary measure, however. As early as the next year, several faculty members were calling for further revisions. The intensity of some of this sentiment is revealed in a "working paper" of the curriculum and instruction committee that was part of a self-study that began in 1969.[10] The document, drafted by Ellis Hollon and eventually adopted in somewhat different form by the committee, refers to the changes as a "so-called 'revision' " and labels the revision "mostly pure farce." The document asserts that the committee is unanimous in the opinion that the total hours for the M.Div., then one hundred hours, should be reduced "by at least fifteen and a maximum of twenty-five hours." The document goes on to argue not only that the total should be reduced but also that the required core should be drastically curtailed to give students more flexibility and freedom.

The work of this self-study committee apparently led to continued reflection on curriculum revision. Two years later, most of the suggestions of the committee were incorporated into the most radical curriculum revision ever made at Southeastern. In 1971 the core was reduced from fifty-six hours to twenty-four hours, a reduction of almost sixty percent. The total number of hours required was also reduced from one hundred to eighty-four. The H-area requirement was reduced to one four-hour general church history course; missions and the church history elective were dropped from the core. In 1978 the church history requirement was increased to six hours—two three-hour courses rather than one four-hour course. Several other changes have been made over the years, with a few hours added to the core, but the curriculum at Southeastern has continued to emphasize freedom and flexibility.

Continuity: John E. Steely

Through much of the period of laying the foundations of the Southeastern tradition and the years of transition, one of the constants was John Steely. Steely came to Southeastern in 1956 from Southern Baptist College in Walnut Ridge, Arkansas, where he had been a faculty member and dean of administration. He was promoted to associate professor in 1958 and to professor in 1963. In Southeastern catalogs, Steely was always listed as a teacher of historical theology. Throughout his tenure, however, he was also a professor of church history, at one time or another teaching most of the church history courses the seminary offered.

Steely was one of the original cast members in the "big course" experiment, teaching the section on the history of doctrine. After that experiment ended, he regularly taught the general church history course and the courses on the early church and medieval periods. After the adoption of a two-course general church history sequence, he taught the first half but not the second. He also took over the Christian Classics course after Shriver left and developed some new church history courses, notably one on the history of women in the early church. One course that Steely rarely taught, perhaps only once, was Baptist history. In light of that fact, ironically, one of his books—*The Baptist Way of Life*, which he co-wrote with Brooks Hays—was used several times as a textbook for Baptist History and Heritage.

Steely was especially valuable to the H area in the mid-1970s. For almost two years after Shriver left and before Glenn Miller came, there was no full-time church history professor at Southeastern. In 1975, George Braswell was elected to the faculty as associate professor of Church History and Missions. Steely and Braswell were the church history faculty for two academic years. They were aided by several visiting professors, including Edward Hughes Pruden, former pastor of First Baptist Church in Washington, D.C., and Bernie Cochran, professor of Religion at Meredith College.

Steely accepted the diverse tasks assigned gladly. He saw himself as a "team player" who wanted to do anything he could to help.[11] His willingness to serve went beyond the classroom. Morris Ashcraft has expressed eloquently this dimension of John Steely:

> In faculty matters no one exceeded John in his knowledge of and involve-
> ment in questions of curriculum and degree. His committee work always was
> done with excellence. He was a leader within the faculty whose quiet but strong
> leadership saved numerous situations. He served the accreditation agencies on
> review committees to other institutions.
>
> Students found Professor Steely always available to help them in their re-
> search and quest for sources. It was a common sight to see him in the seminary
> library guiding students to the sources and instructing them in their research.[12]

New Directions: Glenn Miller and Tom Halbrooks

In the early years of Randall Lolley's tenure as president of Southeastern,
there were many additions to the faculty. None was more colorful and
few were as valuable as Glenn Miller. Miller is a native of Richmond,
Virginia, and a graduate of the University of Richmond, Andover-Newton
Theological School, and Union Theological Seminary in New York. After
leaving Union he taught at St. Mary's Seminary in Maryland and at
Hamilton College before coming to Southeastern in 1976.

In his first two years at Southeastern, Miller was almost the entire
church history faculty. Braswell taught one more history course, then
devoted all his time to missions; Steely taught only one church history
course during Miller's first two years. Thus Miller spent most of his time
teaching basic courses and some courses, such as Baptist history, that
were not his favorites.

Miller's research and teaching have focused on American Christianity
and the modern church in general. He developed courses on selected
topics in the history of Christianity in America, including "American
Revivalism from Jonathan Edwards to Billy Graham," "Religious
Liberty," and "Liberalism and Fundamentalism." A topic of special
interest to him, and the focus of extensive research and writing in the last
few years, is the history of American theological education. When he
taught the course entitled "The Modern Church," Miller focused on the
church in Nazi Germany. Beginning in 1981, he offered this course
regularly every two years for the rest of his tenure at Southeastern.

Miller left Southeastern after the fall 1991 semester to become professor of Church History at Bangor Theological Seminary. He has since
also become the academic dean at that institution. Two excerpts from a

statement of appreciation adopted by the Southeastern faculty express something of their feeling at his departure:

> No member of our community has been more distinctive than Glenn T. Miller. No one who has left us has left a more unfillable place. From his red Vega to his red socks, from his attitude to his vocabulary, from his anecdotes to his avocations, Glenn and the things of Glenn are unique.
>
> Glenn's passion for understanding the history of the church and communicating that understanding to anyone who would stop to learn—whether in a classroom, in the faculty lounge, or standing in the cold outside Stealey—has served to challenge the assumptions and expand the vision of students and colleagues alike.[13]

After two years as the sole full-time church history professor, Miller was joined by a colleague who complemented him both personally and professionally. Tom Halbrooks came to Southeastern in the summer of 1978. A native of Birmingham, Alabama, Halbrooks is a graduate of Samford University, Southern Seminary, and Emory University, where he received his doctorate in 1971. After teaching at Mercer University, Halbrooks served as chair of the division of Humanities and Social Sciences at Southside Community College in Virginia and taught at a Lutheran college in Nebraska.

Halbrooks brought to Southeastern a focus on Baptist history that had been missing since the departure of Pope Duncan. Similarly, his interest in Reformation history filled a gap that had long existed at Southeastern. He developed courses on "English Reform: The Lollards to the Puritans," "The Origins of the Reformed Tradition," and "The Role of Women in Protestantism." The latter course served not only to complement Steely's course on women in the early church, but it also addressed issues important to the growing number of women students at Southeastern.

One of Halbrooks's particular interests is the history of worship. He developed a course on "Worship, Baptism, and Communion in the Reformation" and one on "Worship, Baptism, and Communion among Baptists." The latter became one of Halbrooks's most popular courses. The course is evidence of a very practical bent in his approach to the study of history. Worship in many churches has been enriched by ideas and insights that students have gained from these courses.

Halbrooks is also a talented administrator, with a gift for organization and a dedication to effective execution of policy. During the last few years of his tenure at Southeastern, he served as director of advanced professional studies. He also served as a strong and stable leader of the faculty during some trying times. One aspect of that leadership was the commitment, patience, perseverance, and wisdom he displayed as president of the Southeastern chapter of AAUP during a year in which those qualities were desperately needed. Halbrooks left Southeastern in 1991 and now serves as academic dean and professor of Church History at Baptist Theological Seminary at Richmond.

The most significant development in the teaching of history at Southeastern in the 1980s was the requirement of "Baptist History and Heritage." Baptist history had been required in the first two years of Southeastern's existence, but not in subsequent years. During most years at least one Baptist history course had been offered, but the majority of students did not take it. There had been some sentiment over the years to require it, but not enough to do so. Some faculty members apparently felt that requiring a course in Baptist history was a step toward provincialism and away from a deeper understanding of the broader Christian context.

The requirement of "Baptist History and Heritage" came as part of a curriculum review initiated in 1982. An early step in the process was to settle on the courses that would be required as "Foundational Studies." Apparently there was widespread sentiment from the outset to require a course in Baptist history. The M area, on the other hand, recommended that such a course not be required and that the general church history course continue to give attention to Baptist history and polity.[14]

When the curriculum review committee reported its finding to the faculty, it endorsed the requirement of Baptist history but noted that doing so "may require us to reconsider the hours for general Church History."[15] In the margin of his copy of the report, Morris Ashcraft wrote "strong objection" and "do not cut!" It is not clear whether he was speaking for himself or reporting the sentiment of others. The latter seems most likely.

Tom Halbrooks believes that the overriding factor generating such interest in requiring Baptist history was the "controversy," then in its early stages. According to Halbrooks,

> The Southern Baptist Conventions in 1979 and 1980 and Judge Pressler's "jugular" comment had shown that a battle was on. In that context, we thought it was important to know who we were and who we were not. Lack of knowledge about Baptist history had made people more susceptible to an alternative, and

incorrect, understanding of who Baptists were. We thought that it might help to start requiring Baptist history. There was a strong feeling that we had made a mistake in not requiring it earlier.[16]

Since 1985, H 2142—"Baptist History and Heritage"—has been required of all Baptist students at Southeastern.

Expansion: Delos Miles

During the first three decades of the history of Southeastern, the teaching of evangelism was the responsibility of the "practical" area, "Christianity at Work" (CW) and then M. In 1954 a two-hour course in evangelism, CW 104, was added to the core curriculum. In 1958, however, it was deleted.

For many years, the only evangelism course was CW 134, listed in the Religious Education category. By the 1970s there was considerable sentiment to have more evangelism courses and a professor of evangelism.[17] Toward that end about $400,000 was raised—$300,000 of it from one person—to endow a chair of evangelism. After some delay, in the fall of 1978, John Tresch was given a three-year appointment as a professor of evangelism. Much of the faculty objected to the appointment because Tresch lacked an earned doctorate. During his stay at Southeastern, Tresch developed several new courses. They were listed separately as evangelism courses but were still in the M area.

In 1981 Delos Miles was asked to join the faculty and became the first elected faculty member in evangelism at Southeastern. A native of South Carolina, Miles is a graduate of Furman University, Southeastern Seminary, and San Francisco Theological Seminary, from which he received an S.T.D. in 1973. From 1966 until 1977, he served as director of evangelism for the South Carolina Baptist Convention. From 1978 to 1981, he taught evangelism at Midwestern Baptist Theological Seminary.

When he first joined the faculty, Miles remained in the M area; in 1985, however, he was asked to join the H area, and he accepted the invitation. The principal reason for the shift was to put evangelism and missions in the same area. The area believed that doing so would not only increase efficiency, but would also strengthen both disciplines. Another factor was that the H area was much smaller than the M area. Shifting evangelism would create better balance. Evangelism remained in the H area until 1993, when it became part of the newly formed P area, along with missions and preaching.

Concluding Personal Note

In the spring of 1986, while I was happily employed as a teacher of church history at Golden Gate Theological Seminary, President Randall Lolley called and asked me to come to Wake Forest to meet with the H area and the dean to discuss the possiblity of teaching at Southeastern. I agreed to do so. The meeting went smoothly, with all participants professing to be very impressed with each other. A few weeks later, my wife Margaret and I went to Wake Forest to meet with the faculty, a group of students, and others.

The interviews again went well, with astute questions and substantive dialogue. More striking than the "text" of the faculty interview, however, was a persistent subtext. Many of the members of the faculty seemed not only happy at the prospect of our coming to Southeastern, but also very surprised. The visit of the "Peace Committee" was very fresh in their memories. There was a persistent perception, a correct one as things turned out, that Southeastern would be the first SBC agency to undergo dramatic change as a result of the controversy.

Although no one at Southeastern advised us not to come, others did. We received calls from several states warning us about the perils of doing so. Upon being told that we had decided to accept Southeastern's invitation, some asked us why. As is always the case with such moves, several factors were involved, some of which concerned Margaret's career. Whatever the other factors were, one factor involved our belief that all SBC agencies, including the seminary where we were, would undergo very trying times in the years ahead. The issue was not whether one could avoid the fire, but where and with whom one would be standing when the fire fell. We decided that the best place for us to stand was Southeastern. I still believe we made the right choice.

Notes

[1]The teaching of missions at Southeastern is treated in the chapter by Alan Neely.

[2]*Southeastern Baptist Theological Seminary Bulletin* (1951) 21-22.

[3]*SEBTS Bulletin* (1952) 34-36.

[4]*SEBTS Bulletin* (1952) 39.

[5]Interview with Pope Duncan, 13 January 1994. Unless otherwise indicated, all statements about Duncan's attitudes and actions are based on this interview.

[6]*SEBTS Bulletin* (1957) 47.

[7]Duncan interview.

[8]*SEBTS Bulletin* (1968) 55.

[9]Interview with George Shriver, 14 January 1994.

[10]The document has no title, no date, and no page numbers. Each of the pages has "Hollon" written at the top. The document was discussed and revised at a committee meeting 4 November 1969.

[11]Interview with Donna Steely, 13 January 1994.

[12]Morris Ashcraft, "John Edward Steely," *Perspectives in Religious Studies* 20/4 (Winter 1993): 334.

[13]"In appreciation of Glenn Miller," Statement adopted by the Southeastern faculty, December 1991.

[14]"M Area Minutes," 23 August 1982.

[15]"Curriculum Review Committee," 23 August 1982.

[16]Interview with Tom Halbrooks, 13 January 1994.

[17]The information and conclusions in this discussion are based on an interview with Delos Miles, 14 January 1994.

——————— Chapter 7 ———————

Making Theology Practical:
A Love Letter from the M Area

Robert D. Dale

Some essays are best written out of one's head; other essays can only be crafted from the heart. This is a story of the heart, a love letter. Love letters are written about caring and connection. They are testimonials, the products of persons who gave themselves to, invested themselves in, and were renewed by the love itself. Like that most important love letter of all, the New Testament, love letters are first-hand accounts of one side of an emotional commitment.

Rose-Colored Glasses Can See Accurately After All

Love is blind, according to popular wisdom. But the bias common to love letters does not disqualify them as accurate records of a relationship—as long as the lover resists the temptation to write revisionist history. Frequently history is revisionist, written by the victors to justify their conquests. In that vein, Orwell cynically observed in *1984* that history belongs to the chronicler, and that historians frequently make history over to fit their purposes. But love, when tempered by discipline and the wisdom of time, does not have to romanticize the past.

The rose-colored glasses of love letters do not lend themselves very well to complete chronologies or to technical histories. This subjective account is based primarily on conversations with M-area colleagues who helped to give birth to and to nurture Southeastern and secondarily on review of selected seminary documents. This is my attempt to give a voice to those interviews and that research. Consequently, I have not attempted to catalog the full range of course offerings or to depict all of the contributions of the professors who taught in the M area during

Southeastern's first forty years. Obviously, this space is too restricted and this writer too limited to achieve such lofty goals. Therefore, I have only tried to identify and illustrate three contributions by Southeastern's M area, distinctives that I think have influenced the quality of Southeastern's graduate ministers.

Love at First Sight

First impressions do last. Personally, I felt an attraction of the heart from my earliest introductions to Southeastern. My own first impressions of Southeastern Seminary were based on my contacts with her graduates, serving in ministry up and down the Eastern Seaboard. The southeastern sector of the United States became a regular destination for me during the mid-1970s when I spent five years conducting pastoral leadership conferences for the Sunday School Board across the Southern Baptist Convention. Since those seminars and consultations were mostly sponsored by state conventions or by district associations, I worked a lot with regionalized groups. In some areas, my training groups were homogenous, made up largely of graduates from a single seminary. Over time I noticed distinctive characteristics in these homogenous groups and became fascinated by the combative or frenetic desperation typical of some seminaries' products, the elitist attitudes of others, and the tunnel-vision—"ministry-is-done-inside-a-church-office"—outlookofstillothers. The qualities I saw in Southeastern's graduates were strikingly different and left me intrigued. Ministers who had studied at Southeastern appeared to me to be more confident and serene about their identities, less anxious about ministry performance, more secure in their Christian faith, less brittle personally and professionally, and generally more theologically literate. In short, as local church ministers, Southeasterners were more personally poised, more theologically grace-full, and less guilt-driven professionally. What, I wondered, accounted for these distinctives?

Two types of opportunities—short-term and long-term—to observe the teaching-learning process at Southeastern provided me with helpful impressions and information. During the mid-1970s, I served as a guest lecturer in Southeastern's Doctor of Ministry program on several occasions, spoke at the 1974 Student Conference on Missions and Ministry, and conferred with professors about denominational resources for theological education. Additionally, I taught Pastoral Leadership and Church Ministries at Southeastern from 1977 to 1988. From these vantage points, I observed, probed, and uncovered clues to the soul of the school that could account for the quality of her graduates. I believe I have found at least three distinctives of Southeastern Seminary that positively mark her graduates. These special themes provide the structure for this essay and were factors that the M area strongly endorsed.

Love Is a Partnership

Southeastern was launched on a simple but often neglected idea in Southern Baptist theological education. For ministry to be holistic, education for ministers would be based on the whole rather than the parts. From the beginning, Southeastern's curriculum was integrated and generalized rather than piecemeal and specialized. There were no schools in the new seminary. By design, Southeastern was one school—one school with four blended and complementary areas of instruction for ministry preparation.

Quality theological education, like love, is a partnership of commitment. At Southeastern, the classical divinity disciplines of biblical, historical, and theological studies laid down foundations; practical theological studies built up superstructures. In my eyes, the three classical areas of teaching poured the concrete, and the M area raised the steel. Together, the four areas were deliberately integrated for the sake of students. Perhaps the one-school concept partially explains why Southeastern's graduates reflected inner unity and were less fragmented than some other seminaries' products.

M-area professors, therefore, adopted a bifocal view of seminary education. We saw ourselves as—and functioned as—both practicing theologians and theological practitioners. The only two M-area offerings in the first year's class schedule illustrate this bifocal approach: Dynamics of the Spiritual Life and Preaching in Theory and Practice. Isn't it interesting that the 1952–1953 *Catalog* anticipated course offerings in preaching, teaching, counseling, administration, leadership . . . and living?

The early M-area curriculum grew rapidly but kept its bifocal balance. By 1953–1954, the seminary catalog listed twenty-two "Christianity at Work" courses, including Evangelistic Preaching, Christian Sociology, Church Efficiency, Clinical Training, and Creative Writing. The design and awarding of basic divinity degrees with religious education or church music, the so-called combination degrees, retained the one-school approach.

Southeastern envisioned producing thrice-born ministers—physically born, spiritually reborn, and born once again to the practicality of the Christian gospel. M-area practitioners were in agreement with that founding dream of Southeastern, expressed variously over time. In the January-February 1982 issue of the *Bulletin*, President Lolley cited approvingly his memory of President Sydnor Stealey's frequent description of the seminary as founded on a tripod of education, evangelism, and missions. In a similar vein, Dean Olin T. Binkley, in the January 1953 issue of *Outlook*, depicted Southeastern as a three-sided community of learning, faith, and action. This vision of balance and breadth unified the seminary's teaching task, and the M area enthusiastically supported this educational vision.

The one-school philosophy was demonstrated dramatically when a Doctor of Ministry degree program was inaugurated in the mid-1970s. In contrast to many seminaries' tightly structured doctoral curricula, Southeastern chose to honor the maturity of its doctoral students and to use an integrated study approach informed by the discoveries of adult education. In the twenty-eight hour professional degree, only two colloquia were required of all students. The first colloquium focused on theological method, how theology is done by working ministers. The second colloquium centered on research method, specifically how action research is used in the design and implementation of theologically-based ministry projects. The integrated teaching approach so basic to the Doctor of Ministry program was also evident at the master's level in the interdisciplinary teaching teams. Team-taught M-area courses in family systems and group process illustrate the integration of theory and practice.

Love Is a Constant Conversation

Southeastern established an early and friendly conversation between the "church house" and the "school house." The seminary maintained that dialogue about the ministry of the churches and the ministry of the seminary to those constituent congregations. The result was congregation-focused theological education that incorporated a rich mix of field education, *practica*, field-oriented seminars, adjunctive teachers who were active and successful practitioners, and consultation with the denomination and broader religious community. This ongoing dialogue may also have contributed to the inner coherence of Southeastern's graduate ministers.

At its founding, Southeastern established a unique and pioneering record in field-oriented education. In 1953 Garland A. Hendricks, named "Rural Minister of the Year" by *Progressive Farmer* in 1949 and former North Carolina pastor, moved from Gardner-Webb College to Southeastern to establish a program of field work. Doggedly he taught and traveled. As a result, Hendricks personalized the seminary to churches in the region by meeting face-to-face with church leaders, averaging 80,000 miles each year for twenty-five years. Additionally, he created a link to the sociology department at North Carolina State University that yielded innovative courses in rural church ministry. Robert L. Richardson, an alumnus and a Vanderbilt graduate, returned to Southeastern from teaching posts at Belmont College and Atlantic Christian College in 1973 to teach field education. He served as a stabilizing influence when an even more ambitious approach to field-based supervision was adopted in 1978.

Formation in Ministry provided every Southeastern student an opportunity to practice ministry under the sensitive eye of a skilled field supervisor. Luke B. Smith joined the faculty in 1978 to help spearhead this new teaching initiative. He had taught at Averett College and brought extensive ministry experience in missions and church work. Richardson and Smith created a network of nearly 1000 trained supervisors. An average of 100–125 of the supervisors plus a small group of adjunctive teachers year-by-year launched a generation of young ministers who were even more ready for ministry than their predecessors.

A variety of other teaching approaches kept the conversation between the church and the academy lively. The age-level *practica* in religious education and the traveling seminars in evangelism are two illustrations.

There was, perhaps, no better example of the close relationship of church and seminary than in the high-quality adjunctive teachers the seminary utilized over the years. The M area was the primary beneficiary of these talented ministers' efforts.

Another course that bridged the M area to congregations and their settings was the urban studies seminar taught primarily by Thomas A. Bland. He came to Southeastern in 1956 from the headship of the sociology department at William Jewell College and launched the urban seminar in 1967 in Washington, D.C. Later he made New York City the setting for the course. Bland regularly taught overloads in order to extend the urban experience to students.

Southeastern's faculty and staff reached out to the broader denomination and Christian family through lecturing, consulting, and writing. Formally, Bruce Powers filled a liaison professorship with the Sunday School Board. Informally, M-area professors excelled in a variety of off-campus service. Tom Bland received the North Carolina Baptist Convention's Church Planter of the Year Award in 1986 for his foundational work in beginning several new congregations. During my tenure at Southeastern, four M-area faculty members served as deacon chairs at Wake Forest Baptist Church alone. The church-seminary conversation continued in our private lives as well. Our students knew and appreciated these wider commitments.

Love Blends Gifts

Southeastern's M area deliberately blended the primary functions of ministry: proclaiming the gospel through preaching, teaching, evangelizing, and church music; caring for God's flock as well as reaching out to the community; and leading congregations and ministry agencies. The action-reflection model of theological education was the central element of the M area's efforts in developing the emerging generations of Baptist ministers. Learning-by-doing-and-thinking across the full range of ministry skills readied Southeastern's graduates for more effective and comfortable service in their callings.

The Centrality of Proclaiming the Good News

Preaching was the M area's initial launch pad through M. Ray McKay's impact on the original faculty. McKay, a powerful and inspirational preacher, left Second Baptist Church of Little Rock, Arkansas, to establish basic courses in preaching. Founding President Stealey's early correspondence showed that Southern Baptists felt that Southeastern's faculty selection process was gathering the best of the best. McKay was typical of those recruitment efforts. J. Carroll Trotter, moving from an Alabama pastorate to join McKay in 1955, brought his New Testament expertise, emphasized communication skills through speech, and later helped pioneer videotaped feedback of sermon delivery.

During the late 1960s, two special teachers contributed to the M area's preaching offerings. John W. Carlton, a classicist with Virginia pastorates and previous teaching experience at Southern Baptist Theological Seminary and Duke Divinity School, brought broad theological, psychological, and literary backgrounds to the classroom. Theodore F. Adams, a world-class Baptist, leavened his teaching with gentle strength flowing from thirty-two years of experience as pastor of First Baptist Church in Richmond, Virginia.

The 1980s brought two strong practitioners of preaching to the faculty. Thomas R. McKibbens, pastor of First Baptist Church of Bristol, Virginia, signed on in 1984 and enriched the teaching mix with his training in Baptist history. Roy DeBrand arrived in 1987 from a teaching post at North American Baptist Theological Seminary and stressed a functional and textual approach to preaching.

Religious education was the other plank in the original platform of the first year of teaching at Southeastern. Course work in religious education was offered from the first semester that the fledgling seminary opened her doors. In 1953 Ben C. Fisher, later to lead the Education Commission, commenced teaching religious education. Beginning in 1954, John T. Wayland anchored the seminary's early Christian education efforts and taught practical courses for eighteen years. Wayland was joined by Denton R. Coker and briefly by L. J. Morriss. Thelma Arnote moved from First Baptist Church in Durham, North Carolina, in 1956 to teach religious education and to establish the child care center as a lab school. She brought valuable experience in public school education as well as an eleven-year stint at the Sunday School Board.

During the early 1960s, Robert E. Poerschke joined the Christian education faculty, bringing a wealth of ministry experience in churches, in the Marines, and on campuses. Among his many contributions to the seminary's Christian education curriculum, he pioneered the classroom-plus-practicum approach at Southeastern. J. Colin Harris, a Southeastern and Duke alumnus, came to the faculty from a North Carolina pastorate and taught Christian education creatively, though briefly, in the early 1970s. Bruce P. Powers arrived in 1978 from significant service at the Sunday School Board. He was an expert in denominational resources and educational administration. Additionally, he helped establish the Spring Conference and the computer laboratory, and he published extensively. William P. Clemmons' broad experience in local church leadership, foreign mission service, retreat ministries, writing, and lay ministry stretched Southeastern's Christian education perspectives. His most crucial contribution was designing and offering the most extensive spiritual formation courses in the Southern Baptist Convention.

While evangelism was emphasized and taught at Southeastern from the beginning, it was viewed as a permeating discipline to be included in all courses, regular and adjunctive. Wholesome and balanced courses taught by Denton Coker and others were stressed. In the mid-1970s, one-third of Southeastern's faculty had practical experience on foreign or pioneer missions fields and used that background to encourage church growth. Shortly after I came to the Southeastern faculty, I was in a denominational conference in which Southeastern's effectiveness in evangelism was questioned. As a graduate of Southwestern Baptist Theological Seminary, a school generally accepted as evangelistic, I proposed a simple test. I asked the North Carolina Baptist Convention to sort its baptismal records to see how Southeastern and Southwestern graduates compared. Southeastern graduates' performance in baptisms led the way.

A dual approach to evangelism was adopted in the 1970s. While continuing the permeating philosophy, full-time faculty members were added to teach evangelism as a specialty. John W. Tresch, North Carolina pastor and graduate of Southwestern Baptist Theological Seminary and Vanderbilt, was appointed in 1978 to serve as a residential teacher of evangelism and designed the early course offerings. Delos Miles, Southeastern and San Francisco Theological Seminary alumnus and a war hero, joined the faculty in 1981 after rich experience as pastor, director of evangelism in Virginia and South Carolina, and professor of evangelism at Midwestern

Baptist Theological Seminary. He quickly proved to be the best prac-
titioner of evangelism in Southern Baptist ranks with his prolific writing
in church growth and personal evangelism as well as with his active
preaching and lecturing schedule.

Church music provided another pivotal element to the M area's overall instruction in proclamation skills. President Stealey felt music was
critical for the morale of the campus. Ben S. Johnson, head of the voice
department at William Carey College, began his teaching ministry at
Southeastern in 1956. His contributions to the M area and the seminary
include his down-to-earth nature, the wide range of teaching responsibilities for the many years when he was the only full-time music
professor, and his creative design of the Master of Divinity with Church
Music curriculum. Acclaimed organist H. Max Smith served as artist in
residence in 1959–1960 and as professor of church music until the late
1960s. A variety of other musicians have provided crucial adjunctive
services over the years, also. James W. Good moved from Southern Seminary to Southeastern in 1978. His virtuosity at the organ keyboard is
legendary. C. Michael Hawn joined the faculty in 1982, moving from his
post as minister of music at First Baptist Church in Decatur, Georgia. His
expertise in church music for children and youth, his writing ability, and
his beautiful voice—to say nothing of his gift for "accordion evangelism"—brightened the musical atmosphere of the campus.

The Ministry Resource of Caring Hearts

Pastoral care was an early and strong emphasis in the M area, utilizing
a combination of outstanding faculty members and adjunctive specialists.
Richard K. Young, president of the Southern Baptist Hospital Chaplains'
Association and staff member of the Bowman Gray School of Medicine,
began to offer on-campus and hospital-based course work in 1953. This
combination of classroom and clinical instruction in caring skills became
a distinctive of Southeastern's impact on students and churches. The
Clinical Pastoral Education model of learning under supervision influenced M-area instruction. After 1959, Truman S. Smith, director of
student activities, also taught pastoral care along with his other duties.

A new era of pastoral care instruction dawned with the arrivals of
Richard L. Hester and dean of the faculty Albert L. Meiburg in 1975.

Hester brought a varied background in biblical studies, counseling, pastoral experience, and theological education. His inventive teaching approaches contributed small group supervision, systems thinking, and team teaching to the faculty as well as leadership in educational design. Meiburg had distinguished himself as a theological teacher, clinician, and author. He led significant innovations in adult pedagogy and learning-by-doing. One year during the mid-1980s under Meiburg's leadership, the Southeastern faculty published more theological books and articles than the other Southern Baptist seminary faculties combined.

The Hope of Leadership for the Future

In a creative response to alumni feedback, President Lolley proposed a professorship in leadership. Hester drafted the position description, and Richardson identified me as a candidate. Consequently, I became the first professor of pastoral leadership in Southern Baptist seminaries in 1977. New courses in leader styles, congregational diagnosis, conflict and change management, survival skills, group process, and career assessment were developed. Additionally, I directed the Doctor of Ministry program from 1978 until 1988.

Keeping Your Balance

A full array of professional skills—proclaiming, caring, and leading—is necessary for confident ministry in these demanding times. The action-reflection approach used in Southeastern's M area may have contributed to the balance between the "what" of practicality and "why" of theology in her graduates. I know this range of disciplines created enjoyable interchanges between those of us who taught in the M area.

Love Is Joy

The M-area faculty members worked together well, although our area meetings were often marked by spirited debate. We enjoyed each other, especially at our annual Christmas party. Most of us saw exchanging "white elephant" gifts as an opportunity to palm off plastic flamingos, cast-iron frogs, and garish serving dishes shaped like lobsters. There were exceptions, however. John Carlton always brought the only "good" gift, usually something elegant, and Ben Johnson regularly showed his ingenuity by using the occasion to select his mother-in-law's Christmas gift!

Signing Off

I guess there's only one way to sign a love letter—with a "Love Always" closing. Southeastern, we loved serving Christ through you. Thanks for putting the practical preparation of several generations of your students in our hands. We tried to be good stewards of your trust in us. We will love you always! Signed: the M area.

─────── Chapter 8 ───────

Reflections on Teaching Theology

John W. Eddins, Jr.

The teaching and learning of theology at Southeastern Baptist Theological Seminary prior to 1987 was a dream come true. In this essay I reflect on the dream from my perspective as a teacher who shared in its development, fulfillment, and brokenness during my thirty-six years (1957–1993) at Southeastern Seminary.

The dream began to be realized in the meeting of the Southern Baptist Convention of 1947 in St. Louis, when a committee was formed to study the matter of theological education in light of a proposal for the establishment of new seminaries. During the meeting of the Southern Baptist Convention of 1950 in Chicago, the Convention voted to purchase the campus of Wake Forest College and establish a new seminary to be named "The Southeastern Baptist Theological Seminary, Incorporated."

The Southern Baptist Convention, expressing the dream of some of its leaders, implemented the new vision of a progressive seminary in the East where Baptists had begun their monumental work in the formation of a free church in a free state in colonial America. The campus and spirit of Wake Forest College became the ideal location for a new seminary conceived and birthed by Baptists who desired competent and compassionate pastors and other leaders in the life of the churches and of the larger Christian community. The trustees of the fledgling school, who were accomplished in their chosen professions, sought to give constant support and encouragement to their newly elected President, Dr. Sydnor L. Stealey, and to the faculty, staff, and students. The sharing of the dream and the enfleshment of the vision were also grounded in the adoption and acceptance of the Articles of Faith by each member of the faculty. The Abstract of Principles was taken seriously by the faculty as a confession of faith that provided guidelines for research, teaching, and writing. President Stealey asked me prior to my signing the Articles of

Faith in 1958 if I could accept and live with this doctrinal statement as the context of my work at Southeastern Seminary. With an affirmative response, I interpreted this confessional statement in terms of freedom and responsibility to implement the vision as a sacred trust granted by the churches of the Southern Baptist Convention. To subscribe to another confession of faith from any other source would constitute, for me, a breach of faith with our Baptist people.

Two crucial formative factors in focusing the vision were faculty governance and the design of the curriculum for theological education. Faculty governance, in harmony with the stated purpose of the seminary "to prepare God-called men and women for a variety of Christian ministries," placed the policies and procedures involving academic matters squarely on the shoulders of the faculty. The enthusiastic response of the original faculty to this opportunity to develop a holistic concept of seminary education in which each dimension of the curriculum supplemented and complemented the other was to focus the vision that inspired the faculty and students for almost four decades.

The faculty assumed that all theological students should have a first-rate education in the Bible, church history, theology, ethics, philosophy of religion, Christian education, preaching, pastoral care, worship, evangelism, and missions. The curriculum was designed in four "areas," not departments, with members of each area serving as convener on a rotating basis and representing the area on the Committee on Academic Policy and Procedure. This most significant committee brought their recommendations to the faculty. The faculty also considered issues as a "committee of the whole," which gave the faculty a sense of involvement in the development of the curriculum. The four areas were originally named "The Interpretation of the Bible" (IB area), "The Interpretation of Christianity" (IC area), "Christian Life and Thought" (LT area), and "Christianity at Work" (CW area). Later, the terminology was changed to the "B area," "H area," "T area," and "M area."

The scope of the work in the LT area included systematic theology, ethics, historical theology, and philosophy of religion. Biblical theology was included in the work of the IB area, although some members of the LT area were exceedingly competent in biblical theology. This matter was never a controversial issue among the teachers in these two areas.

In the second year of the seminary, 1952–53, two faculty additions constituted the LT area. They were Olin T. Binkley, Professor of

Christian Sociology and Ethics, and Stewart A. Newman, Professor of Theology and Philosophy of Religion. These two outstanding teachers and scholars caught the vision of the new seminary, and they set the tone for collegiality, competence, and cooperation in the LT area, into which I came in 1957.

Three formative scholars in Professor Binkley's orientation in the field of sociology and ethics were Jesse B. Weatherspoon, William O. Carver, and H. Richard Niebuhr. Binkley sought a solid basis for Christian ethics in biblical ethics interpreted in light of the revelation in the life and teachings of Jesus. He was impatient with philosophical ethics. Through sociology, Binkley related the ethical insights of Christian revelation to some major issues and questions facing humankind. In an interview on 3 January 1994, he described the greatest challenge facing society today as "being in the sphere of reconciliation in race relations."

He observed in the T area (LT area changed to T area in 1968) an excellent balance of research and teaching with a reasonable degree of specialization involving "research translation" from the larger community of theological scholars. Binkley saw the faculty as a whole team of educators working together with a sense of mission. Two of his outstanding books are *The Churches and the Social Conscience* (1948) and *How to Study the Bible* (1969). Professor Binkley became the first Dean of the Faculty in 1958 and the second president of Southeastern Seminary in 1963. He retired from this post in 1974.

Professor Newman brought to the faculty not only his expertise in philosophy of religion and theology but also much-needed knowledge of the life and thought of Baptists in the Southwest and especially in Texas. He described himself, in an interview on 28 December 1993, as a teacher in the tradition of American Personalism as shaped by A. M. Fairbairn, E. S. Brightman, Peter Bertocci, and Georgia Harkness. Newman was the first teacher of systematic theology in the new seminary, and the theological works of W. T. Conner were primary in his classes. Later, he wrote an excellent book on his former teacher, *W. T. Conner: Theologian of the Southwest* (1964). He indicated, however, that his major interests were in the areas of philosophy of religion and philosophical theology. Nevertheless, ecclesiology—especially Baptist ecclesiology—was a burning issue with Newman, and the students flocked to his classes on ecclesiology. He was interpreted as both a caustic and constructive critic of the church as made manifest in the Southern Baptist Convention and shaped by the Landmark movement of the nineteenth century. This ecclesiology has impacted the Sunday School Board of the Southern Baptist Convention until this day. These issues were addressed in *A Free Church Perspective: A Study in Ecclesiology* (1986). Professor Newman taught at Southeastern Seminary until he accepted a teaching post at Campbell University in 1965.

James E. Tull came to the faculty in 1955 and brought to the T area an excellent knowledge of theology, philosophy, and Baptist life and thought. He taught systematic theology and other courses in theology from the perspective of having served as a chaplain in India, Burma, and China during World War II and having engaged in graduate study with Reinhold Neibuhr, Paul Tillich, John Bennett, and Robert Handy. Tull was not a disciple of Barth and Brunner in the debate concerning general revelation and natural theology. He appreciated their emphases on the revelation in Jesus Christ and the Bible as the Word of God, but he had a higher view of the role of reason in the human quest for God and also a more comprehensive view of the scope of revelation.

Professor Tull taught a course in Baptist Theology grounded in the context of his ecumenicity and concern that the first principles of early Baptists were being distorted and eroded in the Southern Baptist Convention. His insightful and penetrating work in Baptist ecclesiology was published under the title of *A History of Southern Baptist Landmarkism in the Light of Historical Baptist Ecclesiology* (1980). An earlier monograph, *Shapers of Baptist Thought* (1972), presented a panorama of diversity among Baptist leaders and scholars from Roger Williams to Walter Rauschenbusch and Martin Luther King, Jr. Professor Tull retired in 1980 and died on 2 March 1989. He was my mentor and dear friend.

In 1956, two additional professors were added to the T area in Christian sociology and ethics and in historical theology. Thomas A. Bland, Professor of Christian Ethics and Sociology, interpreted ethics as a mediating discipline concerned with thinking about the Christian life (theology) and living according to principles and criteria grounded in the Christian revelation (ethics). He rejected the old-line liberal divorce between theology and ethics and affirmed them as integrative disciplines. The influence of Karl Barth, Emil Brunner, Reinhold Niebuhr, H. Richard Niebuhr, Paul Lehmann, and James M. Gustafson in relating ethics to theology and to Christian living shaped Bland's approach to his work.

In an interview on 23 December 1993, Bland observed, "Ethics deals with the character and conduct (being and doing) of humans in context." He stressed a firm biblical foundation oriented in the ethical teachings of Jesus and applied to the crucial contemporary issues of human conduct. Bland described his approach as contextual rather than situational. A pamphlet that he wrote for the Home Mission Board, titled *A Theology for Metropolis* (1977), exhibits this approach to ethics and society.

Professor Bland described members in the T area as colleagues who had the capacity to work together without feeling pressure to conform. Colleagues supported one another and exhibited a basic regard for the expertise and contribution made by each member regardless of age, gender, or length of tenure at Southeastern Seminary. Freedom was given to each partner to explore different approaches and to offer new courses in the curriculum. Significant issues were discussed in a straightforward manner,but an impasse was never reached, before 1987, and fellowship was not broken. Colleagues were not politically or ideologically oriented in the decision-making process, and at times positions were changed in response to additional information and reason. Since the T area generally had a good balance of experienced teachers and newcomers, there was an awareness of good continuity and stability that conveyed a sense of security and well-being. Faculty in the T area balanced their personal and professional goals constructively.

Professor Bland also taught in the M area (Ministry area) and observed that several teachers in the four areas of the faculty offered courses in other areas. The faculty was committed to the concept of one school and one faculty with individual and area "squatter's rights" but not exclusive possession. Many factors contributed to the constructive relationships of faculty in the areas themselves and in the faculty at large. One of the most significant factors was the large degree of faculty participation in the governance of the seminary.

John E. Steely came to the faculty in 1956 in historical theology. Professor Steely was exceedingly devoted to the work in the T area of the faculty as well as to the work of the larger faculty and the seminary. He brought to his teaching ministry superior research-oriented skills and personal warmth. Steely's knowledge of German was outstanding, and he was at home in Hebrew, Greek, Latin, French, and Dutch. He translated seventeen books, to my knowledge, from German and Dutch including works by such notable scholars as Walter Schmithals, Gerhard von Rad, Hans Conzelmann, and E. Flesseman-Von Leer.

Professor Steely had a thorough knowledge of and appreciation for the history of Baptists. Steely and Brooks Hays, former president of the Southern Baptist Convention, wrote *The Baptist Way of Life* (1963). In 1964, he and Stewart A. Newman wrote *The Baptist Advance: The Achievements of the Baptists of North America for a Century and a Half.*

Professor Steely and I taught graduate seminars on the doctrines of the trinity and christology in the Master of Theology degree program, and we collaborated on several other courses. As a younger colleague in theology, I learned from his wisdom and patient labors, and he was my dear friend. He died, before retirement, on Good Friday, 28 March 1986.

In September 1957, I came to the faculty of Southeastern Seminary in the T area as a Special Instructor in Theology. The dream of Southern Baptists had become a reality, and this reality was formed, shaped, and focused into the vision that has been described in its actualization from 1947 to 1957. When I became a part of the T area, the larger faculty, and the seminary family, indeed, I experienced a dream come true! I could feel the excitement of faculty, students, administrative leaders, staff, trustees, and alumni as the seminary family breathed the fresh air of responsible freedom in the joy of learning and teaching the Good News—the Gospel of our Lord Jesus Christ. Frequently, in the evenings and on Saturdays, many members of the faculty were in their offices preparing lectures in a fellowship of learning. This was a heady experience in my introduction to the teaching vocation in the field of theology at the age of thirty-one.

My basic theological perspective was formed in my family of origin and in the local Baptist church of my youth. Studies at Howard College (Samford University) and The Southern Baptist Theological Seminary enabled me to refine my theology in terms of scholarly approaches to the Christian faith. I never experienced a serious conflict between being intelligent and being spiritual.

Given the freedom to define my own terms, I describe my theological perspective as neo-classical. That is, I take the central teachings of the Christian revelation, expressed doctrinally, in the Catholic, Protestant, and free-church traditions and interpret them in light of the revelation in Jesus Christ and in the context of contemporary knowledge and culture. The Bible is my primary source for theology, and my principle of selection is "love in the form of the servant." Although my graduate studies included some neo-orthodox theologians (Karl Barth, Emil Brunner, and Reinhold Niebuhr), I have never been a scholastic neo-orthodox theologian. The assertion that neo-orthodoxy has been my perspective and the perspective of Southeastern Baptist Theological Seminary is simply not accurate. In 1964, I wrote *Theology 136: Systematic Theology* for use by the Seminary Extension Department of the Southern Baptist Convention.

In my reflections on teaching theology at Southeastern Seminary, I remember most vividly the traumatic struggles that many students experienced and expressed concerning their views of the Bible—its origin, nature, meaning, and authority. They expressed fear of the Bible, seeming afraid that if they did not believe views they had been taught by authority figures, they would not be accepted. They had heard that if they did not have a particular view of inspiration and of the Bible, then they did not believe the Bible was the Word of God. Some students who came to the seminary to study the Bible saw that Bible study was dangerous, like touching the ark of the covenant, and it remained for them a closed book.

Since the Bible was my primary source for teaching systematic theology, I steadfastly resisted the view that any theory of inspiration drawn from the tradition of the church should be imposed on the Bible. To postulate any theory about the Bible as the norm for interpreting the Bible is to put the Bible in second place and to proclaim that certain traditions of the church and some individual opinions are superior to Holy Scripture.

Theology is thinking about God, and I have given primary attention to the revelation of God in Jesus Christ with the doctrines of the trinity, christology, and pneumatology at the center. The doctrines of creation, humankind, the church, the Christian life, and eschatology have all been interpreted in light of God.

I understand my task as a teacher of theology as that of giving birth in an academic community to young theologs who, with nurture and nourishment, begin to have a theological life of their own wherein they are enabled with the guidance of the Holy Spirit to use their God-given minds to think for themselves.

Ellis W. Hollon, Jr., was added to the faculty in 1967 in the field of philosophy of religion. Professor Hollon was at home in philosophy, philosophy of religion, and theology. William Temple and Karl Barth were two of the formative thinkers in Hollon's approach to philosophy and theology. His life and work were cut short in a tragic accident, and he died on 8 April 1979. Although his tenure at Southeastern was little more than a decade, he was a dear friend and colleague who left the marks of his thorough scholarship and personal devotion on his colleagues and students.

T. Furman Hewitt came to the faculty in the field of Christian Ethics in 1976 to enlarge the offerings in the sphere of ethics and to complement the work of Professor Bland. In an interview on 21 December 1993, Hewitt described himself as being to the left of some contemporary Baptists in his emphasis on the priesthood of believers, liberty of conscience, soul competence, autonomy of the local church, individual freedom, and authority of the Bible. As an ethicist, he identified with the early Baptists in colonial America who were social and religious reformers. His family of origin (Hewitt), prominent in the Baptist movement in education in the South, molded and focused his views of human behavior in the church and society.

H. Richard Niebuhr and Reinhold Niebuhr were formative scholars in shaping Hewitt's perspective and work in ethics. Although Professor Hewitt taught courses in human sexuality, a dangerous subject for Baptists, he described himself as not being a radical social protester or a thoroughgoing devotee to liberation theology. Hewitt's concern for human welfare was reflected in *A Biblical Approach to the Use and Abuse of Alcohol and other Drugs* (1980).

Professor Hewitt relished his work as a colleague in the T area and in the faculty. He thrived in an atmosphere of gracious acceptance, collegiality, openness, inclusiveness, and diversity. He caught the Southeastern vision and gave his energies to its further fulfillment. Hewitt was a magnetic teacher and friend to a host of students, and his compassion for students and their welfare was commonly known and deeply appreciated.

Claude Y. Stewart came to the faculty in 1978 to join Professor Tull and me in teaching systematic theology. No member of the T area knew him, and, as we reviewed his dossier, we became excited about the possibility of his joining us. Professor Stewart brought additional diversity to our school from his studies in process theology. Stewart's interest in nature as the arena of God's gracious activity was a welcomed enrichment to our theological spectrum. His doctoral dissertation was published in 1983 under the title of *Nature in Grace: A Study in the Theology of Nature*. Process theology did not set well, however, with some extremely conservative and fundamentalist students and trustees, and Stewart came under considerable fire from the radical right. With the threatening storm clouds gathering over him and Southeastern, Professor Stewart resigned from the faculty in December 1986, and theological diversity was greatly diminished.

The death of Professor Ellis W. Hollon, Jr. in April of 1979 created a pressing need for another faculty member in the field of philosophy of religion. Thomas H. Graves arrived in the fall semester of 1979 and began his teaching duties in the spring semester, 1980. In an interview on 14 December 1993, Professor Graves described his perspective in philosophy, theology, and ethics as a dialogical approach in which there is a sharing of issues as mutual confession. He was greatly influenced by Nikolai A. Berdyaev's dialogical method in the dialogue between Christians and Marxists. This dialogical approach differs radically from "apologetics" as proving the truth of Christianity as opposed to the truth in philosophy. Blaise Pascal and Soren Kierkegaard also shaped Graves' approach to religion, philosophy of religion, and theology. The divine wager (Pascal) and the leap of faith (Kierkegaard) involving the whole person were essential in describing religious commitment and experience. Graves insisted that thought was praxis-oriented, including reason but not simply a mental exercise.

According to Graves, the tone of the T area was one of commitment, mutual professional and personal respect, constructive disagreement, openness to one another, inclusiveness, integrity, stability, a remarkable degree of freedom, and a genuine commitment to the church and the churches. When Professor Graves returned from a sabbatical leave in the fall of 1987, he found radical changes in the situation at Southeastern, and he resigned in October of 1987. The Southeastern vision was fast becoming a terrible nightmare for those who built the seminary.

With Professor Tull's retirement, the seminary sought another teacher in theology—a mature, accomplished scholar with profound appreciation for the Baptism tradition. Robert H. Culpepper was elected to the faculty in March 1979 but returned to Japan for one year to complete almost three decades of missionary service. He came to the faculty in 1980 with a high sense of calling and a thorough commitment to being a good teacher of Christian theology.

Professor Culpepper described himself in an interview on 30 December 1993 as more a kerygmatic than an apologetic theologian in teaching systematic theology. He remarked that he was not a disciple of anyone, although the influence of Karl Barth and Emil Brunner partially shaped his theology, especially in the realm of christology. Christology was the key doctrine along with the doctrine of the trinity. Culpepper espoused a high christology with emphasis on the model of Jesus as savior and redeemer firmly grounded in the New Testament. He took the revelation described in the Bible seriously, but Culpepper was not a literalist or a fundamentalist. He advocated and employed the historical-critical study of scripture as long as the biblical material was not ruled out at a pre-suppositional level. His interests in christology and theology resulted in the publication of *Interpreting the Atonement* (1966) and *Evaluating the Charismatic Movement: A Theological and Biblical Appraisal* (1977).

Professor Culpepper rejoiced in what he discovered upon entering the T area, and he became another participant in and shaper of the South-eastern vision. He was pleased to be a team player with colleagues whom he respected in a seminary oriented in faculty governance. The freedom to be himself personally and professionally was most satisfying and chal-lenging to Professor Culpepper.

Professor Morris Ashcraft came to Southeastern Seminary in 1981 as Dean of the Faculty and Professor of Theology. He was already an out-standing leader in theological education in the Southern Baptist Convention and well-known as an excellent teacher, scholar, writer, and preacher in the churches. He gave outstanding guidance in the procure-ment, development, and encouragement of the faculty. Professor Ashcraft also enriched the teaching of systematic theology and other courses in theology while serving as Dean of the Faculty.

In an interview on 20 December 1993, Ashcraft objected to the con-temporary use of terms such as conservative, moderate, and liberal. He interpreted his theological perspective as being in the mainstrean with the "once-for-allness" of the revelation in Jesus Christ described in terms of the incarnation as essential to Christian theology, the Christian life, and the church. For him, "God was in Christ," and this presupposition was the bedrock for theology and practice. This theological approach is well presented in *The Forgiveness of Sin* (1972), *The Will of God* (1980), *Christian Faith and its Beliefs* (1984), and *The Christian Hope* (1988).

Professor Ashcraft knew most of the members of the T area before he came to Southeastern. He described his colleagues in terms of a respectful and fraternal collegiality with an openness and inclusiveness of various theological views without any suspicion or disapproval. He appreciated the openness of students who had not been indoctrinated with Landmarkism and who were willing to learn without demanding that he conform to their beliefs.

Following the adoption and partial implementation of "A Plan of Action" by the board of trustees (March 1987) and a closed meeting of the trustees with President W. Randall Lolley (October 1987), Professor Ashcraft resigned as Dean of the Faculty. He came to Southeastern in time to embrace and enjoy the vision that was now being dismantled and refocused by others from a radically different perspective.

Faculty in the T area had long sought to add to its number teachers of other races and gender. When Dean Ashcraft brought a proposal that Dr. Elizabeth Barnes be added to the faculty as an "Assistant Professor of Theological Studies" with a three-year appointment, the response was one of excitement and delight. Barnes came to the faculty in 1984, bringing needed diversity to the theological offerings with her interests in liberation theology as expressed, in particular, from feminist and black perspectives. During her years at Southeastern, she began to develop a narrative theology, influenced by James Wm. McClendon, and described herself, in an interview on 12 December 1993, as a "narrative-liberationist" or a "liberation-narrativist." Professor Barnes was influenced by Karl Barth, whose thought she examined in her doctoral dissertation later published in 1987 as *An Affront to the Gospel? The Radical Barth and the Southern Baptist Convention*. Barnes focused her teaching on the issue of God's action in the world and the church's responsibility to join that action; the church's faithful discipleship was central in her emphases.

During her work at Southeastern, Professor Barnes taught systematic theology, Christian ethics, philosophy of religion, and a variety of elective courses. Professor Culpepper stood amazed, as did others of us, at her ability to teach effectively in so many fields of study. Barnes became one of the most popular teachers at Southeastern. At the same time, she felt a special burden in being cast as a role model for women and for women in ministry. Following her three-year appointment, Professor Barnes was elected to the faculty, without tenure, as "Assistant Professor of Theology" with a one-vote majority in the Board of Trustees in March 1987.

In the T area, Professor Barnes felt welcome, and she described her relationship as a kind of growing or evolution in which she never experienced opposition. Her feelings of insecurity, lack of confidence, and loneliness were overcome in large measure by the helpfulness of colleagues. Professor Barnes had become a part of the vision of theological education at Southeastern Seminary, but "without tenure" meant that the vision was fading and fading fast.

Following "A Plan of Action" adopted by the trustees in March of 1987, President Lolley and Dean Ashcraft presented to the T area in May 1987 a recommendation to bring Kurt A. Richardson, a doctoral candidate, to the faculty in the field of historical theology. His dossier stated that he was an avowed fundamentalist in his view of the inspiration and authority of the Bible. The members of the T area, with great anguish and soul-searching, opposed the recommendation. Richardson joined the faculty in the fall of 1987.

In my reflections on teaching theology at Southeastern Seminary, I have described the dream that became a reality in a vision enfleshed in the lives of thousands of students, in the churches, and on the mission fields *as I experienced it*. If the reader experienced any part of it, he or she may also give thanks to God and to God's people who provided the rare opportunity for this heavenly feast in theological education and in Christian koinonia.

Shortly before Professor Malcolm O. Tolbert took leave of Wake Forest, following his retirement in 1988, he said something like this to me: "John, my experience at Southeastern has been my Camelot in Christian ministry, and I thank God for it." Yes, for me it was also my Camelot in the forest of Wake, and I am at peace.

———— Chapter 9 ————

"That the World May Believe": The Teaching of Missions, 1952–1988

Alan Neely

"I do not pray for these only, but also for those who believe in me through their word, that they may all be one; . . . so that the world may believe that you have sent me." (John 17:20-21)[1]

In 1834, more than a generation before Baptists in the South founded their first seminary, Baptists in North Carolina opened a college in Wake Forest "to afford our young ministers facilities for obtaining such an education as will qualify them to be able ministers of the New Testament."[2] To be prepared for a New Testament ministry included being equipped for Christian mission in the world. Matthew T. Yates, one of the first and most revered Southern Baptist missionaries to China, was a graduate of Wake Forest College.[3] Many others from the college would follow, including two graduates who later became professors of missions at Southeastern Seminary, John Burder Hipps and George W. Braswell, Jr.

When Southeastern Baptist Theological Seminary began on the campus of Wake Forest College, the faculty and students inherited a missions tradition that had been nurtured and perpetuated in the college for more than a hundred years. Reviewing the history of the two institutions reveals that the new and fledgling theological institution acquired from Wake Forest College not only a magnificent campus but also something far more valuable, a commitment to academic excellence and to the world mission of the church.

The Seminary's Primary Purpose

When the founding trustees considered and approved the original documents that would serve to govern the seminary, the statement defining the institution's *raison d'étre* was unambiguous. Southeastern was established to prepare men and women for "various ministries," including "missionary work at home and abroad."[4] This statement of purpose, therefore, functioned as a guiding principle in selecting the faculty, designing the curriculum, and planning the annual calendar of activities. In all of these, an emphasis on and a commitment to missions is evident.

Readers might reasonably expect that in recounting the history of the teaching of missions at Southeastern Seminary, I would be tempted to claim that the principal factor that influenced the attitude of students toward missions or that inspired some of them to consider missions as a vocation would be the quality and effectiveness of the missions professors. I do not discount the importance of having well-prepared and effective teachers, but it has been my observation that missions classes are a small part of what characterizes the life of a theological institution and determines its ultimate impact on the students. Moreover, the professors of missions—like those in any other discipline—can be unprepared or underprepared, poor communicators, lacking in first-hand experience, colorless, tedious, and generally uninteresting. Yet a missionary spirit and interest can pervade a campus.

Conversely, no matter how able the teachers of missions may be, if there is little or no support by their colleagues and if the attention given to missions is confined to academic discussions in the classrooms, then the interest in and commitment to the Christian mission will be limited. A school's history and tradition, the attitude of the administration and faculty, the place given to missions in the curriculum, in the chapel, and in other campus and off-campus activities will do more to determine students' attitudes than scintillating missions classes. The cumulative impact of seminary life determines whether students see only their own locale or the whole world as their parish.

A Missions Ambience

The missions professors at Southeastern alone did not establish the missions tradition affecting the lives of students. The respect and concern for missions, a concern that permeated the whole of campus life, contributed most to students' attitudes toward and interest in the Christian mission in the world. Even after 1972, when students were no longer required to take any courses in missions, more than sixty percent of them took one or more courses in missions or world religions. Several of the courses, all electives, consistently enrolled fifty to sixty students, and in some cases even more.

A number of factors contributed to this mission ambience: the general respect accorded the discipline by administration and faculty, the times that missions and world religion classes were scheduled, the encouragement and support of what the missions professors proposed and attempted to accomplish, the missions emphasis in the day-to-day activities, and the recognition given to students and alumni who were involved in missionary work.

In contrast to some seminaries and divinity schools, the missions curriculum and faculty at Southeastern were placed in the History area, thus making them a part of the classical theological tradition.[5]

One of the first three professors elected to the faculty was John Burder Hipps, (1884–1967) who—though he was sixty-seven years old when he came to Southeastern—taught full-time for five years and continued to offer an elective course for several semesters thereafter.[6] Though well past his prime, Hipps was a well-known and highly respected missionary who had spent more than a third of a century in China, primarily as a teacher and administrator in the University of Shanghai. He and his wife had returned to the United States in 1949 after the Communists overran China and forced the missionaries to leave. Apparently the Foreign Mission Board (FMB) was not expecting the Hippses to retire, for consideration was given to their going to India to begin Southern Baptist work there.[7] But Hipps was attracted to being a part of the new seminary endeavor at Wake Forest.

Energetic, outspoken, and imposing, Hipps' influence and imprint are clearly visible in the initial shaping and configuration of the school. Missions from the beginning was an integral part of the academic and spiritual life. All students the first year were required to take six hours in missions—a three-hour study in the history of missions, a second three hours in the history of Baptist missions, plus a two-hour course entitled "Dynamics of the Spiritual Life"—all taught by J. B. Hipps.[8]

This arrangement was altered somewhat the second year when students studying for the Bachelor of Divinity could elect a generalized or a specialized program of study. The two programs were identical in that each involved ninety-six hours to complete the degree, fifty-eight of which were required, plus two hours of guided field work. In the specialized program, however, students were expected to choose a vocational field—either pastoral ministry, missionary ministries, or Christian education—and select the additional thirty-six hours of courses in consultation with a faculty advisor.[9]

The chapel schedule included six missionary days a year, days when the time allotted for the service was extended and well-known missions spokespersons were brought to inform and challenge the students to be involved in the Christian mission. Of course, a number of students came to seminary already committed to being missionaries, but others considered missions as a vocation after they arrived in Wake Forest. Hipps later wrote that during the second year of the seminary's life, thirty of the 217 students were missions volunteers.[10] Those who manifested an interest in missions received special attention from professors, and those who became missionaries were featured regularly on the cover and/or in the pages of the *Outlook*.[11] This practice continued from 1951 to 1988.

Despite Hipps' prestige and leverage, however, as the faculty grew, the number of hours in missions a student was required to take was reduced. Nonetheless, every student was exposed to the formal study of the subject. For several years, students were expected to take twelve hours in what was designated as the Historical Interpretation of Christianity, that is, six hours in church history and six hours of missions.[12] Not until 1971–1972, when the core curriculum—courses all students were required to take—was reduced from fifty-six to twenty-four hours, were the missions courses made electives. By that time, the character and the milieu of the school were firmly established.

Missionary Days

As already noted, six Missionary Days were included in the first year's calendar. In the second and succeeding years, however, the number was reduced to five and later to four. On those days the time for the chapel worship was extended, and prominent individuals who exemplified what it meant to be in missions were invited to speak—persons such as Baker James Cauthen, Elmer West, Cornell Goerner, and Keith Parks of the Foreign Mission Board; Courts Redford, Arthur Rutledge, and Hugo Culpepper of the Home Mission Board (HMB); Alma Hunt, Carolyn Weatherford, and Catherine Allen of the Woman's Missionary Union; Congressman Walter Judd (a former missionary to China); George Webber of the East Harlem Protestant Project; Eugene Nida and Robert Bratcher of the American Bible Society; Chester Jump of the American Baptist Foreign Mission Society; J. C. Hoekendijk of Union Seminary (NY); and a steady flow of missionaries, among them David Mein from Brazil, George Hays and Robert Culpepper from Japan, Sarah Bivins from Israel, Charles Allen, Jr., from Colombia, and Zebedee Moss from Kenya.[13]

Though I cannot pinpoint the precise time when the decision was made regarding the giving of "invitations" on Mission Days—that is, inviting students to come forward at the conclusion of the service and publicly declare themselves to be mission volunteers—I am satisfied that it was in the first two or three years in the life of the school. Missionary Days were important events, widely publicized and well attended. Neither the administration nor the faculty, however, wanted these occasions used to pressure and manipulate the students. It was agreed, therefore, that invitations for students to make public decisions about missionary service would be given only on the last Missionary Day of the year. With a few notable exceptions, this was the practice[14] until the late 1970s when the faculty committee in charge of Missionary Days decided to leave decisions regarding invitations to the individual speakers.

Equipping for Mission

From the time Southeastern began, missions was integral to the life of the school. Missionaries were esteemed, as was the missionary vocation, and equipping students for mission was considered a fundamental responsibility of the institution. This was true during the entire period from 1951 through 1988. In an article that President Lolley wrote for the *Outlook* in 1979, for example, he reviewed the various components that contributed to making missions a reality on the campus and not simply a slogan.[15] From September of 1978 until November of 1979, he noted, thirty-four Southeasterners were appointed as missionaries by the Foreign Mission Board. After repeated requests to the FMB and extended negotiations, the board agreed to name Roger Thompson, an alumnus who was a mission volunteer, as a full-time liaison on the campus.[16] Seven of the thirty-six elected faculty members, Lolley pointed out, had served as SBC missionaries: B. Elmo Scoggin, Malcolm Tolbert, Archie Nations, George Braswell, Alan Neely, William Clemmons, and Robert Culpepper. In addition, Luke Smith had been an associate in the personnel department of the Foreign Mission Board for several years. The Fletcher Visiting Professorship had begun, and the seminary had set aside three fully and beautifully furnished residences for furloughing missionaries, available to them at no cost. The missions curriculum included not only courses in mission history and theology but also *practica* in church planting and world religions, off-campus studies, and traveling seminars in home and foreign missions. It is difficult to imagine how more emphasis could have been given to missions or how the exposure to missionaries could have been greater.

Student Missions and Ministry Conferences

In 1958, in cooperation with the two mission boards, missions conferences for college and professional school students were initiated and continued each year. Ordinarily held in late February, they were fashioned not as recruiting mechanisms for the seminary but rather as opportunities for college and professional school students to meet and hear missionaries, talk with mission board personnel, and learn what was involved in the missionary vocation—all in a setting and with a program designed specifically for university-age students.

The commitment to missions of the faculty and seminarians who planned these events was profound, and the persons who were invited to lead them were renowned. For some reason or reasons, the average number of college students who came to these conferences—in comparison with the number who attended similar meetings at other seminaries—was relatively small, usually 200 and hardly ever more than 300, including the seminarians who attended. The other five seminaries meanwhile boasted of "hundreds and hundreds" coming to their conferences, and one or two consistently drew one thousand or more. It was bewildering and frustrating, and repeated efforts were made to increase attendance. Outside consultants were brought in, meetings were held with Baptist campus chaplains individually and as a group, dates for the conference were reconsidered, and the programs were revamped more than once. But the "Student Missions and Ministry" conferences never attracted large numbers. Doubtless they served a needed purpose and affected the lives of many who participated, but it is questionable whether this was the best approach and whether the overall result was commensurate with the investment of time, energy, and funds.

Professors of Missions

During the first thirty-seven years of Southeastern's history, five persons were elected to the faculty as professors of missions: J. B. Hipps (1951), E. Luther Copeland (1956), Emily K. Lansdell (1959), George W. Braswell, Jr. (1974), and Alan Preston Neely (1976).

J. B. Hipps

Hipps, as I have already indicated, though advanced in age, was a robust and potent influence in the school's beginning. A native of Spring Creek in Madison County, North Carolina, he graduated from Mars Hill College and Wake Forest College (B.A.), Southern Baptist Theological Seminary (Th.M.), Union Theological Seminary (S.T.M.), and Columbia University (M.A.). After completing his degree at Wake Forest College, he worked for three years as the principal of a Home Mission Board mountain school in Pennington Gap, Virginia. There he made his decision to enter the ministry; he enrolled in The Southern Baptist Seminary in Louisville in the fall of 1910.[17]

Hipps grew up in an area of North Carolina where a strong anti-missions movement was prevalent, and he often said that he never saw a missionary until three young women appointed by the Northern Presbyterian Board to work in North Carolina mountain schools stayed for a period of time in the Hippses' home.

His first encounter with a "missionary atmosphere," he recalled, was at Mars Hill and Wake Forest colleges. While in Wake Forest he was a member of a small circle that prayed for missionaries and studied together the life of Matthew T. Yates. Three of the five in that group later became foreign missionaries, including J. B. Hipps.[18] His decision to volunteer for missions, however, was made not at Wake Forest but at Southern Seminary, a result, Hipps said, of the influence of three his professors: John R. Sampey in Old Testament, A. T. Robertson in New Testament, and W. O. Carver in Missions. According to Hipps, these three convinced him that "the Bible was a missionary book" from beginning to end, and what they said "was confirmed by the missionary addresses" he heard in chapel, especially on Missionary Days, "and the total impact of missions in the seminary."[19] Thirty-eight years later, Hipps attempted to inculcate that same spirit into the life of Southeastern Seminary.

Though not a theological liberal in the classical sense, J. B. Hipps was unusually progressive and was of an independent mind. At the time of his first missionary furlough in 1920, for example, against the advice and without the approval of the Foreign Mission Board, he accepted a fellowship to study at Union Seminary in New York, a decision that made him suspect with the Foreign Mission Board staff. When Hipps earlier had requested someone at the board to write for him a recommendation to Union, his request was denied. The board refused to approve Hipps' proposal that he spend his furlough at Union Seminary because of the liberal reputation of the school. Hipps nonetheless went on to Union without FMB support.[20]

The year he spent in New York was clearly influential in his overall theological formation, for he studied with several of the most eminent figures in American theological education—teachers such as William Adams Brown in theology, Julius A. Bewer in Old Testament, Daniel J. Fleming in missions, Robert E. Hume in comparative religions, Harry Emerson Fosdick in practical theology, and J. H. Oldham, a visiting professor from England and the editor of the *International Review of Missions.*[21]

Regardless of any shortcomings Hipps may have had because of his age or lack of extensive formal study in the field of missions,[22] his ecumenical spirit, broad-minded theology, and comprehensive world view helped set a direction for Southeastern different from that of most—if not all—Southern Baptist seminaries.

Edwin Luther Copeland

In 1954, while he (b. 1916) and his family were in the United States on a missionary furlough from Japan, Luther Copeland was a guest professor at Southern Seminary in Louisville. During that year he had what appeared to be a chance encounter in Maryland with one of his former professors, Edward McDowell. As it turned out, however, the meeting was crucial in what later occurred. McDowell had left Louisville in 1952 to come to Southeastern, and he was excited about the future of the school. He told Copeland that if he ever decided to come back to the United States permanently, he, McDowell, would be pleased to recommend him as a member of the Southeastern faculty. Copeland already had an invitation to remain at Southern Seminary, but he and his wife Louise were committed to returning to Japan. Two years later, however, one of Copeland's daughters developed a health problem that made it necessary for the family to come back to the United States. He wrote to McDowell about the situation and soon received an invitation to join the Southeastern faculty. Copeland was elected associate professor of Missions in the spring of 1956 and began his work in the fall semester.

Born in Drennen, West Virginia, Copeland was a graduate of Mars Hill College and Furman University (B.A.), Southern Baptist Theological Seminary (Th.M.), and Yale University (Ph.D.).[23] During his student days he served as pastor of several churches in North Carolina, Indiana, and Connecticut, and from 1948 to 1956 he and Louise were Southern Baptist missionaries to Japan. He served first as professor of Christianity in the Seinan Gakuin University, Fukuoka, and later as the school's chancellor.

At Yale, Copeland had studied with the leading American mission historian, Kenneth Scott Latourette. His dissertation, written under

Latourette's direction, was on "The Crisis of Protestant Missions to Japan, 1889–1900."[24]

Copeland was, therefore, eminently qualified to teach missions, probably more qualified than any other missions professor in Southern Baptist history. In the succeeding years, no one, not even J. B. Hipps, did more to shape the missions image at Southeastern than he. Though soft-spoken, Copeland is intense, able, and resolute. His long tenure (1956–1975), knowledge, willingness to innovate, and his ecumenical approach brought continuity, experience, and scholarship to the position.

In his nearly twenty years at Southeastern, Copeland's stature and reputation grew. Though Hugo Culpepper, who later taught at Southern Seminary, and Francis DuBose at Golden Gate were highly regarded in their own right, Copeland, I believe, was the most widely known and re-spected mission scholar among Southern Baptists. Like Hipps, Copeland believed that missions should be a part of the ongoing life of the school, neither more nor less important than Bible, theology, or the practical subjects. He believed missions should be taught from an ecumenical per-spective. "I never offered a course in the history of Baptist missions," he said, "because such a study could be easily distorted and could disregard what the whole church has done."[25] Second, he believed that the study of missions should avoid any trace of paternalism or ethnocentrism, and for this reason he gave more attention to what national Christians accom-plished—Japanese, Chinese, Nigerians, and Brazilians, for example—than to anything the missionaries achieved.

After Copeland came to Southeastern, the number and range of courses expanded markedly. In addition to the two-hour study on the dynamics of the spiritual life, Hipps had offered seven courses: two in the history of Christian missions and one each in comparative religion, the history and practices of foreign missions, the history of Baptist missions, Christianity and world problems, and (SBC) home missions. Copeland developed his own array of courses while experimenting with his colleagues in the teaching of church history. For a few years, 1957–1961, he and the professors of church history—Pope Duncan and John Steely—jointly offered a series of courses in which they made an attempt to integrate the history of missions with the history of Christianity. The effort, though admirable in theory, did not prove to be satisfactory. Only the more gifted students were able to synthesize the materials, while the less qualified complained and finally rebelled. Copeland's explanation for the failure was that the courses were never truly team-taught. Each professor came in on the day he or she was assigned, gave a lecture, and then left it to the students to correlate the mass of information they were being given. Most of them were either unable or unwilling to do it.[26]

Two years after his arrival at Southeastern, Copeland proposed a course entitled "The History of the Ecumenical Movement," and he discovered what many Southern Baptist professors have encountered across the years: if the course subject sounds too radical—in this case the title would have been perceived as a direct assault on Southern Baptist Landmarkism—forget it, or change the wording. So, "The History of the Ecumenical Movement" became "A History of Christian Cooperation in Modern Times,"[27] a title intentionally benign, but a course that served an important purpose—namely, to introduce students to one of the most significant ecclesial and missiological developments of the twentieth century.[28]

Copeland also developed what came to be called Mission Area Studies, courses concentrating on mission history in various parts of the world: Asia, Africa, Latin America, the Near East, and Europe. He, of course, taught the area study on missions in Asia and began offering two Th.M. research seminars: Christianity and non-Christian religions, and Missions and Theology.

Two other courses that Copeland led in generating deserve mention. Copeland and Thomas Bland, professor of Christian Ethics and Sociology, believed that Southeastern students needed to move beyond the prevailing Southern Baptist rural mentality and come to terms with what was happening in urban America. Therefore, they offered for the first time in 1967 what became an influential and popular summer offering, the "Seminar on Urban Studies," a five-week academic and field-oriented experience in Washington, D.C. Not only was this a new venture in Southern Baptist theological education, but it also represented a unique example of interagency cooperation. The seminar was jointly sponsored by the HMB, which contributed substantially in money and personnel, the D.C. Baptist Convention, which virtually seconded James Duncan of their staff to work out the logistics for the course, and Southeastern Seminary. Copeland, Bland, and Emanuel Carlson of the Baptist Joint Committee on Public Affairs were the teaching team.

The second important course that Copeland initiated was the Practicum in Home Missions, "a combination of academic study and field missionary experiences" conducted in the early years in New England and New York in cooperation with the Home Mission Board. Seminarians enrolling for this study spent twelve weeks on the field engaged usually in some form of "church planting." The number of sites to which students were sent in subsequent years, after Copeland left Southeastern and George Braswell assumed responsibility for the course, was expanded significantly.

Like others, Copeland received a minimum of sabbatical leaves during his time at Southeastern, one in 1963–1964 when he was a Fulbright Research Professor at the Banaras Hindu University in India, and a second in 1969–1970 when he was at the University of Chicago studying world religions with Mircea Eliade and missions with R. Pierce Beaver.

Besides dozens of articles, chapters in books, and monographs, Copeland has published three books: *Christianity and World Religions* (1963), *Frontiers of Advance* (1964), and *World Mission and World Survival* (1985).

After the fall semester of 1975, at the age of sixty, Copeland resigned his position as professor of Missions and World Religions to return to Japan as chancellor of the Seinan Gakuin University, the school he had left to come to Southeastern.[29]

Emily K. Lansdell

Shortly after Luther Copeland began his career at Southeastern, an attempt was made to secure an additional professor of Missions. Negotiations were begun with William Shinto, a second-generation Japanese-American and a graduate of Baylor University, who was completing a doctorate in missions under Herbert Jackson at Southern Seminary. Shinto finally agreed to come for a year as a visiting professor (1958–1959), but he was unwilling to leave his work with the American Baptist Convention in California. The decision was then made to invite Emily K. Lansdell (1913–1973), former missionary to China and head of the Carver School of Missions in Louisville, Kentucky. She was elected professor of Missions to begin her work in the fall semester of 1959. Her time at Southeastern, though brief, was significant for two reasons. First, she was the second woman elected to a Southern Baptist seminary faculty to teach a subject other than religious education or music.[30] Second, her impact on women seminarians was profound.

Educationally, Lansdell was well prepared. A graduate of Coker College (B.A.), Duke University (M.A. in English Literature), and Yale University (M.A. in Oriental Studies), she also did graduate studies at the University of Georgia, the W.M.U. Training School in Louisville, and Columbia University's College of Chinese Studies. Mercer University had honored her with an LL.D. She served as a Southern Baptist missionary to China from 1943 until 1951[31] and was president of the Carver School of Missions and Social Studies from 1951 to 1958. Before going to China she taught at Campbell College (North Carolina). As a missionary, she, like Hipps, was a member of the faculty of the University of Shanghai.

Though endowed with formidable administrative skills, Lansdell encountered difficulty as a seminary teacher. A part of the problem stemmed from the fact that in addition to offering courses not only in the history of religions and the principles and practice of foreign missions, she was also made a member of the teaching team engaged in the effort to incorporate the history of missions and church history. These integrated courses, however, attempted too much, for they included not only general church history but also the history of doctrine and the history of missions. Moreover, Copeland and Lansdell were responsible for the section on the history of Eastern Orthodox Christianity. It was an overwhelming task, and, as already noted, the whole undertaking failed. When, therefore, in 1962 Lansdell married J. B. Weatherspoon, who was emeritus professor of Preaching at Southern Seminary and a visiting professor at Southeastern, she resigned. She continued to live in Raleigh after Weatherspoon died in 1965, but she later returned to her home state of Georgia, where she taught for a few years at Georgia Southwestern College in Americus. She died on 10 June 1973 while undergoing treatment for cancer and was buried in the Hephzibah Cemetery, Hephzibah, Georgia.[32]

George W. Braswell, Jr.

For more than ten years after Emily Lansdell's resignation, the second position in missions was filled by visiting professors, that is until 1974 when George W. Braswell, Jr. (b. 1936), was elected associate professor of Church History and Missions. A native of Emporia, Virginia, Braswell is a graduate of Wake Forest College (B.A.), Yale Divinity School (B.D.), Southeastern Seminary (D.Min.), and the University of North Carolina at Chapel Hill (M.A. and Ph.D.).

While studying for the doctorate of ministry degree, Braswell was a visiting instructor in missions at Southeastern and was enrolled in an M.A. program in Cultural Anthropology at the University of North Carolina at Chapel Hill. He received the D.Min. and M.A. the same year and his Ph.D. in Anthropology after returning to Southeastern in 1974.

Braswell was also pastor of the Cullowhee Baptist Church on the campus of Western Carolina University in Cullowhee, North Carolina, from 1962 until 1967, when he and his wife Joan were appointed to begin Southern Baptist work in Iran. In an interview in 1990, Braswell said, "There had never been any other Baptist missionaries in Iran. We were to build some good relationships of trust," hoping the time would come when "we could introduce Southern Baptist missionaries in the country to start churches. Our task was to lay the foundation, to till the soil, and start from scratch."[33]

For a brief period Braswell served as associate director of the Armaghan Institute, a cultural center and language school sponsored by the Presbyterian Church U. S. A., and for four years he was professor of English and Comparative Religions in the Islamic Theological School of the University of Teheran. In addition to his teaching in the Islamic seminary, Braswell taught history for one year in the Damavand College, a Presbyterian four-year liberal arts college for women in Teheran.

Capitalizing on the strong U.S. presence in Iran at that time, Joan and George Braswell began a Baptist fellowship group in their home to minister to U.S. military personnel and oil workers, a gathering that eventually became a church of some four hundred members.

After his first furlough, when he and his family returned to Iran in 1973, Braswell resumed his work with Muslims. The following January, however, he received a call from Southeastern inviting him to return as a permanent member of the faculty. Explaining his decision to accept the invitation, Braswell said:

> Just having arrived in Teheran, we were still living in the hotel, still looking for
> some place to live. I got word from the Foreign Mission Board that my father
> had been seriously burned. Our kids were in school, so . . . I got the first plane
> out and rushed back. He died about 12 hours after I arrived in Richmond. So,

when this call came from Southeastern, I thought to myself about my call and commitment to Iran. I loved the people, and I truly felt called there. But, this was a chance to teach World Mission in seminary. I feel quite sure that my father's death and leaving my mother alone were partial factors, but we definitely felt a strong call to come to Southeastern.[34]

This sense of calling has not diminished, Braswell says, and he has continued at Southeastern, one of seven of the pre-1988 faculty to remain. He has a strong emotional attachment to Wake Forest, where he met Joan, where they went to school together, and where they have reared their children. In 1994 he will complete twenty years as a Southeastern professor. Though in many respects an individualist, Braswell thinks his own thoughts, does his own work independently and effectively, and is regarded as a first-rate teacher.

Like Luther Copeland, Braswell developed several new and original courses: "Anthropology and Middle East Religions," "Major Personalities in World Religions," three "encounter" courses (in Buddhism, Hinduism, and Islam), and two *practica*—one in world religions that concentrated on Hindu, Buddhist, Muslim, Jewish, and Bahá'i religious groups in the United States; and another in American religions that focused on the Church of Latter Day Saints, Jehovah's Witnesses, Christian Science, the Unification Church, the Way International, Hare Krishna, and the Worldwide Church of God. Both of these *practica* involve academic and field experience in which the students meet with leaders and members of the various religious groups and engage them in extensive dialogue. Braswell has likewise continued the summer practicum in home missions initiated by Luther Copeland.

Author of a number of journal articles, Braswell has also published three books: *To Ride a Magic Carpet* (1977), *Understanding World Religions* (1983), and *Understanding Sectarian Groups in America* (1986). He received a special award by the Interfaith Witness Department of the Home Mission Board in 1986 for his "outstanding contribution in helping Southern Baptists understand world religions," and he also received the Southeastern Seminary Citation for Faculty Excellence in 1987.

Alan Neely

In October 1975 my family and I were living temporarily in South Carolina, on medical leave from Cali, Colombia, where my wife Virginia and I were Southern Baptist missionaries. Sometime that month I received a call from the Southeastern Seminary dean, Albert L. Meiburg, inquiring if I might be available to teach during the spring semester of 1976. He said that Luther Copeland had resigned and that Ellis Hollon, professor of Philosophy of Religion, was on leave. Meiburg indicated that he would like to discuss the possibility of my teaching at least one course in missions and another in philosophy of religion.

Though I had never met Albert Meiburg, Randall Lolley, nor any other Southeastern professor, except Luther Copeland, I knew the reputation of the school and believed it to be the kind of environment I would find challenging and stimulating.[35] It was not, however, an easy or simple decision, for it meant leaving my family in South Carolina, traveling back and forth each week to Wake Forest, and developing two new courses. A meeting with Dean Meiburg, John Steely, and George Braswell—as well as a lengthy conversation with Luther Copeland, who was in the last stages of leaving for Japan—was reassuring, and, though my wife and I were aware of the difficulty of what I was about to undertake, we both believed it was the right thing to do.

That first semester at Southeastern was one of the most rewarding teaching experiences of my life, and had it been possible for us to return to South America, developments at Southeastern would have presented me with an agonizing choice. My family and I had spent more than twelve years in Latin America. Our facility in the language, the quality of students we had at the International Baptist Seminary in Cali, our friends and colleagues there, nationals and missionaries, the excitement of living in a bicultural environment, and the conviction that we were where we were supposed to be—all had led us to believe that our calling was to be missionaries.

That assurance was shaken by two realities. however. First, we learned that it was not advisable for us to go back to Colombia at that time. Then, almost simultaneously, President Lolley informed me that the members of the History area—John Steely and George Braswell—as well as Dean Meiburg, had recommended me to fill the post vacated by

Luther Copeland. I was acutely aware that I could not replace Copeland, but it was an tremendous honor to be asked.

Because of a nagging sense of inadequacy,[36] I am satisfied that had it not been for the irrepressible conviction that God had made it possible for me to be at Southeastern and that God was leading me to remain there, I likely would have accepted one of two other positions I was offered that spring—one with a state convention and another with an agency of the U.S. government. I sought the counsel of my wife and a few of my closest friends. In late spring I had a long conversation in Richmond with John Ratliff—a New Mexico member of the Foreign Mission Board, a former missionary to Honduras and Peru, and a long-time friend. I told him about everything: my desire to return to Colombia, the pain even of thinking about resigning from the Foreign Mission Board, the positive experience I was having at Southeastern, and the possibility of going to work for a state convention. Then I told Jack about the government offer, about what I was being asked to do and how much money I would make—more than I had ever imagined earning. His response was direct, gentle, and perceptive. "You can't go back to Colombia now," he said. "You see yourself basically as a missionary and a teacher. How does that fit you to work for a state convention? The job with the government? . . . Hmmm. It sounds more like a temptation to me than a calling." This was possibly the best and most affirming counsel I ever received, and I felt he was right. Distinguishing between a temptation and calling is not easy, but from that moment, it seemed to me that the decision was made.

The trustees elected me by ballot shortly after the close of the 1976 spring semester, and—between teaching a summer course, making a trip to Cali, Colombia, to say goodbye to friends and colleagues and retrieve our personal effects, and finally moving my family from South Carolina to Wake Forest—we settled in and began twelve demanding and gratifying years at Southeastern Seminary.

I cannot evaluate my work there; it would be inappropriate for me to try. I can, however, recount some of the details. Like Copeland, I taught my classes from an ecumenical perspective, primarily because this was the only way I had ever taught missions. I knew of no other way to teach missions truthfully and make the classes interesting. The histories of Southern Baptist missions I had studied virtually ignored what non-

Southern Baptists had done; they were little more than inventories of names, places, and dates—hardly the stuff to keep students awake.

During six of the twelve years that we had lived in Latin America, one of my assignments—besides teaching full-time in the seminary—involved traveling to every country where Southern Baptists had missionaries and studying in depth the nature and quality of missionary work, not only of Southern Baptists, but of other missions as well. I had, therefore, become aware of the pernicious effects of missionary paternalism, of North American neo-colonialism, of the superficiality of a lot of so-called evangelism, and of the careless use of funds at times by missionaries and nationals alike. I fervently believed that nationalizing mission work was not only advisable but also inevitable. Why not encourage and allow the nationals to do their own planning, make their own decisions, and financially support their work? This was, I knew, the only sensible way to do missions. But it meant that the missionaries would not be the Baptist leaders in Brazil, Nigeria, Japan, or anywhere else, and that the time would come when they would either go somewhere else or return home. This was not a radical theory in 1976, but it certainly was not the prevailing Southern Baptist mission practice.

The type of seminarian I wanted to see volunteer for missions, therefore, was one who knew the history of missions, had a sound philosophy and theology of mission, and was secure enough to work with the nationals—preferably work *under* the nationals or come home. I probably overemphasized this during my first years in Wake Forest, but nonetheless we had a steady stream of graduates as well as special students (medical personnel, agriculturalists, and others) who were appointed by the mission boards.

Prior to the beginning of the 1977–1978 school year, George Braswell and I revised somewhat the missions curriculum, adding several new courses, some of which, regretfully, we never were able to teach. Braswell's "Cross-Cultural Communication of the Gospel," however, attracted a large number of students, and the course became a staple in the annual offerings, as did his January and summer *practica*. I introduced two or three courses that should be mentioned, one because of the controversy associated with it, and the others because of the momentous impact they made on me and, I believe, on the students as well.

The course that incited controversy was entitled "The Theology of Liberation," described as "an investigation of the antecedents, origins, and development of liberation theology with special attention given to the question of the oppression-oppressive relationship" as identified and analyzed by theological spokespersons in Latin America, Africa, and Asia. Liberation theology had become already a critical issue in Latin America and was evident in other areas of the world as well. It would have been irresponsible not to deal with it. Yet no sooner had I begun teaching the course than it became obvious that one did not have to look outside the United States for examples of oppressive relationships. Plenty of them were here: the way women, blacks, chicanos, the poor, and the powerless were treated. Moreover, beginning in 1980, it appeared to me that the whole national and international policy of our government was biased against the poor and oppressed. It was also evident that in the United States, many of our attitudes and actions as professing Christians often contributed to these injustices. Even in the seminary our sexist language was insensitive and oppressive. As the area of discourse increased, so did the criticism, but it came largely from a few detractors outside, most of whom had been attacking Southeastern for years. Never once was I called upon by the administration or the faculty to defend or cease what I was doing. The level of trust and the wholesome degree of academic freedom remained constant.

A second course that attracted a growing number of students was in a sense a later version of one of J. B. Hipps' offerings. Instead of "Christianity and World Problems," which was his title, I called the course "World Human Need and the Christian Response." This study was not limited to lectures. In addition to three hours of class time, students were expected to devote two hours every week to meeting human need, preferably in an institutionalized setting where they could be supervised and evaluated. The class members as well as the professor would work during the semester in a homeless shelter, a drug rehabilitation center, an emergency care center, a "clothes closet," or a soup kitchen. This hands-on contact was central in class discussions and proved to be the most effective learning tool I have ever used. I continued to offer this course at Princeton Theological Seminary after going there in 1988.

During my time at Southeastern, both George Braswell and I offered several off-campus and international missions traveling seminars. Also, every year, beginning in 1978, I took a large group of students to the January seminars at the Overseas Ministries Study Center located in Ventnor, New Jersey, and later in New Haven, Connecticut. These were extraordinary, profound ecumenical mission experiences for all of us. Not only did the seminars open the world to the students, they provided an opportunity for us to spend quality time together while being exposed to some of the world's leading missions teachers and practitioners.

Visiting and Part-time Professors

Other than the elected missions faculty, Southeastern has utilized from the mid-1950s visiting and part-time professors of missions. In 1955–1956, for example, B. Elmo Scoggin, furloughing Southern Baptist missionary from Israel, taught two courses in missions. After he was elected to the faculty in 1956, he continued to teach Principles and Practices in Foreign Missions as well as Missions in the Near East—a course that eventually became the Europe, Africa, and Near East Area Study. In fact, Scoggin taught one or more missions courses every year until the fall of 1964. The area study, however, was assigned in 1963–1964 to I. N. Patterson, missionary to Nigeria, who was a visiting professor of missions.

Both Scoggin and Patterson became closely identified with the teaching of missions. Patterson was at Southeastern 1963–1964 and returned in 1967, continuing as visiting professor of Missions until 1974.

Others who served in this capacity besides William Shinto (1958–1959), B. Elmo Scoggin (1955–1956), and I. N. Patterson, were David Mein from Brazil (1965–1966), George Braswell from Iran (1972–1973), Dwight D. Baker from Israel (1974–1975), Donald E. Rice and Nelson Tilton of the HMB, Roy Godwin of the D.C. convention (1978–1979), and John D. Cave (former missionary to Argentina and North Carolina pastor [1979–1981]).

The Fletcher Visiting Professors of Missions

Early in 1978 a representative of the Fletcher Foundation of Raleigh indicated to President Lolley that A. J. Fletcher, well-known philanthropist, benefactor of numerous educational institutions, and founder of a major insurance company and of the Capital Broadcasting Company of Raleigh, was interested in establishing a trust that would fund a visiting professor of Missions. The endowment would be in memory of Fletcher's parents, the Reverend James Floyd Fletcher and Mrs. Louise Barker Fletcher, who served for many years as missionaries in Ashe County, North Carolina, and New River County, Virginia. An agreement was soon reached, and the trust fund was established, naming Southeastern Baptist Seminary as the beneficiary.[37]

The faculty and the administration were of one mind that the Fletcher professors should be both practitioners and theoreticians of missions and identified either with home or foreign missions.

In the first eight years, those invited represented a healthy balance. Phillip E. Rodgerson, Secretary of the Department of Missions of the Virginia Baptist General Association, was the first Fletcher visiting professor. He was followed by E. Luther Copeland (Japan), Marion G. Fray (South Africa), Bishop Stephen C. Neill (India), Nancy A. Curtis (WMU Director for North Carolina), Donald E. Hammer (HMB), Anne Thomas Neil (Nigeria and Ghana), Edna Frances Dawkins (FMB), Anne P. Rosser (Virginia pastor), Nathan Corbitt (Kenya), Ronald Hill (Thailand), John Shepard (Japan), Lloyd Whyte (HMB), Daniel Carro (Argentina), Margaret Fairburn (Liberia), Helen E. Falls (New Orleans Baptist Seminary), Nell Magee (Student Department of the Sunday School Board), C. B. Hastings (HMB), and Jack Hancox (Haiti).

Transition

When I returned from sabbatical leave in Argentina in the summer of 1983, it appeared to me that the whole milieu in the seminary had changed. Something seemed to have happened, for the atmosphere and mood were different. Invariably in my classes there were two or more students who obviously were not there to learn. They were argumentative, accusative, and sometimes insolent. Some, I later discovered, were secretly taping my lectures. The campus became less and less an environment of learning and more and more a field of combat. Between 1983 and 1987, conditions deteriorated. Obviously, the character and direction of the seminary were being radically altered.[38] Despite having been a Southern Baptist all my life and having done all my ministry with Southern Baptists, increasingly I felt that either Southern Baptists did not know me any longer or I did not know Southern Baptists. Perhaps both of us had changed.

A week after President Lolley and Dean Morris Ashcraft resigned, I received a call from the chair of a search committee at Princeton Theological Seminary, and a few months later I was elected to the chair of Ecumenics and Mission. Leaving Southeastern was one of the most painful experiences of my life. It meant leaving our children who, though grown, were living in the Raleigh-Durham area. It meant leaving our grandchildren, our home, and friends. It meant turning loose of a dream, but the time at Princeton has been exceptionally rewarding and happy, and for that I thank God and those who have received us so graciously.

Since 1988 I have read accusations more than once that the faculty at Southeastern prior to 1988 did not believe the Bible, did not support missions, and did not practice evangelism. Anyone genuinely acquainted with the school from 1951 until 1988 or who has taken the time to study the record will know better. Nothing else can and nothing else needs to be said.

Notes

[1]This prayer by Jesus in its entirety epitomizes the Christian mission, and it describes the mission spirit that characterized Southeastern Seminary from its inception. It was the text I chose fortuitously for the first homily I gave in Binkley Chapel after being elected to the faculty.

[2]From the founding resolution establishing Wake Forest College, approved by the North Carolina Baptist State Convention, 4 August 1832.

[3]Yates and his wife Eliza E. M. Yates were appointed by the newly formed SBC Foreign Mission Board in 1846, and they arrived in Shanghai, China, the following year.

[4]The full statement was: "The primary purpose of Southeastern Baptist Theological Seminary is to prepare men and women for Christian leadership in various ministries. This includes preaching and pastoral care, *missionary work at home and abroad*, the ministry of religious education, the teaching of religion and allied subjects in secondary schools and colleges, religious leadership on college campuses, the chaplaincy, social services, and such other forms of religious work as require specialized techniques." *Southeastern Baptist Theological Seminary Bulletin* (1952) 15. Emphasis is mine.

[5]I mention this for two reasons. Missions courses in a few schools have been placed in the field of theology. More commonly, missions has been assigned to history or to the practical area. Putting missions in the History area was a strategic decision. In some theological circles, courses in the practice of ministry have been considered subordinate to Bible, theology, and history. I do not, however, share this point of view.

[6]Except in the case of President Randall Lolley, Dean Albert Meiburg, Dean Morris Ashcraft, and Bishop Stephen A. Neill, I have not included titles for two reasons: (1)they

clutter the text, and (2) all of the elected professors of missions at Southeastern had doctorates. In two cases they were honorary, that of J. B. Hipps and Emily Lansdell, but each had exceptional academic preparation besides years of mission experience.

[7]John Burder Hipps, *Fifty Years in Christian Missions* (Raleigh NC: Edwards & Broughton, 1966) 124–25.

[8]*Southeastern Baptist Theological Seminary Bulletin* (1951) 21–22. Students were also required to take six hours in Church History. One thing that continually changes in an academic institution is the curriculum, and this is surely evident in the history of Southeastern. In 1956 the core curriculum was reduced to sixty-eight hours, twelve of which had to be taken in Church History and Missions. In 1970 the core curriculum was fifty-six hours and the following year was reduced drastically to twenty-four hours. No course in missions was required from that time until 1982, when certain vocational tracks required some courses in missions or world religions.

[9]*Southeastern Baptist Theological Seminary Bulletin* (1952) 37–38. Missionary Ministries included courses in Missions and Evangelism, Missions and Christian Education, Missions and the Christian Life, Missions and Christian Literature, and Missions and Social Service.

[10]*Southeastern Seminary Bulletin* 2/3 (May 1953): 7. [Editor's note: the *Southeastern Seminary Bulletin* was a publication containing seminary news and occasionally scholarly material during the early years of the school, before the emergence of the *Outlook*. It is not to be confused with the *Southeastern Baptist Theological Seminary Bulletin*, the seminary catalog, which is always referred to in *Servant Songs* by year(s) and page number(s). See also chapter 5 in this book, especially note 5.]

[11]*Outlook* 17 (May-June 1967): 2. The names and pictures of graduates or persons who had attended Southeastern who were appointed as missionaries were always included, and issues were sometimes dedicated to missionary alumni "serving around the world." The July-August 1962 issue contains sixty-seven of their pictures plus stories of other Southeasterners who were missionaries. In a 1967 issue the editor wrote that 132 individuals who had attended Southeastern were serving as missionaries, eighty-six of whom were graduates.

[12]*SEBTS Bulletin* (1952) 37–38.

[13]The list of Missionary Day speakers I have been able to compile is complete except for the years 1951–1959. It appears to me that from the beginning there was an imbalance in that a relatively small number of missionaries spoke on Missionary Days in comparison to the better known and more prestigious figures such as agency heads and prominent pastors.

[14]Some speakers, such as Baker James Cauthen, would ignore the policy and call the students to come forward. As I remember, this happened only one time during my first years at Southeastern, and shortly thereafter the policy was changed.

[15]*Outlook* 29 (November-December 1979): 2.

[16]Roger and Susan Thompson subsequently went as FMB missionaries to Ecuador where later, in 1983, he was killed in a plane crash.

[17]Hipps, *Fifty Years in Christian Missions*, 28-31.

[18]Ibid., 36–37.

[19]Ibid., 37–38.

[20]Ibid., 51. He was required to come to Richmond and submit to an inquiry into his theological views conducted by T. B. Ray, educational secretary for the board. Hipps, however, was able to satisfy the Secretary that he had no cause for concern. I have wondered if the results of the inquiry would have been different had Ray examined Hipps after his year of study at Union rather than before.

[21]Ibid., 49. Hume, a former missionary to India, was one of the speakers at the first Parliament of the World's Religions held in Chicago in August and September of 1893. Oldham was a recognized ecumenical leader who had been a major participant in the historic 1910 missions conference in Edinburgh as well as in the formation of the International Missionary Council, a precursor to the World Council of Churches.

[22]Hipps was not academically prepared to teach missions, and he had not taught missions. His major field of study and teaching experience had been in Old Testament, and his students at Southeastern soon discovered the two books he used as the primary sources for his lectures. What he lacked in knowledge, however, he compensated for in vigor and commitment. He loved missions and inspired others to love missions—or at least compelled them to accord missions a central role in the life of the school. His only published works, written after his retirement, are an autobiography, *Fifty Years in Christian Missions* (1966), cited above, and a more skillfully composed *History of the University of Shanghai* (Raleigh NC: Board of Founders of the University of Shanghai, 1964).

[23]During his tenure at Southeastern, Copeland continued to prepare himself. He studied in the Boston University School of Theology in 1960; in the Banaras Hindu University, Banaras, India, 1963–1964; and in the University of Chicago, 1969–1970.

[24]Ann Arbor MI: University Microfilms, 1965.

[25]Interview with Luther Copeland, Raleigh, NC, 3 January 1994.

[26]Ibid.

[27]I had a similar experience in 1977 when I was asked by President Lolley to represent Southeastern on the program committee that was planning the first Convocation of Women in Ministry. I went to Nashville for the first meeting of the committee, met Catherine Allen of the WMU, who was the chairperson, and learned from her that because of the vociferous objections of some SBC reactionaries "from across the river"— meaning from Arkansas, Texas, and Oklahoma—the name of the convocation was being changed to "Women in Church Related-Vocations."

[28]William Estep began offering a graduate seminar on the ecumenical movement at Southwestern Seminary earlier, but I believe he was more negative in his assessment of ecumenism than Copeland.

[29]*Outlook* 25 (January-February 1976).

[30]Helen E. Falls (A.B., M.A., Ed.D.) was elected to teach missions at the New Orleans Baptist Seminary in 1953.

[31]She, like J. B. Hipps, had been forced to leave China in 1949, but she remained under Foreign Mission Board appointment until she resigned in 1951.

[32]*Outlook* 22 (May-June 1973): 9.

[33]"Profile: Professor George E. [*sic*] Braswell, Jr.," *Outlook* 39 (Winter 1990): 6.

[34]Ibid., 7.

[35]Two of Southeastern's first faculty members had been my professors at Southwestern Seminary—Stewart A. Newman and Robert T. Daniel—but Newman had gone to Campbell University, and Daniel had died. My only contact with the school had been in the summer of 1959. I was finishing a dissertation, and my wife, two daughters, and I spent several weeks in Wake Forest. Luther and Louise Copeland were away, and they graciously allowed us to live in their home.

[36]I knew that simply having been a missionary did not qualify me to be a professor of missions, and though I had taught missions for twelve years in Cali as well as when I was a graduate student at Southwestern Seminary, my formal preparation and dissertation were in philosophy of religion, not in missions. Also at the time I thought there was a difference in teaching in a seminary in a third-world country and in a seminary in the United States. I felt positive about my classes in the spring of 1976, but I wondered if I could measure up, what use I would have of Spanish in Wake Forest, and—even more daunting—how I could ever finish a Ph.D. dissertation for the American University that was due in 1977.

[37]The Fletcher endowment was not turned over to the seminary. Rather, each year the seminary was required to make a proposal to the Fletcher Foundation. Beginning in 1980, however, the money requested to fund the visiting professorship was always granted and has amounted to some $12,000 annually.

[38]It would be a mistake to leave the impression that after 1982 all was bad and that life was grim. Until October of 1987, we all had many positive experiences punctuated by a number of entertaining incidents. Most of us were delighted when one of Paul Pressler's minions—who happened to be a seminarian from Mark Corts' church in Winston-Salem—was caught by the Wake Forest police sneaking around town in the middle of the night ripping down Mondale-Ferraro posters—as if their staying up would have made any difference.

Likewise, we were amused by the crescendo of objections coming from outside critics to Glenn Miller's "Lottie Moon Auction"—an annual event that not only enlivened an otherwise prosaic Christmas ritual but also raised a sizable amount of money for the foreign missions offering. It seems that some of the brethren in certain southern states considered an auction tantamount to Catholic bingo, and they were not about to sit around and see Lottie's name desecrated. So, they leaned hard on President Lolley to put a stop to the affair. It did not occur to those purists that doing something tangible to support missions honored the memory of Southern Baptists' only saint more than did snuffing out a fun-time at the seminary.

Chapter 10

Women at Southeastern Seminary

Donna M. Forrester

Through my eyes and those of most other women who experienced it, Southeastern Seminary seemed a rare and wonderful place. We are not always aware of how good something really is until it has been taken away or until we ourselves have gone away and have had other experiences that clarify our perspective. Southeastern was that kind of place for many women who came through its doors as students, spouses, staff, or faculty.

Having had other experiences with seminaries and churches prior to my coming to Southeastern, I quickly became aware of how special Southeastern was. Southeastern was not perfect in any respect; it had its flaws and limitations just like the human beings who were the life blood pumping through its halls and classrooms. Southeastern was the best of the best, though, if one measured its willingness to hear and take seriously the concerns of those who came to study and live out their vocations there.

Of course, no one feminist perspective exists of Southeastern during the days that preceded its demise. Every woman would have her own story of who Southeastern was and how her life was changed or enriched by people and events experienced in that place. Each brought her own story as she walked into a part of Southeastern's history, and each took away a unique story as a result of the blending of lives and stories during our time there.

The reader will find in these next few pages only one of hundreds of stories that could be told. This is also only a part of my story. It would be impossible to record or even to recall all of the details that make up this one perspective. Long after this assignment is done, I will remember many events and people that were an integral part of this story and wish I had mentioned them. I apologize ahead of time for the omission. My attempt is to relate a small part of the role of women at Southeastern and one woman's perspective of the crisis there in the 1980s.

My tenure at Southeastern Seminary began in January 1979, when I entered the Doctor of Ministry program. My choice of Southeastern had less to do with convenience than with the openness of the D.Min. program. Unlike some other seminaries, Southeastern's program was open enough to be tailored to fit the particular gifts of the individual. This was particularly exciting to me as a woman because my gifts and history did not exactly fit the mold that other D.Min. programs would have forced me into. This was also an appealing aspect for other women even in the other degree programs. The call of God to women was never an issue. From the first day as a graduate student, I felt accepted as a full participant in the life of the seminary. That acceptance came from the administration, the faculty, and from other students as well.

Professor Richard Hester requested that I serve with him as his graduate fellow. I made jokes about the title that was given to all graduate assistants regardless of their gender. While I was aware that the term "fellow" had other meanings and did not necessarily refer to a person's gender, it was still fun to poke and prod a little to raise consciousness about the subtleties of gender bias in our culture. With very few exceptions, I found the faculty and administration willing to be prodded, and they were open to learning and growing in their own understandings of issues related to women. This attitude impressed me most—not that everyone jumped to my cadence and changed their opinions, but that they were willing to be open and to hear the concerns of someone else's experiences. I ran into this time and again at Southeastern.

As a woman graduate fellow, I had the opportunity to encounter a larger number of students and have at least some impact on their impressions of women in ministry. Assisting Dick Hester with the basic pastoral care classes was particularly fun because of the way the classes were designed. Two hours of class time and two hours of group time each week gave me the opportunity to be a consistent presence as a woman in ministry, and gave some students an experience they had never before encountered. Of course, some students, particularly males, had never worked with a woman in that kind of role. Because of their limited experience, they did not know how to relate to a woman in such a setting. Learning of the support of the professor in particular and the faculty in general allowed them to stretch their experience and their understanding. I had many conversations with students who reported to me that their opinions about women had changed to a more open and accepting stance because of the women they had encountered at Southeastern.

Such experiences are most often untold and impossible to measure, but they have a positive ripple-effect, especially through former students who are now pastors and other church leaders and have the opportunity to influence many others about women in ministry.

Having finished the Doctor of Ministry degree in May of 1981, I faced the same problem that most women in ministry face—finding a place to use the gifts and abilities that God had given and that had been so well prepared at seminary. With all the wonderful qualities of the free church tradition, some devastating drawbacks still exist for women in ministry. The seminaries have a distinct disadvantage in trying to suggest competent women to church search committees. Old habits are hard to break, and, without ever having experienced women in pastoral positions, many churches are afraid to try to introduce a woman to their congregations. Instead, these churches seem content with the status quo. Even churches that profess to be supportive of women in ministry do not have a very good track record of hiring women for pastoral positions.

Most women at Southeastern faced the reality sooner or later. The reactions to that hurdle were as varied as the individuals. Some of them turned to other denominations for pastoral roles, while some entered other church positions in hopes of moving up or helping to change the perspectives of church people everywhere. A few were fortunate enough to find pastoral positions in smaller churches and began the process of effecting positive change in the Baptist churches across the Southeast.

Emotionally, the reactions were just as varied. Some women reacted with anger and began to fight the injustices and inequities of their plight. Others fought with unquenchable determination to do the very best they could in positions within churches and kept their hope of effecting change in the process.

The Women in Ministry group and the Women's Resource Center at the seminary were wonderful support systems for women who were dealing with these issues. These resources were also helpful for the men who were supportive and who would have the opportunities in the future to make a difference for women.

During my time as a D.Min. student, some important pieces to my vocational puzzle began to fall into place. As an M.Div. student at Southern Seminary in Louisville, Kentucky, I faced a number of personal tragedies that greatly affected my perspective on life and ministry. Understanding those events through my own journey in pastoral counseling had a powerfully positive impact on my life. As I worked through my D.Min. degree, I became convinced that God was calling me to assist other seminarians in understanding and dealing with their journeys. I did my D.Min. project on "Preventive Pastoral Care with Seminary Students." In that experience, I was privileged to walk with a group of twelve students through their first year of seminary. Because of that journey I became even more convinced that the seminary had the responsibility to offer students the chance to learn from their life experiences as well as from their activities in the classroom. It is more and more obvious that there is a direct correlation between the mental health of the minister and the health and well-being of the church. My passion to help seminary students and my conviction that this was an incredible need among students did not wane, even though I had to face reality when I finished my degree and move on into other areas. I found it difficult to leave that calling hanging in the balance, not knowing if I would ever have the chance to make a difference in an area where I felt called and gifted to make an impact.

Having a previous profession that I could rely on to help me make ends meet gave me an advantage that most of my women colleagues did not have. While I was working on my D.Min. degree, I had worked full-time as a psychiatric nurse/therapist in an alcoholism treatment center in Raleigh. It was a wonderful place to work that allowed me flexible hours to do my course work and my writing. It also provided invaluable experience in preparing me for things to come.

When I finished my degree work, the treatment center offered me a clinical coordinator's position, which I took. I was often frustrated, though, that I was not using all the skills and gifts that I had spent so much time improving. I was especially frustrated that I was not working with the seminary students whom I loved and in whom I had so much investment. Even though I was gainfully employed and very appreciative of my job, I was still frustrated.

I prayed daily that God would lead me to the place where I could best serve God and use my gifts. While I knew that I was learning much from working with addictions, I also knew that this field was not what I had spent my life preparing for. I prayed long and hard and sometimes felt that my prayers were hitting the ceiling and bouncing around the room.

One December night I was particularly depressed about my situation, and through my tears I prayed a prayer that let go of something I had been hanging on to for many years. When I was a mere child at G.A. camp, I had been moved by the story of a missionary to China and had gone to the front at the end of the service to commit my life to missions. When I entered seminary after nursing school, everyone thought that I was the perfect candidate for medical missions. China was not open at that time, so I had a terrible fear that God was going to call me to Africa to be a medical missionary. I did not want to be a medical missionary, and I especially did not want to be called to Africa.

In my painfully depressed state on this December night, I finally let that go. I remember telling God that I would go wherever he sent me because I knew that I could not be any more miserable or frustrated than I was at that moment. I said, "I'll even go to Africa if that is where you want me to go." What happened to me in that moment seemed strange and a little frightening at first. I told very few people of this experience. I heard God say to me, "I needed to know that you were willing to go to Africa, because what I have for you to do may be more difficult than going to Africa." I did not know what that meant, but I got up off my knees with a sense of peace I had not experienced in a long time.

That December of 1983 I received two very important phone calls, the first from Dick Hester and the second from Bob Richardson. Both of these men told me that the seminary had decided to create a position of chaplain to the seminary community, and they wanted my permission to submit my name. I was thrilled and anxious—thrilled because it was a possible opportunity to do what I so much wanted to do with my ministry, and anxious because I knew that there were so many qualified people out there who could do a wonderful job. Some time after the first of the year I heard from Dr. Jerry Niswonger, assistant to the president for student development. Jerry told me that there had been a committee of faculty, staff, and students that had taken sixty resumes and narrowed the field to five persons for Jerry to interview. He conveyed to me that I was the last of the five he was interviewing. Unknown to both of us, each of us felt after our first meeting that this was the right match both for Southeastern and for me. A second interview convinced him that he was ready to recommend me to the president to be the first chaplain at Southeastern. Jerry commented that he was a little surprised that a boy from Missouri (himself) would recommend a woman to be the first chaplain, but after two lengthy interviews he was certain that I was the right person for the position.

I was very grateful and awed again by the way God works. I was even more convinced that in God's own time, God would see that I had the opportunity to use the gifts I had been given. I still hold on to that conviction. It does not always happen how and when we might want, but God is faithful to hear and care for God's own children.

In May of 1984, before the infamous convention and the ridiculous resolution on women at the Southern Baptist Convention, Jerry Niswonger and I met with President Randall Lolley for about two hours. He listened to my sense of calling to work with seminary students, and I listened to his desire to care for and nurture the students and families that sacrificed so much to answer the call of God to do full-time ministry. At the end of that interview, I had a real sense of God's presence and blessing. I received a phone call followed by a letter offering me the appointment to begin in August of 1984. Dr. Lolley was keenly aware of the growing sentiment in the SBC against women in ministry. He prepared me for the negative publicity that we might get when he made the announcement, but he was ready to stand firm behind his decision. He told me that he wanted to wait and decide at the convention when to announce my appointment. Unfortunately, he did not make the announcement prior to the adoption of that infamous resolution. When the announcement was made during summer school after the convention, he was accused of appointing me just to "thumb his nose" at the convention. The fundamentalists did not want to believe that the appointment had nothing to do with the resolution and chose to use the appointment as fuel for their fire against Dr. Lolley's leadership at Southeastern.

At the opening convocation in the fall of 1984, Dr. Lolley laid his cards face up on the table. He was bold and courageous and left very little question about his support of women in ministry. He gave me his blanket support to establish the office of the chaplain in a way that would fit my gifts and meet the needs of the students. The response to my presence on campus was overwhelmingly positive and supportive. A small group of students known as the Conservative Evangelical Fellowship, fed and supported by the fundamentalists, strongly opposed my appointment. A few of those students were occasionally rude to me on campus, but they could not hold a candle to the support and encouragement that I received from most of the students. The man who was then the student body president made a point of spending time with me and allowing me to walk with him through some difficult times. He consciously decided to lead for my acceptance on campus by letting others knows of his trust in me. His trust in and commitment to women in ministry in general and to me in particular was courageous and appreciated. He was the first of many.

Getting to know students as they allowed me to walk with them in the inner sanctum of their souls was the most precious gift God gave to me in those years. I tried to go where students gathered—the cafeteria, the lounges, The Corner. I found them open and receptive to my presence and my ministry. They responded well to my preaching in chapel. They sought me out, which was the ultimate trust and confidence in my ministry there on campus.

For the first couple of years, my office was located in Mackie Hall. It was a small office out of the way of normal traffic flow. When the Ledford Student Center was built, there was a good deal of discussion about where to locate my office. I fought hard to have my office right off the main entrance where it would be highly visible to students and visitors alike. Some persons had real reservations about whether or not students would want to be seen going into the chaplain's office. While I was sure that was a concern for some, I wanted to give a different message to students. I wanted to encourage students to see the chaplain as a "normal" person for "normal" people. In other words, I did not want to give the impression that people only went to see the chaplain when there was a crisis or a problem. I wanted the students to visit the chaplain because they might want to understand something better, enrich their lives, improve their communication skills, or apply to their lives the learning that takes place outside the classroom. During orientations I would encourage them to learn from their reactions to things and from the demands on their time, because, even though the situations would change, the ways they learned to deal with them would tend to develop as a pattern. I wanted to dispel some of the myths and stigmas about seeking counseling, and I was convinced that hiding the chaplain's office in a corner would only encourage those misconceptions. After much discussion, the chaplain's office was placed off the main lobby directly across from Student Affairs. That decision proved to be a good one. After the initial impact of the visibility of the office, the students seemed to take pride in others knowing that they were seeing the chaplain. Soon an almost two-week waiting period was required for a regular, non-emergency appointment. The response was overwhelming.

Interestingly enough, there were some differing responses from females to my style of ministry on campus. After I had been there for a while, some of the women felt that I was not taking a strong enough role on campus in promoting women's causes. I was a little surprised at first to hear that criticism. I soon realized, however, that women were as different from each other as they were from men. We all had our own styles of dealing with the women-in-ministry issues. While some women were very verbal and issue-oriented, calling each indication of gender bias to light, I happened to believe that my best chance of having an impact on resistant souls in that community was to do it with love, tenderness, and lots of patience. My style is to invite people to grow and take a look at their biases rather than to point them out directly. As the women and I got to know each other more, we grew to respect and appreciate the differences and to realize that we needed each other and each other's perspective to make the greatest impact on campus. As time went on, the understanding became more comfortable and the difference a non-issue.

The impact of having a woman as chaplain cannot be calculated accurately. I am sure I never heard many conversations regarding a female presence in that role. I am equally sure that all of those conversations were not positive. I am, however, aware of a few stories that are worth sharing—stories that students shared with me or with other faculty or administrators. The purpose of telling these stories is to show some of the impact that the seminary in general and Dr. Lolley in particular made in deciding not only to support women in ministry but also to stand behind that support with a strong, influential appointment. It is easy to have a theory or opinion about women in ministry even though a person may have never experienced a woman in a pastoral role. Most of the time, a direct experience makes a big difference either positively or negatively. A good female role model can soften the crustiest old soul, while a bad female role model can devastate the cause for years to come. Dr. Lolley took a risk, and I think these stories will bear out that it was a risk worth taking.

One student made it clear when he walked into my office that he did not believe that a woman should be in my position. He told me that the only reason that he was there was that his marriage was about to come apart and he did not have enough money to go anywhere else for help. He came with his wife, who was hurt, angry, and about to give up. He was willing to make a covenant of openness and commitment because his marriage was so important to him. We had several sessions together before he began to let down his guard. He started opening up and sharing his hurts, struggles, and feelings—which is the very thing his wife had been wanting for years. The two of them began communicating at an intimate level they had never before achieved. He became a new man, and they fell in love all over again.

He called me at home one night after a significant session where he had really opened his deepest self to his wife in my presence. He told me again that when he first came to me he had no confidence in counseling in general and in a woman chaplain in particular and that he came only to appease his wife. He told me that he had learned a lot of things about himself and about ministry. He thanked me for being willing to stand present to his negative energy so that he and his wife could get to a new place with each other. He had changed his mind about women ministers and said that he had decided to leave it to God to call whomever God deemed fit and gifted for ministry.

That man is now the pastor of a congregation that is fortunate—not because he changed his mind about women in ministry, although I think that was very beneficial, but because their pastor is a person who knows the value of being a real person as well as a minister. He knows the value of human growth in relationships, and he will be a better preacher and pastor because he was willing to stretch beyond his comfort zone and allow himself to grow.

Another student allowed me to walk through the valley of the darkest shadow with him and his wife as they lost their eight-month-old daughter to Sudden Infant Death Syndrome. It was a painful experience for the entire community, but in his pain and need he discovered that his beliefs about women in ministry had been challenged and changed.

The experiences of these students, along with those of many others, were possible because the seminary took a stand that was courageous and prophetic toward women in ministry. The benefits of such a decision cannot be calculated. The stories are endless, and the real benefits will be realized for generations to come.

It was no wonder, then, that when it became obvious that the leadership of the convention had serious intentions of taking over Southeastern, the seminary's stance on women in ministry was one of their major targets. The most vulnerable target for them was Professor Elizabeth Barnes, who taught theology and was well-loved and respected by students. I was a presidential appointment, and, as long as President Lolley was there, they could not get to me. Elizabeth was not a tenured faculty member, however, and therefore was quite vulnerable. Her election to the faculty after having served as an appointed professor was nothing less than miraculous. Only because one trustee left his hospital room and took a flight to North Carolina to be at that particular vote was she elected. We were all elated, but we were aware, as was Dr. Barnes, that she would never receive tenure at Southeastern. Her gifts and abilities as a teacher were outstanding. She was creative and innovative, but to the trustees she was just the wrong gender.

The decisions that the trustees made time and time again only proved to solidify the students, faculty, and administration and gave us all a cause for which to take a stand. The trustee decisions polarized the students into three camps. Some students were obviously supportive of the trustees and of their destructive tactics and did not mind verbalizing their feelings in equally destructive ways in the classrooms and in other forums. Others were obviously supportive of the faculty and administration and made that support known in sometimes helpful and sometimes insensitive ways. Still others tried, often unsuccessfully, to stay out of the controversy and in the middle. Most of them found that hard, if not impossible, to do unless they buried their heads in the sand— which a few seemed to accomplish. It was a very painful time for almost everyone, and students responded to that pain in many different ways.

Both positive and negative responses became noticeable. In watching students and colleagues deal with the crisis around us, I came to a new understanding of the verse that says, "all things work together for good for those who love God, who are called according to his purpose" (Rom 8:28 NRSV). It was sometimes difficult to find anything positive in what was happening during those days. All of us were hurting and angry about the demise of our school and about the lives that were being torn asunder.

The grief that consumed the campus was evident when we walked onto its historic grounds. It was in the air, in the classrooms, in relationships. Just as we had grieved at other times in our lives, we went through stages, and all of us were not at the same place at the same time. If one walked across campus or spent some time in the faculty lounge or the student lounges, one could quickly detect the gamut of feelings and stages being expressed. Some of us were so angry that the anger seemed to consume all our responses and dominate our conversations. People were often impatient with each other and short tempered then. Others were depressed and found it difficult to get motivated to teach or to learn. Assignments were difficult to complete, and students often found themselves daydreaming and not able to give their studies their best shot. Everyone was preoccupied, and this preoccupation showed in different ways for different people.

It was a tough and painful time. I think it is safe to say, on one hand, that academics suffered during those days of turmoil. I think it is also safe to say, on the other hand, that a different kind of learning was happening on that campus because of the events that were taking place—learning that was very positive and useful for the future. Students, faculty, and staff learned what it means to fight for freedom and integrity and take a possibly risky and costly stand for one's faith. I will cherish that type of learning and how it taught me to look for the positive instead of staying angry and being consumed by the negative.

Under the guidance of God and with the advantage of the clearer perspective of time, I can see many positive things that happened during those days. Two positive results should not go unmentioned. A couple of women students started a new tradition at Southeastern that caught on like wildfire. They shared their idea with other students, and together they tied hundreds of yellow ribbons all around the campus in a visible sign of support for faculty and the administration. It was heartwarming to see, profound and moving. The yellow ribbon became a powerful symbol for the rest of our tenure there and still speaks powerfully as it hangs on hundreds of diplomas even now and represents the "Lolley era." The ribbon represented a focused avenue for students, faculty, and administration to make a statement without having to say a word.

Another very positive result of that tough time has to do with learning the value of taking a stand for integrity and freedom. Most of us have lived in times and places where our faith has never been questioned. We have never had to fight for what we believe or take a stand that is risky. During the tragedy at Southeastern many of us had to put our very calling on the line and our jobs in jeopardy when we dared to go against the trustees and the fundamentalist leaders who called the shots. While this was painful and often quite frightening, there was a sense of power and freedom in taking such a stand. Several of my colleagues resigned from their positions at Southeastern, not because they had better offers in other places but because they could not in good conscience work for an administration that they felt was not trustworthy and whose agenda was so vastly different from anything they had been associated with before. I was fortunate in that God led me to a wonderful position where I could use my gifts and at the same time find healing from my grief.

One of my closest colleagues, Woody Catoe, was one of those who made a decision to resign without having a specific place to live out his calling. When he resigned as the director of student affairs, he did not have a job. He and I talked long and hard about the decisions that we were making. I remember well his telling me about the conversation that he had with his children, who had known no other life than their dad working for the seminary that he loved. When he explained to them the reasons for his decision to resign with no job offer, they learned a lesson about their father and about true faith and integrity. They were very proud of him and became very involved in the family's decisions about how their lives would be changed by that event.

Such freedom and integrity is something that one can only talk about until one's life is on the line. Then an experience forces us to back up what we have only thought was true. Then we know what it means to take a stand and be truly free. Jesus has tried to tell us through the ages that the truth sets us free. Some of us know this fact now in ways that we had never before understood. We have felt freedom burning deep within, and it is a memory and understanding that no one can ever take from us. Yellow ribbons and the words "freedom" and "integrity" bring a smile now to many faces. They are tangible symbols of an intangible joy, a joy that is the gift of God.

I have reflected many times in the last four years about my time at Southeastern. I know that God called me there for a specific purpose. I often think about the painful prayer time I had before going to Southeastern, and now I know what God was trying to tell me about how difficult that assignment would be for me. It was very painful to see that wonderful seminary changed so drastically and a very close-knit community torn apart. It was hard to leave a ministry that I felt I was so specifically called to do. When I went to Southeastern I planned to live out my ministry and retire there. I was grieved to bury that dream, and it has taken me years to work through my grief. I have learned that God does not work on my timetable, though, and has a much larger vision and knowledge about what is best for me. I have learned to trust and to hope that what does not make sense to me now will one day be clearer. I have learned that I understand God's will most often in retrospect instead of ahead of time or at the very moment. Most often I venture out on faith and trust because God has led me through the valley in the past, and I know that God will be with me if I stay open and receptive to that divine leading.

My life has gone on, and God has blessed me beyond words with a good position in a wonderful congregation. I am doing theological education day in and day out with people who are seeking to follow the path of Jesus Christ our Lord. I am offering a new and different role model to children who are growing up with the knowledge that a woman in ministry is not something new or strange. I am practicing pastoral care and counseling with people who live and work the best they know how in the world in which they live. I am seeking to be open to God's leading and trying to be quiet enough to hear the voice of God speak to me.

I am who I am because of the five years I spent at Southeastern as the chaplain. I may never know the full impact of that ministry on my life or on the lives of those whom I encountered while I was there, but I have learned to trust the Creator to carry me from day to day and to tell me what I need to know in order to do God's work in this moment. I have learned that when God calls us, male or female, into service, God will provide what we need to do that ministry even if it is not what we think we need or what we might want. I have also learned that I need to rely more on *charis* ("grace")and less on my own understanding.

I am very grateful for the experiences at Southeastern that have taught me so much. I am even more grateful for the relationships that I established there that sustain me today and help me know what Christian community is all about. It is difficult for me to be thankful for events that caused such pain. I do not believe that what happened at Southeastern was the will of God. I do believe that even in the midst of pain and destruction "all things work together for good for those who love

God, who are called according to his purpose." On that belief, I go forward into an unknown future, knowing who has called me and who will guide me.

―――――― Chapter 11 ――――――

Southeastern:
Reflections on a Mission

Glenn T. Miller

The editor asked me to write on Southeastern's place in the larger context of American theological education. Our story consists of four concentric circles, with Southeastern at the center. The first circle is the Southern Baptist Convention, the second the Sunbelt, the third the national background, and the fourth the historical development of American theological education. The seminary's location at the center of these circles symbolizes the reason for its eventual fate.

A Convention School

Viewed from one perspective, the story is easy to tell. Southeastern began as part of a post-World War II expansion of Southern Baptist theological education. During this period of growth, the Southern Baptist seminary-system went from two poorly financed seminaries to six fiscally healthy institutions. Today those seminaries educate approximately one-half of American Protestant seminary students. Thus, Southeastern was part of the most dynamic expansion of seminary education in the convention's— and perhaps in the nation's—history.

Southeastern's sense of mission developed in the nexus of this half-century of dynamic growth. A progressive development of the school's mastery of the art of theological education matched the school's numerical expansion. Thus, Southeastern's administrators gained abilities to adjust the school's life to new realities. The seminary's presidents developed their capacity to train and work with the board of trustees, and the faculty gained proficiency in teaching an increasingly diverse student body.

This steady increase in educational sophistication was not without cost. Behind the calm wording of the faculty minutes, the historian can still detect the disagreements engendered by the school's numerical and intellectual growth. If poverty and deprivation cause dissension in some quarters, prosperity was the foundation of many of Southeastern's internal conflicts.

Southeastern's adjustment to its growth was not evolutionary. The rate of change at Southeastern overran the capacity of the school to adjust to its environment. The altered role of the faculty in the school's administration illustrates these painful adaptations. When Paige Patterson became president, the faculty still contained members who remembered a time when a faculty committee of the whole administered Southeastern. In my own tenure at the school (1976–1991), Southeastern's faculty had to conform to the administrative professionalism of the Lolley presidency. Each step toward a new administrative stance, no matter how demanded by the situation, created resistance.

Growth provided many of Southeastern's most creative moments. Since the student body was expanding, for example, Southeastern could provide a place for women and for some people of color without displacing other constituencies. Growth also supported the expansion of the faculty. Perhaps most important, growth fueled the optimism of the Lolley years. Despite debates and occasional setbacks, many believed that Southeastern was moving toward a golden age. The financial restrictions of the Binkley and Stealey presidencies were not part of the cost of doing business in the Southeast. Those exigencies were the historic price paid for the school's success under Lolley.

Expansion also enabled the school to put the 1960s Bultmannian controversy behind it. Whatever the merits of the various sides, the Bultmannian debacle cost Southeastern dearly. During a historic period of high enrollment in American theological schools, Southeastern's enrollment pattern was flat. Equally significant, the departure of the Bultmannians reversed a growing tendency for Southeastern to displace Southern as the school of choice for younger, more intellectual Southern Baptists. The internal pressure of the controversy left the faculty chronically divided. Yet, as the school expanded, these trends changed. Southeastern regained its position as an intellectual leader, and the school's electives (the freest in the convention) encouraged students to formulate their own theologies. New faculty appointments made the controversy over Bultmann a memory.

In many ways, the school was a microcosm of the convention. Just as Southeastern was struggling with growth, so the Convention overdosed on its own prosperity. Whatever statistic the historian cites, the SBC was expanding. Membership was up. Giving was up. Baptisms were up. The number of missionaries and missionary fields was up, and self-congratulation was up.

The problem was that the convention operated under a system of governance devised in the 1920s to support a financially troubled denomination on the edge of bankruptcy. To understand this system, a few historical reminders may be useful. When the convention founded the Cooperative Program in 1925, railroads bound together the nation. Many trips, even within the South, took a day or more to complete. The long distance telephone was in its infancy, and important information was often telegraphed, especially to rural and small-town areas. Radio was only beginning to establish national networks.

The 1925 convention system reflected these realities. Those who contributed and sent messengers to the annual meeting constituted the convention. Since attendance was time-consuming and expensive, the real power in the convention naturally devolved on the pastors of the largest and richest congregations. This was a small group. Before the convention's president made appointments to boards and agencies, he consulted with this group's leading members and with various state convention officials. Since the convention was small and homogeneous, this system worked and worked well. While the system overlooked many people with excellent leadership and other skills, it also insured that those appointed were competent supporters of the convention's goals.

After World War II, this convention system came to reflect less and less the realities of the churches' lives. The new work in the northern states added many smaller state conventions and churches to the Southern Baptist Convention's roles. What these new constituencies' fair share of governance ought to be was not clear, especially since the new people were not in the "old-boy" network. At the same time, the expansion of the work at home and abroad weakened the sense of connection between ordinary believers and the convention's enterprises. In 1945 one might easily handle the Woman's Missionary Union's list of missionary birthdays at breakfast grace; by 1990, few recognized all the names or places.

The small number of people in the actual leadership of the convention masked the disagreements within the larger body. From the end of the Second World War onward, the convention experienced many controversies over issues ranging from racial justice to theological stance. Although these occasionally resulted in shifts within the convention's ruling elite, the leadership absorbed many blows that might have destroyed a weaker organization. The racial controversies of the 1950s, for example, might have provoked a major shift in leadership, but they did not, nor did the heated 1960s discussion of Ralph Elliott's understanding of Genesis. Prosperity created caution.

In retrospect, what amazes me is that the 1920s convention system lasted as long as it did. The need for formal constitutional revision was evident in the 1950s, but both leaders and supporters operated on the principle that what is not broken should not be repaired. Since the convention worked, no one noted its flaws or asked how the convention could make the system more representative. For Southeastern, a school preoccupied by its own growth, the convention question seemed distant. Only in the early 1980s, when the conservatives had found a new way to power, did the faculty wake up to the dangers in the Southern Baptist cooperative system. By then, the opportunity for prophetic scholarship had passed; the only option was to try to ride out the storm.

The Sunbelt

When the convention founded Southeastern, some of its advocates hoped that the school might serve the South's rural constituency that was just beginning to hire seminary graduates. Although convention leaders had flirted with Richmond and Washington, D.C., as locations for the new school, the Wake Forest location seemed ideal for this more specific mission. Southeastern was not alone in seeking to serve rural America. Since the 1890s, progressive Christians of many denominations had made the improvement of the rural church a major commitment. Schools as diverse as Duke, Drew, Andover-Newton, and Yale were strong centers for the preparation of modern leaders for the rural church. Those interested in the rural church had their own journals, organizations, and courses in seminaries, and they read each other's studies. Although no formal organization existed, those involved with the rural church formed the Rural Church Movement, a loose confederation of seminary professors, teachers, and denominational leaders. American Christians had a rural as well as an urban social gospel.

The Rural Church Movement progressivism had certain characteristics. Like all progressives, the advocates of the Rural Church Movement believed passionately in the power of education to transform human life. The alliance between the minister and the teacher was the foundation of future social advance. For their part, pastors must advocate education in church and out of church. Pastors were to encourage young people to attend the state university; they were to encourage young ministers to go to seminary. All churches were to have a modern church school with well-trained teachers.

The progressives' passion for education extended to science. Human beings had an obligation to know all that they could about their world, and this meant fearlessness in the face of scientific conclusions. In the 1920s, for example, rural progressives at Wake Forest and Duke helped to defeat legislation that would have prohibited the teaching of evolution in the public schools.

The Rural Church Movement had a genuine admiration for rural religious traditions. Especially in the South, rural church progressives tended to be agrarians who had a deep appreciation of country life and values. Unlike their urban counterparts, for example, rural progressives continued to find religious strength in the traditions of the protracted meeting and of special times of grace. Rural Church advocates believed that the democracy and individualism of rural Southern people were sources of the region's strength. The rural church movement peaked before liberation theology became popular. Otherwise the movement's leaders might have spoken of rural religious life as the praxis that formed a foundation for religious and social reflection. Within this framework of traditional rural piety, the churches could combat and try to eliminate such historic evils as racial segregation and lynching.

As I get more perspective on Southeastern, I am more convinced that this rural social gospel provided much of the foundation of Southeastern's progressive tradition. Up until the Patterson-Bush administration, most Southeastern faculty served as interim pastors of small rural congregations with between fifty and one hundred attending. It was common knowledge that many were not interested in serving larger congregations, no matter what the compensation. Faculty frequently used examples from life in rural churches in class.

When the school was founded, the mission to rural areas was socially coherent. Yet every passing year made it less so. Southerners of both races moved off the farms in large numbers and settled in the cities or the suburbs. There was also an educational revolution. The World War II generation went to high school, their children went to college, and their grandchildren to graduate school. People who traveled some fifty or sixty miles to work and participated in country life as a hobby often composed the rural church.

Technology created a post-World War II South that was neither bound to agriculture nor to textiles. The air conditioner, the automobile, and the military created the Sunbelt. Air-conditioning made possible sustained intellectual and physical work throughout the long, hot Southern summers. The automobile and the interstate highway system encouraged the growth of Southern cities, and federal military spending increased the tax base. Unlike the older Southern industrialism, based on cheap labor, the new industries required a more educated work force.

Southeastern's responses to the new Sunbelt were institutionally complex. The school's original interest in sociology (a mark of the Rural Church Movement) waned. Yet pastoral psychology (a more important specialty to a middle-class and urban constituency) never had strong faculty support despite the innovative program developed by Richard Hester and Albert Meiberg. In a similar way, the school had difficulty developing substantial support for programs in urban ministry. The school segregated the excellent urban ministry program taught by Thomas Bland in the summer term. Urban ministry courses never had a significant influence on the school's curriculum.

All Southern Baptist schools (except Golden Gate) had to struggle with the problems and opportunities created by the Sunbelt. Yet the new situation may have affected Southeastern more deeply than the other Southern Baptist seminaries that were located in large cities where urban and suburban churches surrounded them. These city churches were an important part of their educational mix. While students in these schools often served as pastors of rural churches, the urban church was a continual presence in their education, a source of role models and adjunctive faculty. These churches appear to have both mediated and moderated social changes as they influenced the seminaries. Southeastern had no urban buffer to protect it from social change.

That the Sunbelt became a center of a new religious and political conservatism should not have surprised anyone. Many industries in the South were part of a new wave of capitalism in the United States. The new economy seemed, as did the earlier industrial revolution, to create wealth almost from nothing. Moreover, the region was close to the military. Southerners not only disproportionately served in the armed forces, but many of the nation's largest military bases were there. The region also had religious and theological issues that had not been resolved earlier. Unlike the North, the South had not experienced an intense fundamentalist-modernist controversy. Many Southern church members were only partly aware of the issues that had so agitated their northern counterparts. As long as the discussion of such matters as evolution and biblical criticism took place among the traditional southern elite, those issues caused little trouble. When these issues became linked to political causes, they became explosive. After all, North Carolina, not a deep South state, elected Jesse Helms.

Southeastern's agrarian progressivism found itself flanked by new social forces. The traditional strength of agrarian progressivism lay in the alliance between school teachers, church leaders, and small-town professionals. This social class was no longer in power in the South or the Southeast, and the new social order was far less definite or focused. A characteristic faculty statement during the takeover years (1985–1990) was that "The new trustees are not our kind of people." In the good old days, deans of Baptist colleges, judges on the state bench, and leaders of such industries as agricultural products served on the seminary's board. We relied on an elite that was losing throughout the Southeast.

The National Situation: A Difficult Context

The last fifty years tried some human souls. In 1950 American religious organizations were in the midst of a period of major growth, a boom. New members joined, congregations erected church buildings in the newly constructed suburbs, and giving to religious institutions poor since the 1920s reached new levels. Theologically, the tragic fundamentalist-modernist controversy of the 1920s had finally started to heal.

Conservatives, led by such progressive evangelicals as Carl Henry and Billy Graham, entered the larger discussion in more open and creative ways. Old fundamentalism was becoming new evangelicalism. Liberalism also took a new course. Despite (or because of) the worldwide economic and political crisis, the theological renaissance of the 1930s and 1940s put the Bible back in the center of theological discussion. The ecumenical movement was bringing Christians closer together.

From the beginning, the new directions of the 1950s intoxicated Southeastern. Neo-orthodox theology was almost a mark of the school's identity. As in other Southern seminaries, neo-orthodox thought was the bridge that spanned the distance between the conservatism and the newer, more modern streams of thought. Thus such Old Testament professors as Leo Green and John Durham used critical biblical methods while retaining their firm basis in traditional Christian affirmations. The biblical theology movement enlivened almost every department.

Unfortunately, the Southern style of neo-orthodoxy favored at Southeastern began to pass from the national scene in the early 1970s. Why this change occurred when it did is not entirely clear, but the tumult of the 1960s was partially responsible. The civil rights and antiwar movement had changed the theological questions, especially for many younger faculty members, and the continuing crises in Latin America suggested other new avenues. Mainstream theology became a succession of particularities when black theology, feminist theology, and liberation theology joined Moltmann's theology of hope. In addition, various forms of neo-liberalism, often based on Whitehead's process thought, became popular.

Theological change was not only to Southeastern's left. On the right, neo-evangelicalism, which had been moving toward a greater accommodation with other theological positions, acquired new visibility. In part, this was because of tensions within the new evangelical movement itself. Evangelical biblical scholars had begun to flirt with mild biblical criticism and to explore many new social issues from their own theological perspective. One result was a massive debate within evangelicalism that led to such fine distinctions as those drawn in the Chicago Statement on Inerrancy. Interestingly enough, these changes occurred when the schools that hired these scholars received accreditation from the Association of Theological Schools in the United States and Canada.

Simultaneously, the more evangelical churches in America began to outstrip the mainstream churches in growth and in financial support. In part, the expansion of conservative churches was due to the general popularity of conservative positions in the country. After all, only Jimmy Carter, a very conservative Democrat, broke the Republican lock on the White House that began with Nixon's 1968 election, and Carter only served one term. The problems were deeper, however. The mainstream churches, despite their self-proclaimed accommodation to culture, appeared tied to yesterday's America. They lost members in record numbers. In contrast, conservative churches, spurred by aggressive evangelism, appealed to many members of the newer elite. These churches softened their fundamentalism enough to be popular, but they retained enough of their traditions to be an alternative.

The changes in the teaching of religion in colleges and universities were equally significant. Beginning sometime in the 1960s, the teaching of religion became one more secular discipline with its own methodology and its own secular commitments. In a sense, religious studies became more analogous to Near Eastern or Asian studies than to theology. The typical religious studies department thus combined specialists in different religions and experts in different approaches to religion.

The secularization of religious studies further eroded Southeastern's position. Part of the appeal of the type of neo-orthodox theology taught at the school was its ability to promote dialogue with the broader stream of religious option. Yale graduate Olin Binkley was one symbol of this openness, as was the number of non-Southern Baptist doctorates held by members of the faculty. As university departments of religion moved left and as mainstream theology became more isolated, however, Southeastern's dialogue became a monologue.

In short, it was a bad time for the center, and if anything united Southeastern intellectually, it was commitment to a centrist position. Some faculty members, notably Alan Neely in missions and Elizabeth Barnes in theology, introduced some of the newer directions on the left. Others, especially Glenn Miller and Bob Culpepper, talked with the right. Yet the school's general theological stance involved SEBTS in an intellectual struggle on two fronts. Unwilling to embrace the newer forms of liberal theology, Southeastern appeared to those on the left as never quite intellectually respectable or current. Therefore natural alliances with the religion departments of the senior Baptist colleges were never firm. To those on the right, Southeastern appeared unwilling to admit that anything new had occurred in conservative theology. Despite real intellectual affinities with some neo-evangelical theologians, especially those at Fuller Seminary in California, the faculty tended to go its own way.

If these theological issues were not allies of other social and political forces, Southeastern's commitment to a centrist theology would have been a virtue. After all, such important religious thinkers as Robert Bellah called for a renewal of centrist thought in both church and state. Someone needed to speak for those who wanted to retain both the habits of their hearts and the use of their minds. Yet Southeastern was in the midst of social and political movements that made centrism impossible or at least very difficult. The rise of a militant new conservatism, strongest among white southerners, created an atmosphere that made the center an uncomfortable place to be. Issues such as abortion, women's rights, and the place of religion in public life demanded quick ideological answers—yes's and no's. Although individual faculty members could give answers, the institution as a whole could not.

The seminary's centrism confused the attempts of the faculty to deal with outside agencies. Southeastern's faculty with very few exceptions expected the Association of Theological Schools to step into the dispute and at least to affirm the faculty's reading of the situation. The problem was that American theological education was largely at another place. The more classical mainstream schools were accustomed to battles between special interest groups, ranging from feminist and black caucuses to gay liberation organizations. Representatives of these schools tended to interpret Southeastern in terms of their own experience. Also representatives of conservative schools could not understand why so many Southeastern professors acted as if the appointment of someone with their points of view made the school less scholarly. If anything, the experience of many conservative leaders with pressure from organized groups among the constituency was more like that of the mainstream than it was like Southeastern's travail.

Southeastern's position in the center may also explain one of its unnoted tragedies. In the past, attacks on seminary teachers led to the Baptist colleges inviting some (at least the most threatened) to join their faculties. This had been the pattern after the unpleasantness at Southern in the 1950s and reached back to the Whitsitt case at the turn of the century. This time, however, no state Baptist school offered to serve as the Lone Ranger, and the sting of that rejection was the most bitter pill that many Southeastern professors had to swallow.

The Larger Historical Context

Southeastern Seminary, although it opened in 1951, stood in a long theological tradition that reached back to Southern Seminary and beyond it to nineteenth-century Princeton. In that sense, the seminary was part of a larger family of institutions that had certain common characteristics: strong denominational affiliations, a sense of the seminary as an intellectual center for the churches, and a definite confession of faith. While schools of this type are not immune to theological and social change, their strength is their capacity to transmit a tradition—a common body of agreements and disagreements or, to use MacIntyre's wonderful word, "arguments" from generation to generation.

During my years at Southeastern, I had little doubt that the Princetonian tradition, as modified by James P. Boyce at Southern, deeply influenced the school. Like all Princetonian-style schools, Southeastern was responsive to changes in the denominational winds and sought to be a supportive partner of the churches. The place was Baptist to the core. Those who, like myself, had received much of our training outside the denomination, felt smothered by Baptist perspectives on everything from church administration to systematic theology. When we tried to introduce some variety, as when we used more liturgical services in chapel, the effect was unreal—somewhat like children playing church.

My own experience before and after teaching at Southeastern also made me aware of the Abstract of Principles' influence on the seminary. Neither of the seminaries where I studied (Andover-Newton and Union) had a confessional standard. Their professors' own research and at times, I suspect, personal preferences determined their theological stance. In contrast, Southeastern's faculty felt that the Abstract was a covenant that bound them together.

The best analogy for the role of the Abstract is a fence. The area within the fence was an area of freedom. Within this boundary, individual teachers had the right to adopt any method of biblical or theological inquiry that was in harmony with and not contrary to the Abstract. This allowed considerable freedom, and faculty exercised it. Hence some advocated different styles of biblical study, and a number adopted different theological stances. The Abstract served to remind people of a responsibility to their larger theological heritage. The school taught within the framework of loyalty to Baptist life and principles.

Southeastern's broad understanding of confessionalism was typical of schools in the Southern-Princetonian tradition. From the founding of Princeton onward, confessional schools had followed a loose constructionist policy on their foundational documents. Faculty held to the confession as good words and sound doctrine that were in accord with Holy Scripture, but these words were different from those of Holy Scripture. Professors were always to judge doctrine by the confession's (in our case, the Abstract's) affirmation of the Bible. Anything else would have been circular reasoning of the worst sort.

Much of the unpleasant character of the controversy came from the fact that the conservative party wanted to redefine the terms of subscription. Almost all confessional schools have passed through at least one such crisis in their history. Princeton, the flagship of American denominational schools, passed through such crises in the 1830s and 1930s. The first was part of the Old School-New School division of the Presbyterian Church. In a real sense, this division was a tragedy for American Christianity. The victorious Old School struggled to define confessional identity as subscription to a document in all its details. When difficulties with the Statement on Scripture arose, Charles Hodge and his successors developed the Princeton doctrine of the inerrancy of the autographs. They hoped this restatement of the doctrine would be sufficient to protect the Westminster Confession's position on the issue. Ironically, the constant need for redefinition weakened the principle of allegiance to a confession. By the 1920s this more narrow confessionalism was in trouble.

In the 1920s struggle, President Ross Stevenson pulled Princeton Seminary back toward its original, broadly confessional position. Despite the undisputed brilliance of such thinkers as Machen, the tradition appeared headed toward a cultural sectarianism. By the 1930s Princeton was a center for the exploration of the newer orthodox theologies of Emil Brunner and Karl Barth.

Southern Baptists have not had such struggles over their confessional heritage. For one thing, Boyce's original proposal that a Southern Baptist seminary be supported by an explicit confession of faith was rejected in favor of the idea of an Abstract of Principles. The shift was not cosmetic. In the popular Common Sense philosophy of the day, principles guided inquirers into truth; they were not necessarily the truth itself. One of the most important events in Southern Baptist theological education happened in private. James P. Boyce was a student and disciple of the Old School

Presbyterian theologian, Charles Hodge, and he taught Hodge's theology until his death. Yet, although Boyce was the major architect of the seminary, its first president, and its guiding spirit, Boyce did not write the seminary's Abstract. The Trustees assigned that task to John A. Broadus and William Williams. Despite Southern's similarities to the Old School citadel, Baptists did not want Princeton South.

Southeastern followed the Southern Seminary understanding of the Princeton tradition. The Abstract was an effective fence; the administration faithfully asked people about whether they could teach in accord with and not contrary to it, and conscience did the rest. In short, it worked the way a confession ought to work. The Baptist character of the school was inviolate, as was the general direction of the institution.

If one use of the Abstract was to keep the school within the fence, its other use was to fence out external pressures. The founders hoped the Abstract might buffer the school against attacks from without. Yet the Abstract failed to provide this needed protection. In a sense, this failure was not atypical of American confessional seminaries. Confessions are most effective in shaping the internal character of an institution, not in regulating relationships to other bodies.

Concluding Postscript

At a party for the retirement of a colleague, Thomas Graves called Southeastern a Camelot. The image suggested new opportunities, creative energy, and almost unlimited potential. Unfortunately, that Camelot never existed. When we examine Southeastern in its context, we see that it was a school that was often in more tension with its environment than its faculty and administration supposed. If these conflicts do not explain the conservative takeover, they do help us to understand why the school in the forest of Wake was unable to survive the onslaught.

To me, Southeastern remains a parable of American Christianity in the last half of the twentieth century. The story of that period is the collapse of the center and its replacement by a host of competing special interest groups. To the left, these groups are identified with such issues as nationality, race, and gender, and to the right with such public issues as prayer in public schools, abortion, and federal regulation. As in other periods when the center in America has not held, both sides appeal to the same God and the same Bible. Southeastern's fate was to be caught in the middle at a time when extremism was no vice.

What then will become of a centrist stance in theological education? Once the current passion for reform, left and right, recedes, someone will have to reclaim the territory that lies between them. Since the maelstrom of the present has sucked schools like Southeastern into its maw, those times will require new beginnings and a new spirit.

——————— Chapter 12 ———————

Southeastern and New Beginnings in Theological Education

Thomas H. Graves

Introduction: The Seed Bed

The term "seminary" literally means "seed bed." Southeastern Seminary proved to be a valuable "seed bed," germinating the promise of several innovative endeavors in theological education including Baptist Theological Seminary at Richmond. The roots of new and creative efforts in theological education were grounded in the rich soil of the place that was Southeastern. It was there, more than anywhere else, that the dream for free and faithful ministerial education for Baptists was kept alive.

Why Southeastern should have been the one Southern Baptist seminary to oppose dramatically the fundamentalist takeover of its trustees and why Southeastern should have been the "seed bed" of so many new ventures are questions related to the basic character of the school itself. First, the school from its founding had highly regarded the role of the faculty and developed a much less hierarchical administrative structure than its sister institutions. The faculty had control over significant areas of seminary life such as the deanship, admissions, chapel worship and speakers, and guest lecturers.

Second, because the school had no Ph.D. program there was not the possibility for inbreeding of the faculty. In fact, the diversity of faculty backgrounds assured that the school would find it difficult to march in lockstep with traditional patterns.

Third, the school lacked from its beginning an undue allegiance to denominational leadership. A diverse faculty, jealous of its powers, led by a school president who wielded significantly less power than presidents at other schools, made Southeastern much less malleable to denominational control and much more productive of ideas that might run counter to denominational pressures.

One other factor that differentiated Southeastern and made it possible for planned, rational, and concerted resistance to fundamentalist pressures was the simplification of the seminary's structure within a single school. There was no separate meeting of Theology, Music, or Christian Education faculties. At Southeastern the faculty as a whole made decisions for the life of the school. Consequently, when a time of resistance came, the faculty was able to respond as a single unit. For whatever reasons, the faculty and administration of Southeastern was enabled to speak with clarity and courage.

Each of these influences meant that the faculty of Southeastern was at the forefront of the battle. At Southeastern, it was not a denominational conflict relegated to administrators, trustees, and denominational officers. The fact of the faculty's centrality at Southeastern obviously affected the concerns of the community. The resulting focus was in large part on the task of education, teaching, and the classroom. The issue was one of whether the freedom of the classroom and the scholarship of the teacher would be allowed to operate within the environment of Southern Baptist life. In this atmosphere the question could be asked: Are there options to what is available in Southern Baptist life? The issue was raised early at Southeastern, and the ability to articulate the question made it possible to seek options in Baptist theological education.

The Early Efforts: Wake Forest and Duke

Informal conversations between the faculty members of Southeastern and persons outside the school concerning a new home for the Southeastern tradition were numerous and varied. Contacts were made with persons in places such as Mercer University, Stetson University, Furman University, and the University of Richmond. The possible options that arose from the demise of Southeastern were surprising in their variety and number. For example, Averett College in Danville, Virginia, seriously studied a plan to implement a master of divinity program very early in the conflict.

One of the earliest attempts to establish a new center for theological education in the region once served by Southeastern occurred in relation to Wake Forest University. Randall Lolley announced his intention to resign on 22 October 1987. In mid-November Mike Queen met with Tom Hearn, president of Wake Forest; Ed Wilson, provost; and William Joyner, vice-president for development. Queen, the pastor of First Baptist Church, Wilmington, North Carolina, was a Southeastern graduate and president of the Wake Forest Ministerial Alumni Council. Queen assembled the ad hoc committee on Wake Forest University Divinity School and wrote in a memo to each committee member: "With recent events in the SBC and particularly at Southeastern Baptist Seminary in old Wake Forest, the future of Baptist theological education on the east coast seems in doubt."[1] Several persons with close ties to Southeastern served on the committee, including Bob Spinks, recently resigned vice-president for development at Southeastern; Tom Halbrooks, professor at Southeastern; and Tom Graves, a former professor at Southeastern. The group scheduled a meeting for 16–17 December 1987 for the purpose of sharing a vision for theological education with Tom Hearn and other representatives of Wake Forest University.

In the discussion, the events at Southeastern were central. It was noted that the cry for options was coming from the grass roots level. Churches "are now asking, 'where will we get our preachers?' Over 50 resolutions of support have been received by SEBTS from churches and associations."[2] Particularly when calculating the financial support for a new school, the alumni and donors to Southeastern were mentioned frequently. The ad hoc committee argued that Southeastern's "alienated constituency will not support 'fundamentalism' but will support a divinity school based on historic Baptist principles."[3]

In response to the interest expressed by the ad hoc committee, Hearn appointed a committee to investigate the establishment of a divinity school at Wake Forest. One of the initial steps taken by this study committee was to survey moderate Baptists in the southeast. In June of 1988 a questionnaire was mailed to the 3,155 paid subscribers to *SBC Today* in Virginia, North Carolina, South Carolina, and Georgia. The 1,119 responses, a 35.5% response rate, seemed to demonstrate the high level of interest in the possibility of an alternative school. Among the findings were the following: (1) 73% felt there was a need for another divinity school in the Southeast; (2) 72% felt it was desirable that the school be affiliated with a university; (3) 59% supported the establishment of a divinity school at Wake Forest; (4) 92% stated that preparing pastors for churches is the most important objective of a new divinity school.[4] In

April 1989, as a result of the study committee's work, the Wake Forest board of trustees approved the concept of a divinity school pending the availability of necessary financing.

Another early attempt to establish an alternative for Baptist theological education in the region was a discussion with the administration of Duke Divinity School. The faculties of Southeastern and Duke maintained close contact through the years, holding an annual dinner and discussion. There was a great deal of personal contact between the two schools because of Southeastern faculty members who had studied or taught at Duke or who lived in Durham. Soon after Lolley's resignation, Max Rogers, professor of Old Testament at Southeastern and a Durham resident, contacted Dean Dennis Campbell of the Duke Divinity School to inquire about the use of the Duke library should a new Baptist seminary be established nearby. Dean Campbell seemed receptive to further discussions and asked to meet with a group of Southeastern faculty and representatives of the Alliance of Baptists. On 26 May 1988, Campbell met again with Rogers and other Southeastern faculty John Eddins and Alan Neely. Also included in the discussion was Mahan Siler, chair of the Alliance of Baptists' committee on theological education.

As the discussions continued, the Alliance's committee offered two proposals. One called for the establishment of a Baptist seminary in affiliation with Duke. The faculty of the new seminary would be "adequate to offer the full range of courses necessary to provide a theological education for contemporary ministers."[5] The proposal envisioned a relationship with Duke in which the library resources of Duke would be available to the new Baptist seminary, where there would be limited cross-registration between the two schools, and where class schedules would be coordinated to facilitate cooperation. A second option proposed by Alliance leaders was that a Center of Baptist Studies be established for students enrolled at Duke. The faculty and staff of the Center would offer approximately one-third of the M.Div. curriculum to Baptist students enrolled at Duke.

Campbell responded to these possibilities in September 1988 with the warning that Duke simply could not accommodate the additional enrollment being projected by the establishment of a separate seminary: "our library simply could not accommodate another seminary's students. . . . We cannot service 100 to 200 more students." Neither was the Duke faculty eager to relinquish control over a significant portion of its curriculum. Nevertheless, to scale back the size of the Duke response was not to diminish the desire on the part of Duke faculty and administration to do something to fill the vacuum left by Southeastern.

Efforts now proceeded through continued contact between persons at Duke and the theological education committee of the Alliance as well as through the formation of the ad hoc Baptist House of Studies committee. A proposal for a house of studies was put forward by Russell Richey, associate dean of Duke Divinity School. It was received well by the study committee and by the representatives of Duke. Richey envisioned a Baptist Studies program that would recruit, advise, and locate suitable placements for Baptist students at Duke. A committee on Baptist Studies would advise the Duke curriculum committee concerning courses that would serve the need of Baptist students. Richey's plan received support from both the Duke faculty and from the ad hoc Baptist House of Studies committee. In the spring of 1990 the Alliance voted to encourage the program at Duke. Though smaller in scope than the original proposals, the possibilities of this program at Duke offered a real hope to those seeking options for Baptist ministerial students.

In the spring of 1992, Furman Hewitt, formerly professor of Christian Ethics at Southeastern, was named interim director of the Duke program. Hewitt accepted the position with a strong desire to "create a Baptist community of learning and fellowship in the ecumenical context of a nationally regarded divinity school."[6] In part, the spirit of Southeastern is finding expression within the Divinity School at Duke.

Baptist Theological Seminary at Richmond

The beginnings of the programs at Wake Forest and Duke were exciting, yet with the delay in getting the Wake Forest school begun and with the downsizing of the Duke proposals, there remained a strong desire to foster possibilities for Baptist theological education elsewhere. Many desired a quicker response on a larger scale.

The Alliance of Baptists stands as the group that first envisioned the operation of a new seminary in Richmond. The story of the Alliance's relation to the Southeastern saga should be clearly recognized. At its very heart the Alliance was driven by those intimately connected with the takeover at Southeastern and those strongly desirous of establishing a place where theological education for Baptists could flourish in a non-fundamentalist environment. As one of its Charter principles, the Alliance was committed to creative theological education. The Alliance understood as well as any group that theological education was the "seed bed" of whatever future Baptists might have.

Specific discussion about the possibilities of a seminary in Richmond can be traced to Alliance discussions concerning not seminary education but rather relationships with American Baptists. These high-level discussions involved key officials in American Baptist life such as John Sundquist and Harold Germer, as well as officers of the Alliance. One item that emerged from the talks was the suggestion from the American Baptist representatives that it might be possible to construct a joint effort in theological education, particularly if it could be tied to efforts underway to strengthen the program supported by American Baptists at the School of Theology at Virginia Union University in Richmond. In the fall of 1988 the board of the Alliance gave its support to discussions with American Baptists to investigate what might be done cooperatively for the cause of Baptist theological education in the south. The idea was fueled by a great deal more than hopes to establish a new school. The possibility of beginning such an effort in conjunction with American Baptists and involving African-American Baptists, since Virginia Union is a largely African-American institution, was a dream bridging two great chasms of Southern Baptist history.

On 30 November 1988 a meeting was held in Charlotte, North Carolina, to discuss possibilities for a joint Alliance-American Baptist venture. Present at the meeting were American Baptist denominational officials Sundquist and Germer; Allix James and John Kinney of the School of Theology at Virginia Union University; Larry Greenfield, president of Colgate-Rochester Divinity School; George Peck, president of Andover-Newton Divinity School; and members of the theological education committee of the Alliance. The Alliance committee was composed of ten persons, four of whom had close personal ties to Southeastern: Anne Neil, Donna Steely, Mahan Siler, and Tom Graves. They were also joined by Morris Ashcraft and Alan Neely, acting director of the Alliance.

In outlining their dreams for a new school, the participants spoke of a need to continue the heritage of Southeastern. In responding to the question of what were the traditions of Southeastern, their answer was:

From its beginning in 1951, Southeastern was ecumenical in spirit and practice, manifested an openness to other theological points of view, has welcomed students from other denominations and utilized faculty (though not elected) who were non-Baptists, emphasized academic integrity, and had for many years been racially and gender inclusive.[7]

Though recognizing the clear link to Southeastern, the participants in the discussion were specific in their desire not to form a "Southeastern in exile." The purpose was to give birth to an institution that would embody innovative approaches to ministerial training, stressing such factors as global learning, spiritual formation, and congregational involvement in theological education. The Charlotte meeting concluded with the naming of a task force composed of Ashcraft, Kinney, Greenfield, Germer, and Neely.

The task force met in Richmond on 3 and 4 January 1989 and was joined by representatives from Union Theological Seminary and Presbyterian School of Christian Education. A vision for the new school grew beyond a relationship with Virginia Union and came to include cooperation with the two other seminaries of Richmond. The task force recommended that the Alliance proceed with the establishment of a seminary in Richmond in cooperation with the other theological schools in the city and that Morris Ashcraft be asked to develop detailed proposals of how such a school might be constituted. On 4 January the task force presented its report, and Randall Lolley was present to speak to a meeting of Richmond pastors about the need to develop new avenues of theological education for Baptists in the Southeast. Notably, in the first public announcement calling for the establishment of a seminary in Richmond, both Randall Lolley and Morris Ashcraft were present and involved. The task force planned to present its final report to the annual gathering of the Alliance scheduled for 1–3 March in Greenville, South Carolina.

In Greenville the report of the task force was opposed by some members of the theological education committee of the Alliance, particularly those with close ties to seminaries other than Southeastern. When the committee report was presented to the Alliance board, there were objections again. When the proposal was presented to the full Alliance, it again met with voices of opposition. In the spring of 1989 it was difficult for many not associated with Southeastern to see the need for a new school. Some persons continued to argue that the events at Southeastern were not the blueprint for future fundamentalist control of Southern

Baptist theological education. After extensive debate, highlighted by an appeal from Elizabeth Barnes of the Southeastern faculty, the proposal to establish a new seminary in Richmond passed with more than ninety percent support.

Upon the school's approval, the Alliance named a provisional board for the Richmond seminary that included former Southeastern professor Alan Neely. At the first meeting of the provisional board in April 1989, Morris Ashcraft, former Southeastern dean, was engaged as the acting president of the seminary. Ashcraft moved temporarily to Richmond and began to construct the foundation of the young school. Ashcraft worked to develop the initial financial reserves of the school, established a relationship with the three seminaries already in Richmond, and found a temporary home for the school's offices in the facilities of Northminster Baptist Church. He acted to establish the legal basis for the school through the adoption of its charter and papers of incorporation. The prestige of the seminary grew immensely under Ashcraft's leadership.

Ashcraft was helped by the work of the Southeastern chapter of the American Association of University Professors (AAUP), which produced a document entitled "A New Vision for Baptist Theological Education." Prepared by the AAUP committee on alternative education chaired by Furman Hewitt, the report stated that the "faculty determined to do what it could to assure that the vision which Southeastern had sought to embody would not die."[8] The report discussed a variety of topics such as governmental structure, doctrinal orientation, admission and evaluation of students, community life, faculty, and trustees. The document meticulously unearthed the relevant material available from accrediting agencies on these subjects and provided a road map for the formation of a new Baptist seminary. What the AAUP had learned in its defense of the Southeastern faculty was well used in the development of a manual for the establishment of a new school. The AAUP committee was composed of Morris Ashcraft, Elizabeth Barnes, John Eddins, Fred Grissom, Dick Hester, Max Rogers, and Furman Hewitt.

In January 1991 Tom Graves accepted the presidency of the seminary at Richmond, coming from the pastorate of St. John's Baptist Church in Charlotte, North Carolina. Graves had previously served on the Southeastern faculty for eight years. The immediate task before the school was threefold: build a faculty, secure facilities, and broaden the base of support.

The most crucial faculty choice was made in securing Tom Halbrooks to serve as dean and professor of Church History. Halbrooks served as an assistant to Ashcraft during his years at Southeastern and was a leader in the faculty's resistance to pressure from the fundamentalist trustees. Halbrooks' acquaintance with accrediting standards and expectations, learned from the drudgery of the struggles at Southeastern, served him well as he developed the academic framework for a new school. Linda McKinnish Bridges, a Ph.D. in New Testament from Southern Seminary, was also added to the full-time faculty in 1991. In addition to others, adjunctive help came from former Southeastern faculty. Bob Dale taught practical theology, and Chevis Horne taught preaching. In the fall of 1991 the school opened for its first classes with thirty-two students and a faculty of seven.

By the fall of 1992 the enrollment had climbed to eighty-six, and three additional faculty members were elected: Glenn Hinson, Isam Ballenger, and Elizabeth Barnes. Hinson was asked to develop the seminary's emphasis in spirituality as well as teach in the areas of worship and church history. Hinson brought to the seminary world-wide renown as a scholar, having served at Southern Seminary for over thirty years. Isam Ballenger, former vice-president of the Foreign Mission Board, had resigned when the board's fundamentalist trustees cut off funding for Ruschlikon Seminary, where Ballenger formerly served as president. Ballenger came to the seminary to teach in the area of missiology and to lead its mission immersion program. Elizabeth Barnes also joined the faculty in 1992 as associate professor of Theology and Ethics. Barnes had served on the faculty of Southeastern since 1987.

The student population in the fall of 1993 grew to 131. Joining the new students were faculty members Sam Balentine and Marilyn Nelson. Balentine had been on the faculty at both Southeastern and Midwestern Baptist Seminaries as professor of Hebrew and Old Testament. Nelson came to Richmond from the D.C. Baptist Convention, where she served as director of Social Ministries. Nelson's responsibilities included providing leadership for the seminary's field-based experience in local congregations. Together with an adjunctive faculty, which now included former Southeasterner John Eddins, Baptist Seminary at Richmond had assembled a Baptist theological faculty second to none.

The hunt for adequate facilities to house the young school in the fall of 1991 was greatly aided by the gracious invitation of Presbyterian

School of Christian Education (PSCE) to locate offices and classrooms in Paisley Hall, which had been the continuing education center for PSCE. In following years the Baptist Seminary at Richmond would increase its leasing arrangements with PSCE to provide additional class-room, office space, and chapel facilities. Arrangements were also made to permit Baptist students to have access to the dorm space of PSCE as well as the cafeteria and bookstore on the PSCE campus. An agreement was reached with Union Theological Seminary (UTS) to pay for the use of its sizable library facilities. The infrastructure of the school was essentially leased from PSCE and UTS, giving the Richmond seminary a basis for accreditation much sooner than would normally be expected for a school so young.

A key need for the school remains the broadening of its base of support. Though the Alliance of Baptists had given birth to the seminary in Richmond, it lacked the financial resources to support the school. The seminary's most crucial task was to secure needed financial support. In the summer of 1991 Randall Lolley agreed to send a letter to alumni/ae of Southeastern inviting them to become honorary alumni/ae of Baptist Theological Seminary at Richmond. That group has now grown in size to almost 1000 persons and provides a core of faithful donors and friends.

A key to the seminary's success was the adoption of the school by the Baptist General Association of Virginia (BGAV). In that process the political network of moderate Baptists in the state provided essential help. Ron Crawford—a Southeastern graduate, trustee of Baptist Theological Seminary at Richmond, and president of the BGAV—was one of the persons crucial in establishing Virginia Baptists' relationship to the seminary. In the fall of 1991 the school was added to the alternative budget of the BGAV. The following year the seminary was named a Shared Ministry of the BGAV. Now the state nominates two persons to serve on the school's board of trustees. A similar process was followed in North Carolina, where the state convention added the school to its alternative budget in the fall of 1993.

The Cooperative Baptist Fellowship (CBF) is the largest denominational group supporting the Richmond seminary. The CBF provides funds for the general operation of the seminary in addition to scholarship assistance for students and other program support for the faculty. Alumni/ae and friends of Southeastern were crucial in the efforts to extend the seminary's range of supporters.

The inclusion of the seminary in the budget of the BGAV opened the door for help from the scholarship funds of the Keesee Fund of Martinsville, Virginia. Again Southeastern connections were central, as Chevis Horne, a former Southeasterner, served on the Keesee board. Becoming an institution eligible for scholarship aid from the Keesee Fund was the biggest financial help in the school's young life, meaning that its Baptist students from North Carolina or Virginia would have most of their tuition paid.

A Vision for the Future

In remembering the good years of Southeastern, one should also be reminded that obsessive nostalgia can be a sign of decadence. The healthiest of situations always point to a renewed and creative future. The roots of the Southeastern tradition run deep at the new Richmond school. The founders of the school insisted, however, that Richmond not serve as a clone of any other place. The hope was that this new school would provide a renewed vision for American theological education. The desire to chart new paths for ministerial training is more important than just the preservation of the Southeastern heritage.

In keeping with the earliest dreams of a new beginning for theological education, Baptist Seminary at Richmond has established its program upon three distinct characteristics: spirituality, globalization, and congregational focus. The emphasis upon spirituality means that each student at the seminary begins with course work on spiritual formation and proceeds to classes on becoming a spiritual guide for others. This focus on the minister's spiritual formation has been strangely absent from much of Protestant theological education and is seen to be a possible key to the spiritual revitalization of the church.

Another focus of the young school is on global experience. Each student is placed at the seminary's expense in a missions situation. Students have traveled to Mexico City, Zimbabwe, Israel, Washington, D.C., and Appalachia to gain an acquaintance with the needs of the world beyond the scope of our comfortable suburban life. Theological education occurs through actual praxis often more thoroughly than in any classroom experience.

A third key component of the school's life is the focus on congregational life. The Richmond seminary is committed to emphasizing the role of the congregation in each of its courses, insisting that the scholarship of the classroom never be out of dialogue with the life of the church. Students are placed in congregational settings where their work is supervised in part by a committee of lay persons, the real experts in congregational life. The seminary sees its task as serving as a resource for congregational life in the region.

Baptist Theological Seminary at Richmond exists because of the turmoil at Southeastern. It was established by persons well acquainted with the Southeastern story. Its future will be different from what was known at Southeastern, for these are different times and the Richmond school is now nourished by so many different streams. Whatever its future, Baptist Theological Seminary at Richmond will forever be indebted to the courage of those brave persons in the forest of Wake who said a loud "no" to Baptist fundamentalism and a clear "yes" to Baptist freedom and sound scholarship.

Notes

[1]Mike Queen, Wilmington NC, to ad hoc committee on Wake Forest University Divinity School, 8 December 1987; transcript in my possession.

[2]"Ad Hoc Committee Responses to Dr. Hearn," Mike Queen, Wilmington NC, to ad hoc committee on Wake Forest University Divinity School, 18 December 1987; transcript in my possession, 1.

[3]Ibid., 2,

[4]"Report of the Divinity School Committee," Wake Forest University (Winston-Salem NC, undated) 2-3.

[5]"Proposal for a Baptist Seminary in Affiliation with Duke University," undated.

[6]Furman Hewitt, "A Word from the Director," *Baptist House of Studies*, 2/2 (Spring 1992): 1.

[7]Minutes of the Special Meeting Regarding Possible New Seminary in Richmond (Charlotte NC, 30 November 1988) 2.

[8]"A New Vision for Baptist Theological Education," The Committee on Alternative Theological Education (Wake Forest NC, 1 March 1989) 1.

Appendixes

WHERE ARE THEY NOW?
(Faculty/Administrative Officers of Southeastern Baptist Theological Seminary 1987–1988)

Faculty

Morris Ashcraft, Dean/Professor of Theology. Retired: now teaching adjunctively at Duke Divinity School, Durham NC.

Samuel E. Balentine, Associate Pastor of Hebrew and Old Testament. Resigned: now a faculty member at the Baptist Theological Seminary at Richmond VA.

Elizabeth B. Barnes, Assistant Professor of Theology. Resigned: now a faculty member at the Baptist Theological Seminary at Richmond VA.

Thomas A. Bland, Sr., Professor of Christian Ethics and Sociology. Retired.

George W. Braswell, Jr., Professor of Missions and World Religions. Remains on the Southeastern Baptist Theological Seminary faculty.

William P. Clemmons, Professor of Christian Education. Resigned: now a faculty member at Northern Baptist Seminary, Lombard IL.

Donald E. Cook, Professor of New Testament. Retired early: now a faculty member at the Divinity School, Gardner-Webb University, Boiling Springs NC.

Robert H. Culpepper, Professor of Theology. Retired: now pastor of Oak Ridge Baptist Church, Kittrell NC.

Robert D. Dale, Professor of Pastoral Leadership and Church Ministries. Resigned: now Assistant Executive Director, Baptist General Association of Virginia, Richmond VA.

Roy E. De Brand, Professor of Preaching. Resigned: now pastor of Franklin Baptist Church, Franklin VA.

John W. Eddins, Jr., Professor of Theology. Retired: now teaching adjunctively at the Presyterian School of Christian Education and at the Baptist Theological Seminary at Richmond VA.

James W. Good, Professor of Church Music. Remains on the Southeastern Baptist Theological Seminary faculty.

Thomas H. Graves, Professor of Philosophy of Religion. Resigned: now president of the Baptist Theological Seminary at Richmond VA.

Fred A. Grissom, Professor of Church History. Remains on the Southeastern Baptist Theological Seminary faculty.

G. Thomas Halbrooks, Professor of Church History. Resigned: now Dean of the Baptist Theological Seminary at Richmond VA.

C. Michael Hawn, Professor of Church Music. Resigned: now a faculty member at Perkins School of Divinity, Southern Methodist University, Dallas TX.

Richard L. Hester, Professor of Pastoral Care and Psychology of Religion. Resigned: now Executive Director, Georgia Association of Pastoral Care, Atlanta GA.

T. Furman Hewitt, Professor of Christian Ethics. Retired early: now Director, Baptist House of Studies, Duke Divinity School, Durham NC. Teaches adjunctively at the Divinity School.

Ben S. Johnson, Professor of Church Music. Remains on the Southeastern Baptist Theological Seminary faculty.

W. Randall Lolley, President. Resigned: now pastor of the First Baptist Church, Greensboro NC.

H. Eugene McLeod, Professor of Bibliography/Librarian. Retired.

Albert L. Meiburg, Professor of Pastoral Theology. Retired: now teaches adjunctively at the Baptist Seminary, Hong Kong.

Delos Miles, Professor of Evangelism. Remains on the Southeastern Baptist Theological Seminary faculty.

Glenn T. Miller, Professor of Church History. Resigned: now a faculty member and dean at Bangor Theological Seminary, Bangor ME.

Archie L. Nations, Professor of New Testament Interpretation. Retired.

Alan Neely, Professor of Missiology. Resigned: now a faculty member at Princeton Theological Seminary, Princeton NJ.

Ben F. Philbeck, Professor of Hebrew and Old Testament. Deceased.

Robert E. Poerschke, Professor of Christian Education. Retired.

Bruce P. Powers, Professor of Christian Education. Remains on the Southeastern Baptist Theological Seminary faculty.

Robert L. Richardson, Jr., Professor of Supervised Ministry. Resigned: now is Staff Chaplain Supervisor, Carolinas Medical Center, Charlotte NC.

Max G. Rogers, Professor of Old Testament. Remains on the Southeastern Baptist Theological Seminary faculty.

Luke B. Smith, Professor of Supervised Ministry. Resigned.

Richard A. Spencer, Professor of New Testament. Resigned: now a faculty member at Appalachian State University, Boone NC.

Malcolm O. Tolbert, Professor of New Testament. Retired.

Administrative Officers

Bernice Ashcraft, Technical Services Librarian. Retired.

Carson Brisson, Registrar/Assistant to the Dean. Resigned: now is Registrar at Union Theological Seminary, Richmond VA.

Rodney V. Byard, Assistant to the President: Communications. Resigned: just completed eighth year as a member of the Wake Forest Town Board.

C. Woody Catoe, Director of Student Development. Resigned: recently completed Ed.D.; associate pastor, Millbrook Baptist Church, Raleigh NC.

Charles T. Dorman, Director, Student/Field Ministries. Retired: serves regularly as an interim pastor.

G. Paul Fletcher, Assistant to the President: Business Affairs. Remains at Southeastern Baptist Theological Seminary as Vice-President of Internal Affairs.

Donna M. Forrester, Chaplain. Resigned: now is associate pastor, First Baptist Church, Greenville SC.

C. T. Harris, Assistant Librarian/Technical Services. Resigned: now is librarian at Wingate College, Wingate NC.

W. David Lee, Director of Management Services. Resigned: now is an officer with Carolina Builders, a construction company, Richmond VA.

Ethel Burton Lee, Associate Director, Student/Field Ministries. Resigned.

Wayne F. Murphy, Director of Planned Giving. Resigned: now a professional financial consultant.

Jerry L. Niswonger, Assistant to the President: Student Development. Resigned: now is pastor, Emporia Baptist Church, Emporia VA.

Jo Sloan Philbeck, Reference Librarian. Remains at Southeastern Baptist Theological Seminary.

W. Robert Spinks, Assistant to the President: Financial Development. Resigned: now is Director of Development, The Divinity School, Wake Forest University, Winston-Salem NC.

Rita A. Vermillion, Circulation Librarian. Remains at Southeastern Baptist Theological Seminary.

Purpose*

The primary purpose of Southeastern Seminary is to prepare men and women for Christian leadership in various ministries. This includes preaching and pastoral care, missionary work at home and abroad, the ministry of religious education, the teaching of religion and allied subjects in secondary schools and colleges, religious leadership on college campuses, the chaplaincy, social service, and such other forms of religious work as require specialized techniques.

Vital to all these areas of service is a full understanding of the origins, content, and history of the Christian faith and its special relevance to the needs of the modern world. Courses of study directed toward such an understanding constitute the Core Curriculum and are regarded as the basic training for all prospective Christian workers.

While the Seminary is conscious of its responsibility to the Southern Baptist Convention, its facilities are open on an equal basis to students of all denominations, and it is the aim of the Seminary to help produce a leadership for the whole Christian movement.

To accomplish these ends, the Seminary proposes to maintain a God-called faculty who are especially qualified by training and experience to offer leadership in maintaining high standards of achievement in the intellectual and spiritual spheres. Appropriate provision will be made for adequate physical facilities and for an excellent library.

In pursuit of these objectives, the faculty are conscious of certain great emphases which undergird the Seminary program of education: (1) A sound knowledge of the Bible; (2) A wholesome and intelligent evangelism; (3) A challenging vision of the world-wide mission of Christianity; (4) A prevailing spiritual dynamic in the lives of students and faculty; (5) A sense of the significance of the local church—urban and rural; and (6) A consecrated scholarship for providing genuine Christian leadership.

*Southeastern Baptist Theological Seminary Bulletin, 1952.

Statement of Purpose*

Southeastern Baptist Theological Seminary seeks to prepare God-called men and women for vocational service in Baptist churches and in other Christian ministries throughout the world. This purpose is implemented through programs of spiritual development, theological studies, and practical preparation in ministry.

Statement of Mission*

Southeastern Baptist Theological Seminary is an institution of higher learning established and supported by the Southern Baptist Convention in order to "contend earnestly for the faith which was once and for all delivered to the saints." The Seminary maintains an administration and faculty of God-called members whose convictions and calling reflect consistent adherence to the institution's Articles of Faith. The Seminary's administration and faculty are qualified by personal commitment to Christ, by academic preparation, and by personal and professional experience to provide guidance in spiritual, intellectual, and practical endeavors. Through its administration and faculty, the Seminary offers a program of instruction which focuses on three primary areas: (1) spiritual development, (2) theological studies, and (3) practical preparation.

I. Spiritual Development—The Seminary seeks to foster spiritual growth in the grace and knowledge of the Lord Jesus Christ as essential preparation for Christian ministry and service. The foundation for spiritual development is an unqualified commitment in obedience and faith to the person and work of the Lord Jesus Christ. Spiritual development also requires seeking and following the Holy Spirit's guidance in the formation of Christian thought and character in the pursuit of one's Christian calling.

II. Theological Studies—The Seminary seeks to prepare men and women for Christian ministry and service by helping them discern, defend, and proclaim God's revealed truth. The Seminary pursues high academic standards in providing courses of study for understanding the Bible and the history, content and contemporary relevance of the Christian Faith. The Seminary is committed to the complete veracity, inerrancy, and infallibility of the Bible as an essential foundation for effective Christian ministry and service.

III. Practical Preparation—The Seminary ephasizes intelligent and intentional evangelism in obedience to the Lord Jesus Christ's commission to make disciples of all nations. Spiritual development in Christlikeness and Bible-based theological studies will produce a compassionate desire to minister to the human suffering caused by indivudual, social and spiritual evils. The Seminary program provides practical preparation for a wide variety of Christian ministries, with special focus on proclaiming the Gospel and extending the ministry of the local church.

Southeastern Baptist Theological Seminary Bulletin, 1992–1993.

Report of the Southern Baptist Convention Peace Committee*

Recommendation 5

We recommend that, in view of the intense public discussions of the last few years, trustees determine the theological positions of the seminary administrators and faculty members in order to guide them in renewing their determination to stand by the Baptist Faith and Message Statement of 1963, to the Glorieta Statement of their intention to work toward reconciliation of the conflict in the Convention, and to their own institutional declarations of faith as the guidelines by which they will teach their students in preparation for Gospel ministry in the churches, mission fields and service to the denomination.

The Bible is a book of redemption, not a book of science, psychology, sociology or economics. But, where the Bible speaks, the Bible speaks truth in all realms of reality and to all fields of knowledge. The Bible, when properly interpreted, is authoritative to all of life.

We call upon Southern Baptist institutions to recognize the great number of Southern Baptists who believe this interpretation of Article I of the Baptist Faith and Message Statement of 1963, and, in the future, to build their professional staffs and faculties from those who clearly reflect such dominant convictions and beliefs held by Southern Baptists at large.

We, as a Peace Committee, recognize and respect those in Southern Baptist life whose view of Scripture differs from this one and pledge to continue to cooperate. We pledge the highest regard, charity and commitment to them in our combined efforts to fulfill the Great Commission and we call upon them to make the same pledge.

[The report includes an introduction and five major sections: I. Sources of the Controversy, II. Findings, III. Conclusions, IV. Recommendations, and V. Acknowledgements.]

Annual of the Southern Baptist Convention, St. Louis MO, 16 June 1987 (Nashville TN: Executive Committee, SBC, 1987) 241.

Contributors

Morris Ashcraft is a graduate of Ouachita Baptist College (B.A) and Southern Baptist Theological Seminary (B.D., Ph.D.). He has also done postdoctoral study at the University of Zurich and the University of Chicago. Ashcraft taught at Southern Baptist Theological Seminary (1951, 1954–1958), Furman University (1958–1959), Midwestern Baptist Theological Seminary (1959–1981), and Southeastern Baptist Theological Seminary (1981–1988), where he was also dean of the faculty. Dr. Ashcraft was the first acting president of Baptist Theological Seminary at Richmond. The author of numerous articles and six books, including the Broadman Bible Commentary on Revelation (1972) and *Christian Faith and its Beliefs* (Broadman, 1984), Ashcraft teaches adjunctively in the Baptist Studies program at Duke University Divinity School and volunteers regularly for Habitat for Humanity.

Thomas A. Bland was professor of Christian Ethics and Sociology at Southeastern Baptist Theological Seminary from 1956 through 1993. A graduate of the University of North Carolina at Chapel Hill (B.S.) and Southern Baptist Theological Seminary (B.D., Th.D.), he also did postdoctoral work at Yale University, UNC-Chapel Hill, and Union Theological Seminary in New York. Additionally, he taught adjunctively at the Baptist Theological Seminary at Ruschlikon, Switzerland. Bland helped to pioneer Southern Baptist work in urban America, and his annual Urban Seminar, which featured field work first in Washington, D.C., and later in New York City, was extremely popular. Among his publications is a chapter in *The Gambling Menace*, edited by Ross Coggins (Broadman, 1966), and two chapters in *Extremism: Left and Right*, edited by Elmer S. West, Jr. (Eerdmans, 1972). During his years at Southeastern, Dr. Bland was also interim pastor of many churches, three of which he helped to start: Holly Hill Baptist Church, Burlington, North Carolina; Greystone Baptist Church, Raleigh, North Carolina; and Woodhaven Baptist Church, Apex, North Carolina. For these efforts he was recognized by the North Carolina Baptist State Convention in 1986 as Church Planter of the Year.

Thomas A. Bland, Jr., is editor of *Servant Songs*. A native of Wake Forest, North Carolina, he is a graduate of Wake Forest University (B.A.), the University of North Carolina at Chapel Hill (M.A., Ph.D.), and Southeastern Baptist Theological Seminary (M.Div. with Languages). His publications include a series of Adult Life and Work Sunday School lessons that he wrote for the North Carolina Baptist newspaper *Biblical Recorder* (April–June 1992). Bland presently serves on the North Carolina Baptist State Convention's General Board and on its Council on Christian Higher Education. He is pastor of Sharpsburg Baptist Church, Sharpsburg, North Carolina.

Donald E. Cook is a graduate of Furman University (B.A.), Southeastern Baptist Theological Seminary (B.D., Th.M.), and Duke University (Ph.D.). He also did postdoctoral study at the Hebrew Union College in Jerusalem. He was professor of New Testament at Southeastern from 1965 through January 1994. Currently he is senior professor of New Testament Interpretation in the Divinity School of Gardner-Webb University, Boiling Springs, North Carolina. Publications over the years include numerous articles and book reviews as well as Sunday School lessons. A very active interim pastor and Bible study teacher over the years, Cook is presently pastor of the Bethany Baptist Church, Baskerville, Virginia.

Robert D. Dale taught pastoral leadership and church ministry at Southeastern Baptist Theological Seminary from 1977 through 1988. From 1978 through 1988, he also directed the D.Min. program there. Dale is a graduate of Southwest Baptist College (A.A.), Oklahoma Baptist University (B.A.), and Southwestern Baptist Theological Seminary (B.D., Ph.D.). Additionally, he has studied at Southern Methodist Univer-sity and the University of Kansas. A nationally recognized authority on church leadership, Dale is the author of many articles and of fifteen books, including *To Dream Again* (Broadman, 1981) and *Keeping the Dream Alive* (Broadman, 1988). Currently he is the assistant executive director for the Baptist General Association of Virginia and director of its Center for Creative Church Leadership Development. He also teaches adjunctively at Baptist Theological Seminary at Richmond.

John W. Eddins, Jr., was professor of Theology at Southeastern Baptist Theological Seminary from 1957 through 1993. A graduate of Auburn

University (B.S.), Samford University (B.A.), and Southern Baptist Theological Seminary (B.D., Th. D.), Eddins has engaged in further study at Duke University, Union Theological Seminary in New York, and the University of North Carolina at Chapel Hill. His publications include numerous Sunday School lessons; a study course for the SBC seminary extension department titled *Theology 136: Systematic Theology* (1964); and many articles, including "Faith and Mission: Love in the Form of a Servant," a compendium of his theology that appeared in the inaugural issue of *Faith and Mission* (Fall 1983). Eddins has been interim pastor of many churches and has taught the annual January Bible Study and Baptist Doctrine Study in diverse places numerous times. He presently teaches adjunctively at the Presbyterian School of Christian Education and at the Baptist Theological Seminary at Richmond.

Donna M. Forrester was the first chaplain at Southeastern Baptist Theological Seminary, serving from 1984 through 1989. She holds the B.S. in Nursing from the University of South Carolina, the M.Div. from Southern Baptist Theological Seminary, and the D.Min. from South-eastern. She also completed a residency in Pastoral Counseling at the School of Pastoral Care at the North Carolina Baptist Hospital in Winston-Salem and is a Certified Family Life Educator through the National Council on Family Relations. Dr. Forrester currently is minister of Pastoral Care and Counseling at First Baptist Church, Greenville, South Carolina.

Thomas H. Graves was professor of Philosophy of Religion at Southeastern Baptist Theological Seminary from 1979 to 1987. A graduate of Vanderbilt University (B.A.), Yale Divinity School (S.T.M.), and Southern Baptist Theological Seminary (M.Div., Ph.D.), he has done additional study at the School of Theology at Claremont, California. Graves has also taught adjunctively at Barton College in Wilson, North Carolina, and at Baptist Theological Seminary of Zimbabwe. His many publications include chapters in *Best Sermons 5*, edited by James W. Cox (Harper-Collins, 1992), and in *The Struggle for the Soul of the SBC*, edited by Walter B. Shurden (Smyth & Helwys, 1993). Additionally, he served as editor of Southeastern Seminary's scholarly journal *Faith and Mission* from 1982 to 1986. Graves has been pastor of several churches, most recently St. John's Baptist Church in Charlotte, North Carolina (1987—

1991). He has been president of Baptist Theological Seminary at Richmond since 1991.

Fred A. Grissom is a graduate of the University of Alabama (B.A.), the University of Chicago (M.Th.), and Southern Baptist Theological Seminary (M.Div., Ph.D.). He has been pastor of churches in Alabama and Kentucky and interim pastor of numerous churches in four other states. His teaching experience includes service at Virginia Intermont College (1979–1981), Golden Gate Baptist Theological Seminary (1981–1986), and Southeastern Baptist Theological Seminary, where he has been professor of Church History since 1987. During the 1990–1991 academic year, Grissom was president of the Southeastern Seminary chapter of the American Association of University Professors (AAUP), which because of numerous faculty resignations and retirements has evolved into a minority—but still prophetic—voice at Southeastern. Grissom has also been editor of *Faith and Mission*. His publications include articles in *Baptist History and Heritage* and *Biblical Illustrator*.

Richard L. Hester was professor of Pastoral Care and Psychology of Religion at Southeastern Baptist Theological Seminary from 1975 through 1991. He was also the first president of the Southeastern chapter of the AAUP, serving from 1987 through 1988. A graduate of Baylor University (B.A.) and Southern Baptist Theological Seminary (B.D., Ph.D.), with postdoctoral work at Duke University, Dr. Hester is a Fellow of the American Association of Pastoral Counselors. He presently is executive director of the Georgia Association for Pastoral Care, which provides pastoral counseling, clinical pastoral education, and training in pastoral counseling.

W. Randall Lolley was president of Southeastern Baptist Theological Seminary from 1974 through March 1988. He holds the A.B. from Samford University, the B.D. and Th.M. from Southeastern, and the Th.D. from Southwestern Baptist Theological Seminary as well as honorary doctorates from Wake Forest, Samford, Campbell, Mercer University, and the University of Richmond. His postdoctoral work has included study at Wake Forest, Furman, Yale, Harvard, Princeton, and the University of Chicago. Lolley's record of denominational service is extensive, including most recently his term as first vice-president of the North Carolina

Baptist State Convention (1989–1991). A nationally renowned pastor and educator, Dr. Lolley has been a member of three White House Conferences (on Race, Family, and Aging) and a member of accreditation visiting teams for the Association of Theological Schools (ATS). His extensive publications include *Bold Preaching of Christ* (Broadman, 1980), which he co-edited. Lolley currently is pastor of First Baptist Church, Greensboro, North Carolina.

Glenn T. Miller was professor of Church History at Southeastern Baptist Theological Seminary from 1976 through 1991. He holds the B.A. from the University of Richmond, the B.D. from Andover-Newton Theological School, and the Ph. D. from Union Theological Seminary in New York. Considered an authority on American religious history and on the history of American theological education, Miller is the author of *Religious Liberty* (Westminster, 1976) and *Piety and Intellect* (Scholars, 1990), among other publications. He presently is professor of Church History and academic dean at Bangor Theological Seminary, Bangor, Maine.

Alan Neely was professor of Missions at Southeastern Baptist Theological Seminary from 1976 through June 1988. A graduate of Baylor University (B.A.), Southwestern Baptist Theological Seminary (B.D., Th.D.), and American University (Ph.D.), Neely and his wife Virginia were foreign missionaries to Colombia, where he was professor of Philosophy of Religion and Missions at the International Baptist Theological Seminary in Cali from 1964 to 1976. The author of many articles in Spanish and English, Neely has translated two books, *A History of the Church in Latin America* by Enrique Dussel (Eerdmans, 1980) and *Worship and Politics* by Raphael Avila (Orbis, 1982). He also edited *Being Baptist Means Freedom* (Alliance of Baptists, 1988) and was for several years editor of Southeastern's scholarly journal *Faith and Mission*. A widely recognized authority on missiology and on lib-eration theology, Dr. Neely is now Henry Winters Luce Professor of Ecumenics and Mission at Princeton Theological Seminary.

Index